Five or Ten Minutes of Blind Confusion:

The Battle of Aiken, South Carolina, February 11, 1865

Other work by Eric J. Wittenberg:

We Ride a Whirlwind: Sherman and Johnston at Bennett Place (2017)

The Union Cavalry Comes of Age: Hartwood Church to Brandy Station, 1863 (Second ed. 2017)

Out Flew the Sabers: The Battle of Brandy Station, June 9, 1863 (with Daniel T. Davis, 2016)

The Second Battle of Winchester: The Confederate Victory that Opened the Door to Gettysburg (with Scott L. Mingus, Sr., 2016)

The Devil's to Pay: John Buford at Gettysburg. A History and Walking Tour (2014)

Protecting the Flank at Gettysburg: The Battles for Brinkerhoff's Ridge and East Cavalry Field (Second Edition, 2013)

The Battle of White Sulphur Springs; Averell Fails to Secure West Virginia (2011)

Gettysburg's Forgotten Cavalry Actions: Farnsworth's Charge, South Cavalry Field and the Battle of Fairfield (Second Edition, 2011)

The Battle of Brandy Station: North America's Largest Cavalry Battle (2010)

Like a Meteor Blazing Brightly: The Short but Controversial Life of Colonel Ulric Dahlgren (2009)

One Continuous Fight: The Retreat from Gettysburg and the Pursuit of Lee's Army of Northern Virginia, July 4-14, 1863 (with J. David Petruzzi and Michael F. Nugent, 2008)

Rush's Lancers: The Sixth Pennsylvania Cavalry in the Civil War (2007)

Plenty of Blame to Go Around: Jeb Stuart's Controversial Ride to Gettysburg (with J. David Petruzzi, 2006)

The Battle of Monroe's Crossroads and the Civil War's Final Campaign (2006)

Little Phil: A Reassessment of the Civil War Leadership of Gen. Philip H. Sheridan (2002)

With Sheridan in the Final Campaign Against Lee (2002)

Glory Enough for All: Sheridan's Second Raid and the Battle of Trevilian Station (2001)

At Custer's Side: The Civil War Writings of James Harvey Kidd (2001)

Under Custer's Command: The Civil War Journal of James Henry Avery (2000)

One of Custer's Wolverines: The Civil War Letters of Brevet Brigadier General James H. Kidd, 6th Michigan Cavalry (2000)

We Have it Damned Hard Out Here: The Civil War Letters of Sgt. Thomas W. Smith, Sixth Pennsylvania Cavalry (1999)

Five or Ten Minutes of Blind Confusion:

The Battle of Aiken, South Carolina, February 11, 1865

Eric J. Wittenberg

Publisher's Cataloging-in-Publication Data
provided by Five Rainbows Cataloging Services

Names: Wittenberg, Eric J., 1961- author. | Sokolosky, Wade, writer of foreword.
Title: Five or ten minutes of blind confusion : the battle of Aiken, South Carolina, February 11, 1865 / Eric J. Wittenberg ; [foreword by] Wade Sokolosky.
Description: Burlington, NC : Fox Run Publishing, 2018. | Includes bibliographical references and index.
Identifiers: LCCN 2018947790 | ISBN 978-1-945602-07-8 (pbk.) | ISBN 978-1-945602-06-1 (hardcover)
Subjects: LCSH: Aiken, Battle of, Aiken, S.C., 1865. | South Carolina--History--Civil War, 1861-1865. | Sherman's March to the Sea. | Sherman's March through the Carolinas. | Wheeler, Joseph, 1836-1906. | Kilpatrick, Judson, 1836-1881. | BISAC: HISTORY / United States / Civil War Period (1850-1877) | HISTORY / United States / State & Local / South (AL, AR, FL, GA, KY, LA, MS, NC, SC, TN, VA, WV)
Classification: LCC F269 .W58 2018 (print) | DDC 973.7/8--dc23.

Cover design by Sandra Miller Linhart
Historical Painting "Ambush: The Battle of Aiken, S.C." by Larry Arnold courtesy of the Artist.

Published by
Fox Run Publishing LLC
2966 South Church Street, #305
Burlington, NC 27215
http://www.foxrunpub.com/

Respectfully dedicated to the horse soldiers of the Union and Confederacy who followed the guidon into battle at Aiken, South Carolina, on February 11, 1865.

Table of Contents

List of Maps

List of Images

Five or Ten Minutes of Blind Confusion
The Battle of Aiken, South Carolina, February 11, 1865

Author's Preface

This is my third book on some aspect of the Civil War in the Carolinas in 1865. My first book on the Civil War in the Carolinas was a study of the March 10, 1865, Battle of Monroe's Crossroads, the last large-scale cavalry battle of the Carolinas Campaign. That morning, nearly 6,000 Confederate horse soldiers pounced on Union cavalry commander Bvt. Maj. Gen. Judson Kilpatrick's sleeping and unprepared camp, scattering the Federals and nearly capturing Kilpatrick, who escaped to a nearby swamp clad only in his nightshirt. Amused Union infantrymen jokingly referred to "Kilpatrick's shirt-tail skedaddle." However, Kilpatrick rallied his troopers; they drove off the Confederate horsemen and slept in their camps that night. The Battle of Monroe's Crossroads must be considered a Union victory as a result.

Monroe's Crossroads marked one of four significant defeats Confederate forces suffered during the Carolinas Campaign, which commenced on February 4, 1865, when Maj. Gen. William T. Sherman's 64,000 soldiers invaded South Carolina with the goal of reaching their ultimate destination 400 miles away—the crucial railroad hub at Goldsboro, North Carolina. Sherman's men punished the South Carolina population, which they blamed for the terrible war that had raged since the shelling of Fort Sumter, South Carolina, nearly four years earlier. As the blue horde swarmed across South Carolina, only a handful of Confederate troops were available to resist them, including the 4,000 Southern cavalrymen of Maj. Gen. Joseph Wheeler's Cavalry Corps of the Army of Tennessee. Obviously, there was little that such a small force could do to hinder the advance of more than 60,000 soldiers.

Along the way, Wheeler harassed his former West Point school chum Kilpatrick and his troopers at every possible opportunity. On February 11, 1865, Wheeler laid a trap for Kilpatrick and his men in the streets of Aiken, South Carolina. Using decoys to draw in the Union troopers, Wheeler ambushed and defeated Kilpatrick's cavalry, driving them nearly five miles until they reached Kilpatrick's main body at Montmorenci, South Carolina. The Confederates nearly captured Kilpatrick during the determined fighting in Aiken. Wheeler's victory over Kilpatrick's men prevented them from reaching and destroying critical Confederate manufacturing facilities at Augusta, Georgia, and Graniteville, South Carolina, and also saved Aiken from the torches and tender mercies of the Northerners. However, in so doing, Wheeler disobeyed direct orders to hold the line for as long as possible at the Edisto River to the south of Columbia, South Carolina, the state capital. Although he defeated Kilpatrick on the battlefield, by disobeying orders Wheeler insured that there were inadequate forces to hold the line of the Edisto, sealing the fate of Columbia, which fell to Sherman's army on February 17, 1865. Much of Columbia's downtown burned to the ground in a great conflagration whipped by gale-force winds.

This is the story of the Battle of Aiken, told in a detailed tactical narrative for the first time. The paucity of reliable Confederate records from the late stage of the war has always made documenting the Carolinas Campaign a challenge. Also, the fighting in Aiken lasted only about an hour. Consequently, cobbling together a detailed narrative is a real challenge for any historian addressing these events. Perhaps these daunting obstacles have prevented anyone from examining this significant Confederate battlefield victory in any detail until now.

This book begins with a description of the opening phases of the Carolinas Campaign and sets the stage for the Battle of Aiken. Two chapters address the opposing forces that tangled at Aiken. A detailed battle narrative follows in the next two chapters, as well as a discussion about the aftermath of the fighting. The conclusion of the book provides some analysis of the battle and places it in its proper historic context. Finally, there are three appendices. The first is an order of battle for the Battle of Aiken. The second addresses all known and identified Confederate casualties at Aiken. The third compares and contrasts the December 4, 1864, Battle of Waynesboro, Georgia, with the Battle of Aiken. At the end, I hope the reader will have a greater understanding of, and appreciation for, the nasty cavalry battle that raged in the streets of Aiken on February 11, 1865.

No project like this is possible without the assistance and generosity of a lot of people. First, and foremost, I am grateful to Mike Alberti of Lexington, South Carolina, who made multiple trips to Aiken to obtain research materials and to photograph the main battlefield for me. Tom Elmore took time out of his busy schedule to give me a tour of the Aiken and Montmorenci portions of the battlefield, and also provided useful sources. Wade Sokolosky offered the fruit of his labors to identify Confederate battle casualties during the Carolinas Campaign and penned the foreword that follows. Dave Powell provided some useful source material, as did J. Keith Jones and Terry

Brasko. Craig Swain not only read and commented on the manuscript for this book, but he also alerted me to the fascinating parallels between the Aiken and Waynesboro battles. He also helped me to better understand the terrain features that the Confederates could have used to hinder Sherman's march through South Carolina. Daniel L. Mallock read and commented upon my manuscript too, helping to make it a better book. Master cartographer Mark Anderson Moore is the first person to map these actions, and his excellent maps improve my work.

All errors of interpretation are solely my own.

This is the second book that I have published with my friends at Fox Run Publishing of Burlington, North Carolina. It also marks the second time that I have worked with editor Heather Ammel, and this is the second time that Heather's guidance and diligent editing have made this the best book it can be. Keith Jones did a fine job of laying out this book and getting it ready for publication.

And, as always, I remain grateful to my long-suffering but much loved wife, Susan Skilken Wittenberg, without whose infinite patience for my need to tell these stories of the American Civil War, none of this would be possible.

Eric J. Wittenberg
Columbus, Ohio

Foreword

More than two decades ago, historian Mark L. Bradley published his seminal work, The Battle of Bentonville: Last Stand in the Carolinas, which remains the definitive study of Maj. Gen. William T. Sherman's 1865 Carolinas Campaign. Bradley's work was groundbreaking because it presented the most detailed analysis of the campaign. However, it is important to note that Bradley's primary focus was on the Battle of Bentonville, and although he introduced the reader to the desperate fighting that occurred in the weeks leading up to the campaign's culminating battle, he only sought to provide a summary of the rest of the campaign.

Fortunately, since the release of *Last Stand in the Carolinas*, other historians have followed in Bradley's footsteps, delving deeper into research and releasing book-length studies on lesser-known battles of the campaign, such as Wise's Forks, Monroe's Crossroads, and Averasboro. One such historian is Eric Wittenberg, a noted author of many superb books on cavalry operations in the Eastern Theater of the Civil War. In 2006, Eric broke this paradigm with the release of *The Battle of Monroe's Crossroads and the Civil War's Final Campaign*, the only complete account about the March 1865 violent cavalry clash in the North Carolina Sandhills. Then, in 2017, Eric followed up with another related study, *We Ride a Whirlwind: Sherman and Johnston at Bennett Place*, providing much needed attention to the drama that unfolded during the war's final days in North Carolina.

Despite the efforts of Bradley, Wittenberg, and others, the South Carolina phase of Sherman's campaign seems to be the one remaining darkroom, where further study is required. Although much has been written about Sherman burning South Carolina's capital, Columbia, and the impact of the general's "hard hand" of war on the state's civilian population, the emphasis on these two specific points has overshadowed the military operations that occurred, creating an oversight regarding important aspects of the campaign. An example is the overlooked Battle of Aiken, South Carolina, fought on February 11, 1865, and despite its significance at the time, the clash is not well known today. This is unfortunate because it was an important battle in the opening weeks of the Carolinas Campaign, setting the tone for the vicious mounted fighting that followed in the coming weeks.

Fortunately, this key cavalry battle in the Palmetto State finally receives its due recognition with the publication of *Five or Ten Minutes of Blind Confusion: The Battle of Aiken, South Carolina, February 11, 1865*. Aiken has deserved a closer look for years, as its role in the campaign was more significant than historians previously realized or have allowed. As Eric reveals, the Battle of Aiken was unusual for the Civil War; it was one of only a handful of strictly urban cavalry engagements that occurred during the war. Ironically, in three of those four battles Sherman's cavalry chieftain, Bvt. Maj. Gen. Judson Kilpatrick, was the Union commander. Additionally, Kilpatrick's noted adversary Maj. Gen. Joseph Wheeler decided to engage his Union counterpart at Aiken with cavalry, saving the important city of Augusta, Georgia, with its vital powder works, arsenal, and other critical depots, as well as the mill town of Graniteville, South Carolina, from what would have assuredly been their destruction.

Five or Ten Minutes begins with a discussion about Sherman's planning for the Carolinas Campaign at Savannah, Georgia, and then follows the Union army's initial movements into South Carolina, which were designed to deceive the Confederates and keep the Southern high command in the dark about Sherman's real intention—Columbia, South Carolina. Because the cavalry possessed the ability to rapidly travel greater distances, these mounted troopers performed a vital role in this chess game of maneuver. Eric's well-researched and fast-paced narrative brings the opposing forces to Aiken, where the stage is set for an ultimate showdown between two brave, veteran cavalry commanders, Generals Kilpatrick and Wheeler, each leading battle-seasoned soldiers and seeking to destroy the other. Eric expertly details the strong characters in both armies while simultaneously exposing their weaknesses.

Five or Ten Minutes is a blow-by-blow account of the battle, continually shifting from the commanders' perspectives to those of the individual soldier in the saddle. Because the battle was fought in an urban setting, eyewitnesses were limited by what the trooper could see and experience in the fighting. Despite such hurdles, Eric has crafted an accurate and detailed account of the tactical setting and fighting as it developed hour by hour, all the while displaying an even-handedness that strikes an appropriate balance by telling the story from both sides, whether good or bad. Complementing the study are numerous photographs, helpful footnotes, and five excellent maps master Civil War cartographer Mark Moore created that fully enhance the reader's understanding of the battle's complex urban nature.

Further, no previous account of the Battle of Aiken has been written with anything approaching such a high level of detail and analysis. With Eric's release of *Five or Ten Minutes*, this important cavalry battle that occurred during the opening phases of the Carolinas Campaign finally gets the attention it rightfully deserves. *Five or Ten Minutes* will remain the definitive work on the battle for years to come.

Wade Sokolosky
Beaufort, North Carolina

CHAPTER ONE

THE CAROLINAS CAMPAIGN BEGINS

Major General William T. Sherman, aged 45, commanded the Union Department of the Mississippi, which encompassed all Union forces east of the Mississippi River and south of Virginia. The West Point-trained Sherman rose to prominence along with his close friend Ulysses S. Grant. Grant was promoted to lieutenant general and commander of all Union armies after his decisive triumph at the Battle of Chattanooga in November 1863. Sherman replaced Grant as commander of the Army of the Tennessee and then as commander of the Department of the Mississippi. Sherman's 1864 campaign to capture the critical railroad city of Atlanta, Georgia, required all summer, but Sherman seized it in September, depriving the Confederacy of that crucial rail hub.[1]

Maj. Gen. William T. Sherman, commander of all Union forces in South Carolina.

(Library of Congress)

"Sherman was tall, lithe, and active, with light brown hair, close-cropped sandy beard and mustache, and every motion and expression indicated eagerness and energy," Maj. Gen. Jacob D. Cox, who commanded one of Sherman's army corps in 1865, recalled. "His head was apt to be bent a little forward as if in earnest or aggressive advance, and his rapid incisive utterance hit off

---

1. Ezra J. Warner, *Generals in Blue: Lives of the Union Commanders* (Baton Rouge: Louisiana State University Press, 1964), 442-443.

the topics of discussion in a sharp and telling way. His opinions usually took a strong and very pronounced form, full of the feeling that was for the moment uppermost, not hesitating even at a little humorous extravagance if it added point to his statement; but in such cases the keen eye took a merry twinkle accentuated by the crow-foot lines in the corner, so that the real geniality and kindliness that underlay the brusque exterior were sufficiently apparent. The general effect was a nature of intense, restless activity, both physical and mental."[2]

Sherman was a brilliant strategist, but he was not a great tactician. "Sherman's own knowledge of his own impulsive nature made him unduly untrustful of his own judgment when under great responsibility in emergencies, and this in spite of his unusual intellectual activity and his great confidence in his deliberately matured judgment," Maj. Gen. John M. Schofield, who commanded one of Sherman's armies, observed. "For this reason Sherman's capacity as a tactician was not by any means equal to his ability as a strategist. He lacked the element of confident boldness or audacity in action which is necessary to gain the greatest results by taking advantage of his adversary's blunders."[3]

After their summer-long campaign to capture Atlanta, Sherman's troops rested for a few weeks to refit and prepare for their next campaign. Then, on November 15, 1864, his army left Atlanta and spent the next five weeks making its legendary March to the Sea. The expedition ended with the surrender of the seaport town of Savannah, Georgia. The most notable organized Confederate resistance came from Maj. Gen. Joseph Wheeler and his 4,100[4] cavalrymen. Union troops bypassed the Confederate garrison at Augusta, Georgia, on their way to Savannah, leaving the town unmolested.[5]

---

2. Jacob D. Cox, *Reminiscences of the Civil War, 2 vols.* (New York: Charles Scribner's Sons, 1900), 2:203
3. John M. Schofield, *Forty-Six Years in the Army* (New York: The Century Co., 1897), 341-342.
4. The Confederates had significant forces available to resist Sherman's advance, but those troops were not led well.
5. The most important gunpowder manufacturing facility in the South was located in Augusta, Georgia. However, Sherman never deemed them important enough to destroy. Historian Theodore P. Savas thinks that was one of the great errors of the Civil War. However, this theory disregards the fact that the one thing Confederate armies did not lack during the final few months of the Civil War was gunpowder. It seems unlikely that the destruction of the powder works would have damaged the Confederate war effort, its adverse affects on civilian morale notwithstanding. See Theodore P. Savas, "The War's Biggest Blunder: William T. Sherman had Many Opportunities to Capture Augusta's Ordnance Complex and Didn't Even Try." *Civil War Times* 56 (August 2017): 30-35.

Sherman believed that the only way to end the Civil War was to break the will of the Southern civilian population, and he intended to do so. His men "made Georgia howl," as he later described it. After fanning out across Georgia like a plague of hungry locusts, the blue-clad hordes arrived at Savannah about five weeks after setting out from Atlanta. Lieutenant General William J. Hardee, the Confederate commander at Savannah, abandoned the city and led his small command into South Carolina on December 20, where it would help to defend the Palmetto State. The next day, the mayor of Savannah surrendered the city, hoping that Sherman would not destroy it, and thus ended an incredible campaign that only foreshadowed what was yet to come in the Carolinas.[6]

With Savannah about to fall, Sherman jotted a letter to Lt. Gen. Ulysses S. Grant, the general-in-chief of the Union armies, proposing his next moves:

> **I left Augusta untouched on purpose, because the enemy will be in doubt as to my objective point, after we cross the Savannah River, whether it be Augusta or Charleston, and will naturally divide his forces. I will then move either on Branchville or Columbia, by any curved line that gives us the best supplies, breaking up in our course as much railroad as possible; then, ignoring Charleston and Augusta both, I would occupy Columbia and Camden, pausing there long enough to observe the effect. I would then strike for the Charleston & Wilmington Railroad, somewhere between the Santee and Cape Fear Rivers, and, if possible, communicate with the fleet under Admiral [John A.] Dahlgren (whom I find a most agreeable gentleman, accommodating himself to our wishes and plans). Then I would favor an attack on Wilmington, in the belief that Porter and Butler will fail in their present undertaking. Charleston is now a mere desolated wreck, and is hardly worth the time it would take to starve it out. Still, I am aware that, historically and politically, much importance is attached to the place, and it may be that, apart from its military importance, both you and the Administration may prefer I should give it more attention; and it would be well for you to give me some general idea on that subject, for otherwise I would treat it as I have expressed, as a point of little importance, after all its railroads leading into the interior**

6. For the best detailed discussion of Sherman's March to the Sea, see Noah Andre Trudeau, *Southern Storm: Sherman's March to the Sea* (New York: Harper, 2007).

> **have been destroyed or occupied by us. But, on the hypothesis of ignoring Charleston and taking Wilmington, I would then favor a movement direct on Raleigh. The game is then up with [Gen. Robert E.] Lee, unless he comes out of Richmond, avoids you and fights me; in which case I should reckon on your being on his heels. Now that Hood is used up by Thomas, I feel disposed to bring the matter to an issue as quick as possible. I feel confident that I can break up the whole railroad system of South Carolina and North Carolina, and be on the Roanoke, either at Raleigh or Weldon, by the time spring fairly opens; and, if you feel confident that you can whip Lee outside of his intrenchments, I feel equally confident that I can handle him in the open country.**
>
> **One reason why I would ignore Charleston is this: that I believe Hardee will reduce the garrison to a small force, with plenty of provisions; I know that the neck back of Charleston can be made impregnable to assault, and we will hardly have time for siege operations.[7]**

The Carolinas were now in Sherman's sights, and he had special plans to punish South Carolina's population, even if those plans did not include assaulting the place where the rebellion began—Charleston.

The same day, Sherman penned a letter to the army's chief of staff, Maj. Gen. Henry W. Halleck, that further outlined his plan:

> **The truth is, the whole army is burning with an insatiable desire to wreak vengeance upon South Carolina. I almost tremble at her fate, but feel that she deserves all that seems in store for her.**
>
> **Many and many a person in Georgia asked me why we did not go to South Carolina; and, when I answered that we were en route for that State, the invariable reply was, "Well, if you will make those people feel the utmost severities of war, we will pardon you for your desolation of Georgia."**

7. William T. Sherman, *Memoirs of Gen. W. T. Sherman,* 2 vols. (New York: Charles L. Webster & Co., 1891), 2:225. Sherman referred to Maj. Gen. Benjamin F. Butler's efforts to capture Fort Fisher, North Carolina, a massive earthen fort that guarded the mouth of the Cape Fear River, which flowed north to Wilmington, and was the last significant seaport remaining open to Confederate blockade runners. He also mentioned Maj. Gen. George H. Thomas's crushing defeat of Gen. John Bell Hood's Army of Tennessee in the December 15-16, 1864, Battle of Nashville.

I look upon Columbia as quite as bad as Charleston, and I doubt if we shall spare the public buildings there as we did at Milledgeville.[8]

Sherman's men blamed the people of South Carolina for the war, and the Federals were determined to punish them for it.

On December 27, Grant authorized Sherman's proposed campaign in the Carolinas:

Without waiting further directions, then, you may make your preparations to start on your northern expedition without delay. Break up the railroads in South and North Carolina, and join the armies operating against Richmond as soon as you can. I will leave out all suggestions about the route you should take, knowing that your information, gained daily in the course of events, will be better than any that can be obtained now.

Lt. Gen. Ulysses S. Grant, general-in-chief, Union forces.

(Library of Congress)

It may not be possible for you to march to the rear of Petersburg; but, failing in this, you could strike either of the sea-coast ports in North Carolina held by us. From there you could take shipping. It would be decidedly preferable, however, if you could march the whole distance.

From the best information I have, you will find no difficulty in supplying your army until you cross the Roanoke. From there here is but a few days' march, and supplies could be collected south of the river to bring you through.[9]

Grant believed that he needed Sherman's army to join him in the trenches around Petersburg, Virginia.

Sherman, however, had other ideas. On January 2, he laid out his plan for Grant.

8. Ibid., 227-228.
9. Sherman, *Memoirs*, 2:238.

HDQRS. MILITARY DIVISION OF THE MISSISSIPPI,
In the Field, Savannah, Ga.,
January 2, 1865.
Lieut. Gen. U. S. GRANT,
City Point:

GENERAL: I have received, by the hands of General Barnard, your note of 26th and letter of 27th December. I herewith inclose to you a copy of a project which I have this morning, in strict confidence, discussed with my immediate commanders. I shall need, however, larger supplies of stores, especially grain. I will inclose to you, with this, letters from General Easton, quartermaster, and Colonel Beckwith, commissary of subsistence, setting forth what will be required, and trust you will forward them with your sanction, so that the necessary steps may be taken at once to enable me to carry out this plan on time. I wrote you very fully on the 24th and have nothing to add to that. Everything here is quiet, and if I can get the necessary supplies in my wagons I shall be ready to start at the time indicated in my project, but until those supplies are in hand I can do nothing; after they are I shall be ready to move with great rapidity. I have heard of the affair at Cape Fear; it has turned out as you will remember I expected. I have furnished General Easton a copy of the dispatch from the Secretary of War. He will retain possession of all cotton here and ship it, as fast as vessels can be had, to New York. I shall immediately send the Seventeenth Corps over to Port Royal by boats to be furnished by Admiral Dahlgren and General Foster, without interfering with General Easton's vessels, to make a lodgment on the railroad at Pocotaligo. General Barnard will remain with me a few days, and I shall send this by a staff officer, who can return on one of the vessels of the supply fleet. I suppose that now that General Butler has got through you can spare them to us.

My report of recent operations is nearly ready and will be sent on in a day or two, as soon as some further subordinate reports come in.

I am, with great respect, very truly, your friend,

W. T. SHERMAN, Major-General.[10]

10. *The War of the Rebellion: A Compilation of the Official Records of the Union and Confederate Armies*, 128 volumes in 3 series (Washington, D.C.: United States Government Printing Office, 1889), vol. 47, part 2, 6-7,

Sherman included his proposal for the coming campaign:

> **Project for January.**
> **Extremely confidential.**
>
> **Right Wing move men and artillery by transports to head of Broad River and Beaufort; get Port Royal Ferry and mass the wing at or in the neighborhood of Pocotaligo.**
>
> **Left Wing and cavalry work slowly across the causeway toward Hardeeville to open a road by which wagons can reach their corps about Broad River; also by a rapid movement of the Left secure Sisters Ferry and out as far as the Augusta road--Robertsville.**
>
> **In the meantime all guns, shot, shells, cotton, &c., to be got to a safe place, easy to guard, and provisions and wagons got ready for another swath, aiming to have our army in hand about the head of Broad River, say Pocotaligo, Robertsville, and Coosawhatchie by the 15th of January.**
>
> **Second. Move with loaded wagons by the roads leading in the direction of Columbia, which afford the best chance of forage and provisions. Howard to be at Pocotaligo 15th of January, and Slocum to be at Robertsville and Kilpatrick at or near Coosawhatchie about same date.**
>
> **General Foster's troops to occupy Savannah, and gun-boats to protect the rivers as soon as Howard gets Pocotaligo.**[11]

This was an extremely ambitious plan made necessary by the lack of sufficient shipping to move Sherman's army to Petersburg by sea. Sherman intended to divide his command into two wings.[12] His cavalry would escort the army's Left Wing and would remain to the

(hereinafter referred to as OR.) All further references are to Series 1 unless otherwise noted. Sherman referred to Rear Admiral John A. Dahlgren, commander of the U.S. Navy's Atlantic Blockading Squadron, which was then operating off the coast of South Carolina around Charleston.

11. Ibid., 7. Sherman referred to Maj. Gen. John G. Foster's Department of the South, consisting primarily of the United States Colored Troops.
12. On January 2, Easton wrote to Quartermaster General of the Army, Maj. Gen. Montgomery Meigs, "Time is a very important consideration, and I suggest that such sail vessels as it may be necessary to use in this work be towed by the steamers in order to save as much time as possible." *OR* 47, 2:8. Thus, the lack of shipping was so severe that Easton was proposing to use sailing vessels to meet the needs of supplying Sherman's force.

left of the army's advance, not in its front. Sherman expected the cavalry to distract Confederate attention from the advance of the Right Wing, which would march for Columbia. On January 5, Sherman declared to his wife, Ellen, "I do think that in the several grand epochs of this war, my name will have a prominent part."[13]

Grant approved the plan, and Sherman spent the month of January preparing himself and his army for the ordeal of marching more than 400 miles through swamps and across numerous major rivers. "Sherman was practically acquainted with the route and the topography of the country, which, like all the Southern seaboard, is low and sandy, with numerous extensive swamps, deep rivers widely swamp-bordered, and only approachable by large causeways, on which the narrow head of a column may be easily resisted by a small force of the enemy," a Federal cavalryman noted, describing the challenges that the army would soon face. "The rivers generally are long, deep, and run nearly parallel with the Savannah, and to avoid frequent and difficult crossings, it would be necessary to march into the interior upon what might be termed ridges between two or more streams until the upper and narrow waters were reached, then cross, moving eastward towards Goldsboro."[14]

Gen. P. G. T. Beauregard, commander of the Military Department of the West.

(Valentine Museum)

Between the South Carolina/ Georgia border and Columbia, Sherman would have to contend with the following major rivers: the Savannah, which served as the state border, the Salkahatchie, the north and south forks of the Edisto, and, finally, the Congaree. Located north of Columbia were the

13. M. A. DeWolfe Howe, ed., *Home Letters of General Sherman* (New York: Charles Scribner's Sons, 1909), 325.

14. "A 10th Ohio Cavalryman," "Campaign Through the Carolinas. From Savannah to Goldsboro With Kilpatrick's Cavalry. Obstacles Overcome. Crossing the Savannah on a Swaying Pontoon Bridge. Hand-to-Hand Fighting. Destroying the Property of a Bloodhound-Keeper," *The National Tribune*, April 28, 1892.

Catawba River, Big Lynch Creek (now known as Lynches River), Little Lynch Creek, and Great Pee Dee and Little Pee Dee Rivers. Each of these rivers and streams flowed diagonally across the state, from northwest to southeast, and each was a significant obstacle, all the while providing an opportunity for the Confederates to defend against attempted river crossings. General P. G. T. Beauregard, the commander of the department that included South Carolina, and who had served in South Carolina for much of the war, recognized the significance of these rivers. He intended to bottle up Sherman's army between the rivers to the south of Columbia. Beauregard knew the choke points where the Confederate forces could contest Sherman's passage.

In December 1864, after the fall of Savannah, Beauregard outlined his thoughts for the defense of South Carolina in a letter to Lt. Gen. William J. Hardee:

> **As already instructed, you should organize all your troops for the field, collecting sufficient transportation, ammunition, and provisions for an active campaign. You must have depots of provisions and forage at several points in the interior of the State. Columbia would be a very suitable point; Florence also, if you expect to move in the direction of North Carolina. Augusta, Mayfield, and Milledgeville must be depots for future operations. Your defensive lines from the Savannah River would be, as already explained to you: First, the Combahee and Salkahatchie to Barnwell Court-House, thence to the Savannah River; second, the Ashepoo and Salkahatchie to Barnwell Court-House, thence to Savannah River; third, Edisto to Branchville, thence across toward Barnwell Court-House; fourth, Edisto and Caw Caw Swamp, or Rantowles Creek; fifth, Edisto and Ashley. Wheeler's cavalry must protect your front toward Savannah River, and your right flank from Barnwell Court-House toward Augusta. At least, the larger portion of his cavalry must be south of that river, to watch the movements and check the progress of any force moving toward Augusta or the interior of Georgia, until the rest of the cavalry and other forces could be sent to give battle to the enemy.**

Beauregard produced a viable plan for the defense of South Carolina that relied on natural obstacles, which many of South Carolina's rivers offered. But he also warned Hardee not to expect significant reinforcements until the remnant of the Army of Tennessee could make its way to South Carolina. Until those reinforcements could arrive, Hardee would have to contend with Sherman with minimal forces. Beauregard intended to delay actions along the natural barriers created by the network of rivers bisecting South Carolina in order to buy sufficient time for the Army of Tennessee to arrive and fall in with his available forces. The question remained whether those troops would arrive in time to permit him to do so.[15]

Sherman recognized that the Confederates had sufficient forces available to defend both Charleston and Augusta; however, the Southerners lacked the necessary troop strength to meet his army in the field. The Confederate cavalry was the only force available with sufficient mobility and numbers to resist Sherman's advancing army in open battle. Sherman later wrote:

> **I had a species of contempt for these scattered and inconsiderable forces, knew that they could hardly delay us an hour; and the only serious question that occurred to me was, would General Lee sit down in Richmond (besieged by General Grant), and permit us, almost unopposed, to pass through the States of South and North Carolina, cutting off and consuming the very supplies on which he depended to feed his army in Virginia, or would he make an effort to escape from General Grant, and endeavor to catch us inland somewhere between Columbia and Raleigh? I knew full well at the time that the broken fragments of Hood's army (which had escaped from Tennessee) were being hurried rapidly across Georgia, by Augusta, to make junction in my front; estimating them at the maximum twenty-five thousand men, and Hardee's, Wheeler's, and Hampton's forces at fifteen thousand, made forty thousand; which, if handled with spirit and energy, would constitute a formidable force, and might make the passage of such rivers as the Santee and Cape Fear a difficult undertaking...Still, it was extremely desirable in one march to reach Goldsboro' in the State of North Carolina (distant four hundred and twenty-five miles), a point of great convenience for ulterior operations, by reason of the two railroads which meet there, coming from the seacoast at Wilmington and Newbern.[16]**

Sherman knew that he had to move carefully and quickly in order to prevent the Army of Tennessee from making a juncture with the other scattered, and generally ineffectual, Confederate forces in his front.

15. *OR* 44, 1009-1010.
16. Sherman, *Memoirs*, 2:271-272.

Sherman made it clear that he had no intention of advancing on Charleston, which was stoutly defended. In a meeting with Lieutenant Commander Stephen B. Luce during the planning phase of the campaign, Sherman declared, "You navy fellows have been hammering away at Charleston for the past three years. But just wait until I get into South Carolina; I will cut her communications, and Charleston will fall into your hands like a ripe pear." Luce later noted, "Charleston fell into our hands just as General Sherman said it would, by severing her communications."[17] Sherman's strategy for his upcoming campaign was brilliant—but was it logistically feasible?

Sherman's army consisted of 60,079 men divided in two separate armies: the Army of the Tennessee, commanded by Maj. Gen. Oliver O. Howard,[18] and the Army of Georgia, commanded by Maj. Gen.

17. Stephen B. Luce, "Naval Administration, III," *Proceedings, U. S. Naval Institute* 29, no. 4 (December 1903), 820.
18. Oliver Otis Howard was born in Leeds, Maine, on November 8, 1830. He studied at an academy in North Yarmouth, Maine, and put himself through Bowdoin College by teaching school during the off seasons. He graduated from Bowdoin in 1850 and was then appointed to West Point, where he graduated in the class of 1854, along with Robert E. Lee's son George Washington Custis Lee, J. E. B. Stuart, Stephen D. Lee, William D. Pender, and Stephen H. Weed. Howard spent most of his pre-war career as a mathematics instructor at West Point, where he served as a first lieutenant of ordnance at the outbreak of the Civil War. He was elected colonel of the 3rd Maine at the end of May 1861 and resigned his regular commission on June 7. Howard commanded a brigade in Samuel P. Heintzelman's division at the First Battle of Bull Run, in Virginia, and was promoted to brigadier general, even though his command was driven from the field in a rout. During the Peninsula Campaign, he commanded a Second 2nd Corps brigade and lost his right arm to a combat wound in Virginia at the Battle of Seven Pines in May 1862. Eighty days later, he returned to duty and commanded the army's rear guard during the retreat from the Second Battle of Bull Run. At Antietam, in Maryland, Howard succeeded to command of the 2nd Division, Second 2nd Corps after Sedgwick was wounded, and he led the division at Fredericksburg, Virginia. On November 29, 1862, he was promoted to major general. On March 31, 1863, he was given command of the Eleventh Corps, which was poorly led and subsequently routed at Chancellorsville, Virginia, and Gettysburg, Pennsylvania, making his command the butt of the entire army's jokes. When the 11th and 12th corps were sent to Chattanooga, Tennessee, that fall, Howard remained in command of his corps, but after the death of Maj. Gen. James B. McPherson, he assumed command of the Army of the Tennessee, which was Sherman's right wing during the Carolinas Campaign. He was commissioned brigadier general in the Regular Army at the end of the war and appointed first commissioner of the Freedmen's Bureau, an organization that became rife with fraud, corruption, and inefficiency under his leadership. He was acquitted by a court of inquiry in 1874 and then helped to found Howard University in Washington, D.C. During the 1870s and 1880s, he served in the Indian Wars, and he was superintendent of West Point for a time. When he was promoted to major general in 1886, he commanded the Division of the East until his retirement in 1894. Howard spent the rest of his life writing, speaking, and engaging in

Maj. Gen. Oliver Otis Howard, commander of the Army of the Tennessee.

(Library of Congress)

Maj. Gen. Henry W. Slocum, commander of the Army of Georgia.

(Library of Congress)

Henry W. Slocum.[19] This estimate does not include the troops of Maj. Gen. John G. Foster's Department of the South, which included Brig. Gen. John Hatch's troops, operating to screen Sherman's right by keeping pressure on Charleston. In addition, a cavalry division numbering approximately 4,500 troopers, commanded by Bvt. Maj. Gen. Judson Kilpatrick, accompanied Sherman's army group and operated with the Left Wing.

religious and educational activities. In 1893, he was awarded the Medal of Honor for bravery at Seven Pines. He died on October 26, 1909. Biographer Ezra J. Warner said Howard's career "must constitute one of the great paradoxes of American military history: no officer entrusted with the field direction of troops has ever equaled Howard's record for surviving so many tactical errors of judgment and disregard of orders, emerging later not only with increased rank, but on one occasion with the thanks of Congress." Warner, *Generals in Blue*, 237-239.

19. Henry Warner Slocum was born on September 27, 1827, at Delphi, Onondaga County, New York. He attended Cazenovia Seminary, taught school for several years, and then entered West Point, graduating in 1852. After serving in Florida in the Seminole Wars and garrison duty in Charleston Harbor, he resigned his commission in 1856 to begin the practice of law, a profession he had prepared himself for during his army career. He served as the county treasurer in Syracuse, New York, as well as a state legislator and as a colonel and artillery instructor in the New York State Militia. On May 21, 1861, he was commissioned colonel of the 27th New York, which fought at the First Battle of Bull Run, where Slocum received a thigh wound. He was promoted to brigadier general of volunteers on August 9, 1861. When he

This campaign offered almost unprecedented logistical challenges. On January 2, Sherman's chief quartermaster wrote to the U.S. Army's chief quartermaster, Maj. Gen. Montgomery Meigs, indicating that Sherman required 60 days' worth of grain for 35,000 animals and rations for 70,000 infantrymen as he prepared to march, as well as shallow-draft steamboats and barges. "The animals of this army are in great jeopardy at present for the want of grain, as but little has as yet arrived, and the animals have been without for several days," Sherman's supply officer, Bvt. Brig. Gen. Langdon C. Easton, recounted. Easton remarked that time was of the essence; the grain for Sherman's animals had to be on hand when the campaign began.[20] Since Sherman intended to march through the interior of South Carolina, there were limited options for the army to be resupplied. The Union army would have to live off the land; it could not halt anywhere without immediately running short on rations. Consequently, Sherman's men would have to keep moving to remain sufficiently supplied for the duration of the campaign.

In addition to 35,000 animals that required subsistence, Sherman's command included 68 guns, about 2,500 wagons, and 600 ambulances. Moving such a large command through deep swamps and across wide rivers only added to the challenges faced by the Union army. Furthermore, the Union cavalry's movements and effectiveness would be severely constrained by these logistical challenges for the coming campaign. Not until the Left Wing and the cavalry reached the town of

returned to duty, he took command of a brigade of Gen. William B. Franklin's division, and when Franklin became a corps commander, Slocum assumed command of the division. On July 25, 1862, he was promoted to major general and led his division through the Peninsula Campaign and at the Second Battle of Bull Run, where he helped to cover rank and Maj. Gen. John Pope's retreat. He took command of the 12th Corps after the Battle of Antietam. The 12th Corps took heavy losses at the Battles of Chancellorsville and Gettysburg. In September 1863, the 11th and 12th corps were ordered to report to Chattanooga, under command of Maj. Gen. Joseph Hooker. Slocum tendered his resignation, but President Abraham Lincoln refused it. He served in the District of Vicksburg for a time in 1864, and then, after the death of Army of the Tennessee commander Maj. Gen. James B. McPherson during the Atlanta Campaign, Slocum was called to join the army as commander of the 20th Corps (which consisted of the combined 11th and 12th corps). During the March to the Sea, Slocum commanded the Army of Georgia and Sherman's Left Wing. On September 28, 1865, he resigned his commission and returned to Syracuse, New York. He lost an election for Secretary of State and moved to Brooklyn, New York, where he resumed practicing law after refusing a commission as colonel in the Regular Army. Slocum served in Congress for three terms as a Democrat and on the Board of Gettysburg Monument Commission. He died on April 14, 1894. Warner, *Generals in Blue*, 451-453. Thus, two of Sherman's army commanders—Howard and Slocum—were refugees from the Army of the Potomac.

20. *OR* 47, 2:8.

Barnwell, South Carolina, where Sherman could rely upon rail lines for supplies, would they be able to live off the land effectively.[21]

Winter weather conditions did not favor an aggressive campaign. "The heavy Winter rains began early in January, which rendered the roads execrable," an officer of the 10th Ohio Cavalry observed, "the rivers became so swollen that all their channels were filled, overflowing the vast extent of rice fields lying along their courses."[22]

"By the 15th of January I was all ready to resume the march," Sherman reported. "Preliminary to this, General Howard, commanding the Right Wing, was ordered to embark his command at Thunderbolt, transport it to Beaufort, S.C., and thence by the 15th of January make a lodgment on the Charleston Railroad, at or near Pocotaligo." The 17th Corps established a supply depot near the mouth of Pocotaligo Creek near Hilton Head, South Carolina. Slocum's Left Wing and Kilpatrick's cavalry received orders to rendezvous near Robertsville and Coosawhatchie, South Carolina, with a depot of supplies at Purrysburg, or Sisters Ferry, in Georgia, on the Savannah River.[23] Sherman massed his army in the area between Savannah, Georgia, and Pocotaligo, South Carolina, a distance of approximately 30 miles, collecting supplies and preparing for the campaign.

Slocum's Left Wing "on the west bank of the river, with the cavalry, were to cross at Sister's Ferry, while Howard should advance from Beaufort to Pocotaligo, driving Hardee's forces over the Combahee River, and occupy the country between that stream and the Coosawatchie," a Union officer recalled. "Howard's movements would thus threaten Charleston, while Slocum looked toward Augusta; so that the enemy would be left in doubt as to Sherman's purpose, though the position of his troops would be the best possible for the

21. On January 21, Sherman told Grant, "Our supplies have come daily, that is, we have never had four days' forage ahead, but I will depend on enough coming to get me out to the neighborhood of Barnwell, where we will find some." *OR* 47, 2: 103. The logistics of the Carolinas Campaign make for a fascinating study. Sherman's army had to build its own roads as it marched, all while being cut off from resupply sources.
22. "A 10th Ohio Cavalryman," "Campaign Through the Carolinas."
23. *OR* 47, 1:18. This plan had to be changed due to the logistical challenges. Instead of becoming a depot, Sisters Ferry became the Left Wing's main crossing point into South Carolina. Lieutenant Commander Stephen Luce led a small group of steamers up the Savannah River to Sisters Ferry to provide logistical support for the Left Wing. "After hearing General Sherman's clear exposition of the military situation, the scales seemed to fall from my eyes….It dawned on me that there were certain fundamental principles underlying military operations…principles of general application whether the operations were on land or at sea," Luce later said. Luce, "Naval Administration, III," 820.

advance upon Columbia, which for the first stage of the campaign was Sherman's objective. The same would be true of Slocum, for Robertsville was only about 30 miles nearly east from Sister's Ferry, and the wagons of each column could therefore be full when communication should be broken with Savannah, which place Gen. Foster was to garrison."[24]

On January 25, Sherman ordered that Maj. Gen. Francis P. Blair, Jr.'s forces demonstrate against the Combahee Ferry and the railroad bridge "across the Salkehatchie, merely to amuse the enemy, who had evidently adopted that river as his defensive line against our supposed objective, the city of Charleston." Hatch's troops of Foster's command then replaced Blair's infantrymen, who continued the demonstration.[25] Sherman personally reconnoitered the line; he noticed that heavy rains had swollen the river so that water stood in the swamps at depths reaching up to twenty feet in some areas for more than a mile. "Not having the remotest intention of approaching Charleston, a comparatively small force was able, by seeming preparations to cross over, to keep in their front a considerable force of the enemy disposed to contest our advance on Charleston."[26]

Kilpatrick's cavalry prepared for its important role in the campaign. Civil War cavalry had three main missions: scouting, screening, and intelligence gathering. Scouting entailed finding marching routes for the army. Screening, a harder task, required interposing the cavalry between the main body of the army and the enemy in an effort to keep the enemy from finding the main body. These were important missions, but no mission was more important than intelligence gathering. "There are no more important duties, which an officer may be called upon to perform, than those of collecting and arranging the information upon which either the general, or daily operations of a campaign must be based," Dennis Hart Mahan, the West Point instructor who had taught both Judson Kilpatrick and Joseph Wheeler, succinctly declared.[27]

William T. Sherman did not use his cavalry in a traditional sense. While Kilpatrick's horsemen operated on the left flank of Slocum's

---

24. "A 10th Ohio Cavalryman," "Campaign of the Carolinas."
25. While this demonstration occurred, the rest of Foster's Department of the South demonstrated on the Stono and Edisto Rivers on the coast. This was part of a rather intricate plan aimed to keep the troops of Maj. Gen. Lafayette McLaws pinned closer to the coast and away from the roads to Columbia. The men of the Department of the South found this duty frustrating.
26. *OR* 47, 1:18.
27. Dennis H. Mahan, *An Elementary Treatise on Advanced-Guard, Out-Post, and Detachment Service of Troops, and the Manner of Posting and Handling Them in the Presence of an Enemy* (New York: John Wiley, 1861), 105.

Left Wing as it made its way across South Carolina, their primary task was to contend with the still-determined Confederate cavalry of Maj. Gen. Joseph Wheeler. Kilpatrick's troopers were to keep Wheeler's men as far away from the Union infantry as possible. Any intelligence gathering was done either by detachments of mounted infantry that Sherman sent out or by specific detachments of cavalry assigned to serve with specific infantry corps. Sherman, apparently, was not concerned about Kilpatrick's command's traditional scouting or screening functions, because his cavalry did not serve this role during the march through South Carolina.

The Union cavalry camps buzzed with anticipation of the impending campaign. "For weeks the utmost activity had prevailed at all points; fresh horses for remounts had been furnished from those captured on the march; the sick and wounded sent to Savannah; the division had been reviewed by Gen. Sherman before his departure; so by the 30th a thousand flags were again floating in the breeze," a captain of the 10th Ohio Cavalry recalled.[28]

Sherman's movements during the opening phases of the campaign were constrained by the logistical problems described herein, as well as by the inclement winter weather. By January 29 the floodwaters had receded and the roads around Savannah had finally dried out sufficiently to allow Sherman to put his army in motion. Slocum's Left Wing troops marched for Sisters Ferry. In the meantime, the 20th Corps left Savannah and marched toward Hardeeville, South Carolina, moving into the open. That, in turn, permitted Howard's 17th Corps to move out of Beaufort, South Carolina, while three divisions of the 15th Corps headed for Pocotaligo. The Right Wing had its wagons loaded and was ready to march. "I therefore directed General Howard to move one corps, the Seventeenth, along the Salkehatchie, as high up as River's Bridge, and the other, the Fifteenth by Hickory Hill, Loper's Cross-Roads, Angley's Post-Office, and Buford's Bridge," Sherman reported. He left one division at Pocotaligo, feinting at the Salkehatchie River railroad bridge and ferry. Sherman intended to turn the enemy flank and force the Confederates to retreat across the Edisto River.[29] Sherman's two wings covered a front nearly 40 miles across.

Sherman's soldiers often built their own roads as they marched. "The whole country was a vast quagmire," an Ohio soldier recorded. "All the roads had to be corduroyed for the passage of the artillery and wagons...For weeks the clothing of the soldiers was saturated with water...The men slept in their soaked garments, lying upon boughs and

28. "A 10th Ohio Cavalryman," "Campaign of the Carolinas."
29. *OR* 47, 1:18-19.

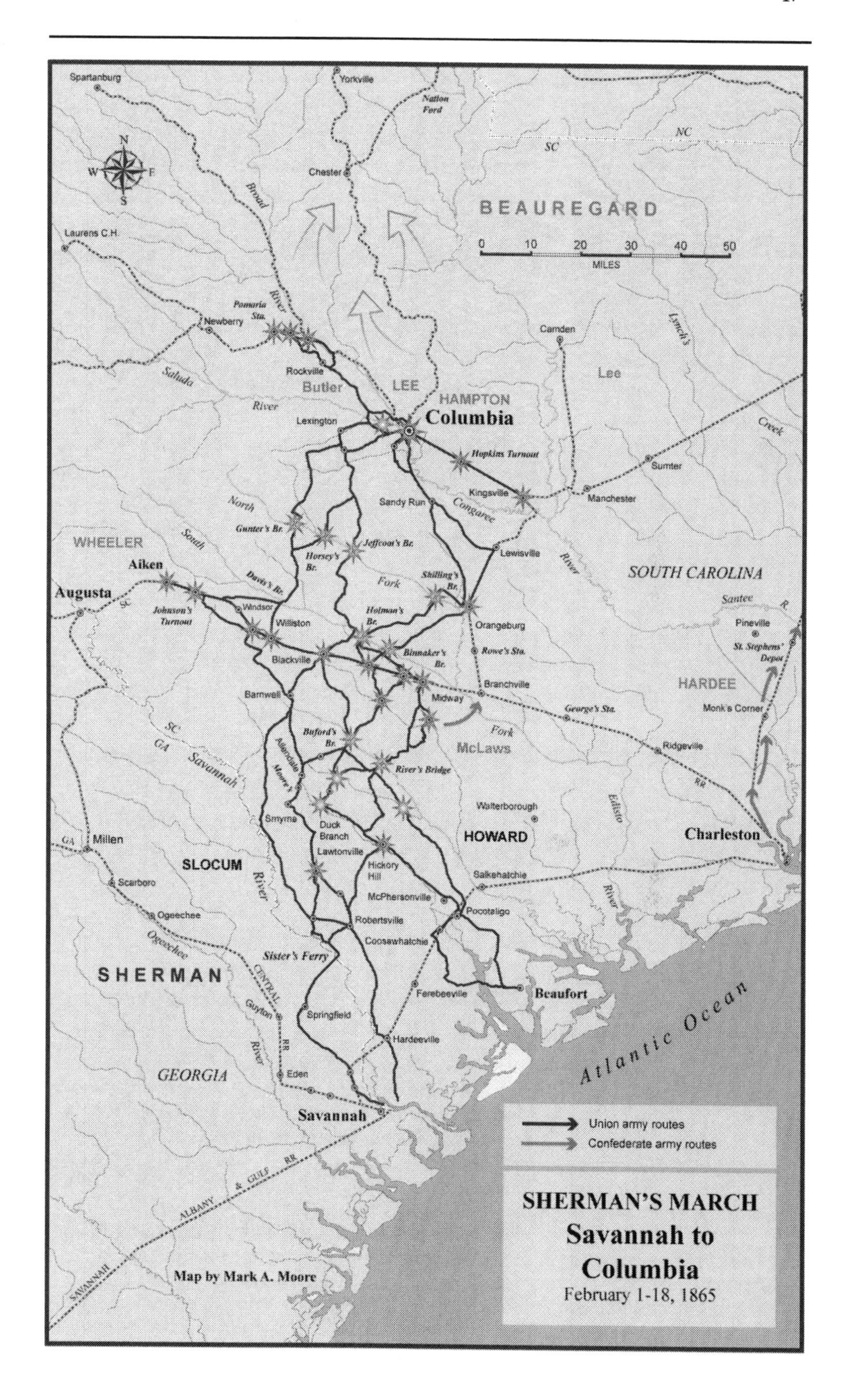
SHERMAN'S MARCH
Savannah to Columbia
February 1-18, 1865
Map by Mark A. Moore
Union army routes
Confederate army routes
BEAUREGARD
0 10 20 30 40 50
MILES
Spartanburg
Yorkville
Nation Ford
NC
SC
Chester
Broad
Laurens C.H.
Pomaria Sta.
Newberry
River
Camden
Lynch's
Lee
Saluda
Rockville
Butler
LEE
HAMPTON
River
Lexington
Columbia
Creek
Hopkins Turnout
Sumter
Kingsville
Manchester
Sandy Run
Congaree
North
Gunter's Br.
Jeffcoat's Br.
Horsey's Br.
Lewisville
WHEELER
South
Aiken
River
Augusta
Davis's Br.
Shilling's Br.
SOUTH CAROLINA
Fork
Santee
Johnson's Turnout
Windsor
Holman's Br.
Orangeburg
Pineville
Williston
St. Stephens' Depot
Binnaker's Br.
Rowe's Sta.
Blackville
HARDEE
Branchville
Barnwell
Midway
George's Sta.
Monk's Corner
Buford's Br.
Fork
SC
GA
Savannah
McLaws
Ridgeville
River's Bridge
RR
Walterborough
Edisto
Smyrna
Duck Branch
HOWARD
Charleston
Millen
Lawtonville
SLOCUM
Hickory Hill
Salkehatchie
Scarboro
River
McPhersonville
Ogeechee
Pocotaligo
Robertsville
Ogeechee
Coosawhatchie
Sister's Ferry
SHERMAN
CENTRAL
Ferebeeville
Beaufort
Guyton
Springfield
Atlantic Ocean
River
RR
Hardeeville
GEORGIA
Eden
Savannah
ALBANY & GULF RR
SAVANNAH

logs. The immense toil and labor of moving...under such conditions cannot be conceived. The endurance of the soldiers was marvelous. Day after day they pushed on, cheerful and patient, counting no obstacle too great to be overcome, and with a faith in 'Uncle Billy' that was measureless."[30]

A trooper of the 9th Ohio Cavalry described the process: low ground was "made passable by cutting small trees, trimming off the limbs and laying them side by side across the road. These lying in the mud and water were not very solid so that occasionally a horse's hoof would slip between the logs and over the log he would go likely breaking his leg."[31] This was hard, arduous work and fraught with danger. Their efforts prompted Confederate Gen. Joseph E. Johnston to later admiringly declare that "when I heard that Sherman had not only started, but was marching through those very swamps at the rate of thirteen miles a day, making corduroy road every foot of the way, I made up my mind that there was no such army since the days of Julius Caesar."[32]

The weather had been cold for about a week, with a slight snowfall, making the passage of the army's wagons and artillery easier. Kilpatrick's troopers marched at daylight on January 30, passing through Savannah, moving to the left, and taking the river road toward Sisters Ferry. The Union horsemen arrived there about noon the next day, capturing two small boats and securing the ferry with little opposition.[33]

"The actual invasion of South Carolina has begun," Maj. George W. Nichols, one of Sherman's staff officers, wrote in his diary on February 1. "The well known sight of columns of black smoke meets our gaze again; this time houses are burning, and South Carolina has commenced to pay an installment, long overdue, on her debt to justice and humanity. With the help of God, we will have principal and interest before we leave her borders."[34] Sherman's notorious

30. Wilbur F. Hinman, *The Story of the Sherman Brigade, the Camp, the March, the Bivouac, the Battle and How the Boys Lived and Died During Four Years of Active Field Service* (Alliance, OH: privately published, 1897), 909.
31. J. H. McKeever, ed., *He Rode with Sherman from Atlanta to the Sea* (Aberdeen, SD: McKeever Press, 1947), 22.
32. Michael C. Garber, Jr. "Reminiscences of the Burning of Columbia, South Carolina," *Indiana Magazine of History*, Vol. 11, No. 4 (1915), 287.
33. "A 10th Ohio Cavalryman," "Campaign of the Carolinas." According to Lieutenant Commander Luce, while planning the Carolinas Campaign, Sherman indicated that he wanted a gunboat available to him to protect his pontoons across the Savannah River. Luce, "Naval Administration, III," 820.
34. George Ward Nichols, *The Story of the Great March, from the Diary of a Staff Officer* (New York: Harper & Bros., 1865), 131.

"bummers"—foragers—fanned out across the countryside, pillaging as they went.[35]

"After reaching the State of South Carolina, it seemed as if the enemy were invading the State from all directions—north, south, east and west," one of Wheeler's troopers lamented. "It was a difficult matter to calculate when and where we would meet the next marching column. We would meet and check them temporarily, when we would be threatened by another. It seemed that the enemy were making an effort to cover every community in the whole State, still exhibiting their propensity to burn and destroy."[36]

"Wheeler's cavalry [had]... felled trees, burned bridges, and made obstructions to impede our march," Sherman recalled. "But so well organized were our pioneer battalions, and so strong and intelligent our men, that obstructions seemed only to quicken their progress. Felled trees were removed and bridges rebuilt by the heads of columns before the rear could close up."[37]

Maj. Gen. Lafayette McLaws, commander of a division in Hardee's Department.

(Library of Congress)

About 5,000 veteran Confederate troops under Maj. Gen. Lafayette McLaws held the line of the Salkehatchie River in force. Approximately 2,100 of McLaws's men, commanded by Col. George P. Harrison, consisting of both infantry and artillery, were entrenched at Rivers and Buford's Bridges.[38] The only way to get to the main bridge was across a

35. For a detailed discussion of the work done by Sherman's bummers, see Elmore, *Carnival of Destruction*, 82-98.
36. George B. Guild, *A Brief Narrative of the Fourth Tennessee Cavalry, Wheeler's Corps, Army of Tennessee* (Nashville, TN: privately published, 1913), 113-114.
37. Rev. G. S. Bradley, *The Star Corps; Or, Notes of an Army Chaplain, During Sherman's Famous "March to the Sea"* (Milwaukee, WI: Jermain & Brightman, 1865), 255.
38. *OR* 47, 2:1069.

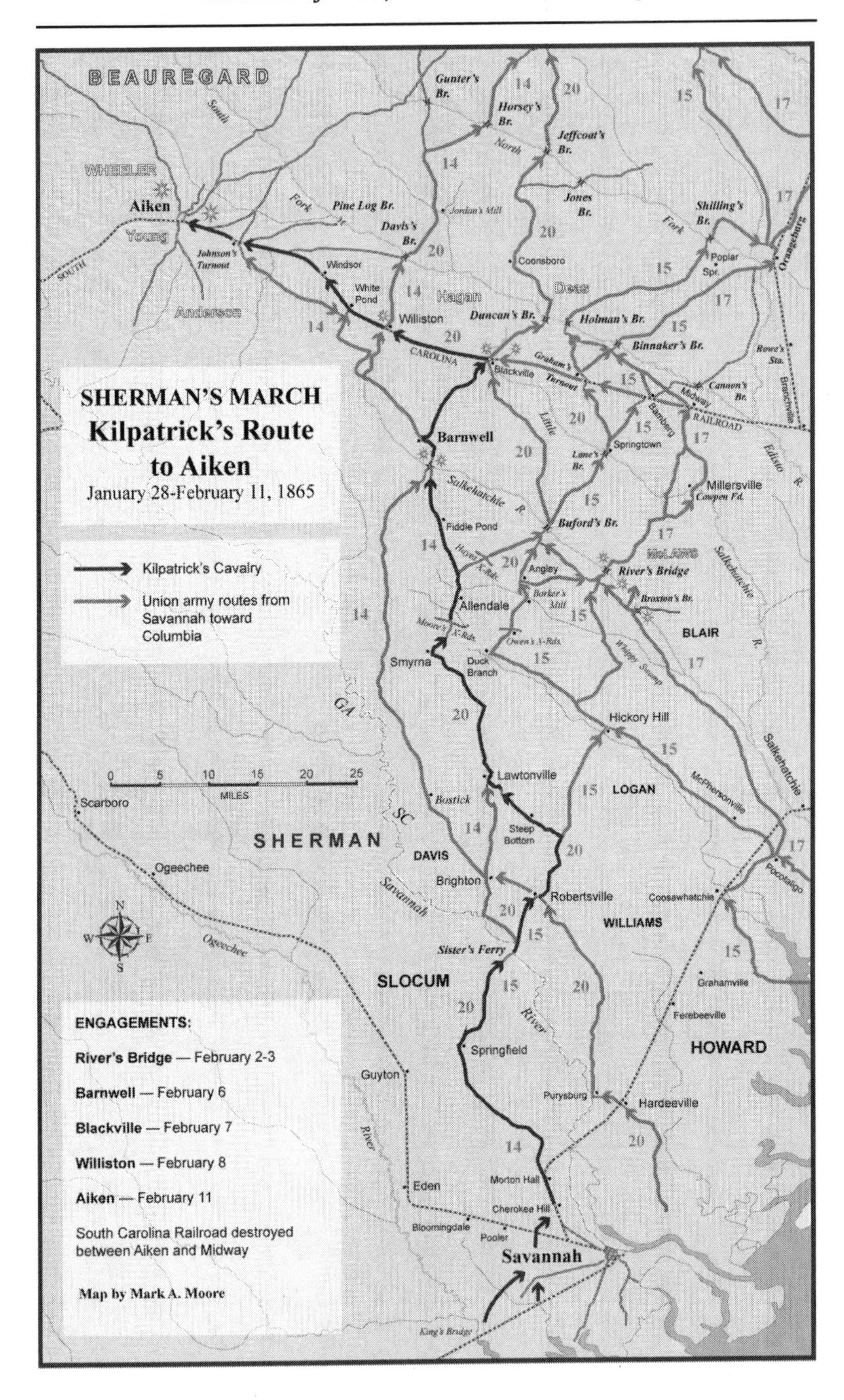
SHERMAN'S MARCH
Kilpatrick's Route
to Aiken
January 28-February 11, 1865
Kilpatrick's Cavalry
Union army routes from Savannah toward Columbia
ENGAGEMENTS:
River's Bridge — February 2-3
Barnwell — February 6
Blackville — February 7
Williston — February 8
Aiken — February 11
South Carolina Railroad destroyed between Aiken and Midway
Map by Mark A. Moore
BEAUREGARD
WHEELER
Young
Anderson
Hagan
Dean
McLAWS
SHERMAN
SLOCUM
DAVIS
LOGAN
WILLIAMS
BLAIR
HOWARD
Aiken
Johnson's Turnout
Windsor
White Pond
Williston
Blackville
Barnwell
Fiddle Pond
Allendale
Smyrna
Duck Branch
Lawtonville
Bostick
Steep Bottom
Brighton
Robertsville
Sister's Ferry
Springfield
Guyton
Eden
Purysburg
Hardeeville
Morton Hall
Cherokee Hill
Bloomingdale
Pooler
Savannah
King's Bridge
Scarboro
Ogeechee
Hickory Hill
McPhersonville
Pocotaligo
Coosawhatchie
Grahamville
Ferebeeville
Springtown
Millersville
Midway
Bamberg
Orangeburg
Coonsboro
Poplar Spr.
Gunter's Br.
Horsey's Br.
Jeffcoat's Br.
Jones Br.
Shilling's Br.
Pine Log Br.
Davis's Br.
Duncan's Br.
Holman's Br.
Binnaker's Br.
Cannon's Br.
Graham's Turnout
Lane's Br.
Buford's Br.
River's Bridge
Broxton's Br.
Angley
Barker's Mill
Owen's X-Rds.
Moore's X-Rds.
Hayes' X-Rds.
Rowe's Sta.
Branchville
SOUTH CAROLINA RAILROAD
0 5 10 15 20 25
MILES
GA
SC
N
W
E
S

causeway "built of logs and dirt where there are bridges, of which there are thirteen in number from twenty to forty feet long, many of them spanning considerable bodies of water."[39]

"We encountered [Maj. Gen. Joseph] Wheeler's [Confederate] cavalry, which had obstructed the road by felling trees, but our men picked these up and threw them aside, so that this obstruction hardly delayed us an hour," the Federal commander explained.[40] Sherman ordered the 17th Corps of the Right Wing to take Rivers Bridge and the 15th Corps, also of the Right Wing, to capture Buford's Bridge.

Two regiments of Georgia infantry of Colonel George P. Harrison, Jr.'s brigade of McLaws's division, numbering 565 effectives, as well as the 3rd Arkansas Cavalry, defended Rivers Bridge. These well-entrenched troops repulsed a direct Union assault down the narrow causeway through thick swamp on February 2. "The fighting in the dense woods and along the causeways was close and murderous for such few numbers," the historian of the 3rd Arkansas Cavalry remembered. Lieutenant James P. Morgan, 3rd Arkansas Cavalry, was mortally wounded in this fighting, while Lt. Col. Marzaime J. Henderson and Maj. William Blackwell, of the same regiment, were severely wounded.[41] Several gray-clad horse soldiers were killed.[42]

On February 3, two divisions of the 17th Corps flanked the Confederate defenders out of their position at Rivers Bridge "by crossing the swamp, nearly three miles wide, with water varying from knee to shoulder deep. The weather was bitter cold, and Generals [Joseph A.] Mower and [Giles A.] Smith led their divisions in person, on foot, waded the swamp, made a lodgment below the bridge, and turned on the rebel brigade which guarded it, driving it in confusion and disorder toward Branchville," Sherman recounted. Wheeler's troopers resisted Sherman's advance, which was precisely what Sherman did not want. Mounted Confederate troopers of the 8th and 10th Texas Cavalry charged the infantry repeatedly but failed to halt their advance. The Union infantry drove the Confederates away at the cost of one officer and 17 men killed, with 70 men wounded. The retreating Southern horse soldiers burned the bridges and causeways at

39. Andrew J. Boies, *Record of the Thirty-Third Massachusetts Volunteer Infantry, from Aug. 1862 to Aug. 1865* (Fitchburg, MA: Sentinel Printing Co., 1880), 111.

40. Sherman, *Memoirs*, 2:272.

41. There is now a battlefield state park on the site of this fighting, and Lieutenant Morgan of the 3rd Arkansas rests in the park's Confederate cemetery.

42. Calvin L. Collier, *The War Child's Children: The Story of the Third Regiment, Arkansas Cavalry, Confederate States Army* (Little Rock, AR: privately published, 1965), 127.

Cowpens Ford before retiring to Graham's Station on the South Carolina Railroad.[43]

Captain Asbury Z. Gatch commanded Company L of the 9th Ohio Cavalry. That night he penned a remarkable letter to his wife. "The duties, privations and hardships of soldiering are one of the most arduous and trying character," he wrote. "But it is my conviction after 13 months experience in the Service, 12 in the field, that there is no duty so trying, no intolerable and no exposure that bears so sensibly upon the Constitution. And so much disheartens and overwhelms one at the separation from the loved ones from home. I can endure the weary march. I can relish the can food. I can face the shot strengthened by the hope that I will escape its fury. But I can not endure this long separation from those who are dearer to me than life itself." Gatch's eloquence spoke for the war-weary men of both sides.[44]

On the afternoon of February 3, after working night and day to complete the pontoons across the Savannah River, the Federal cavalry made their way down to the riverbank and began crossing on a pontoon bridge that evening. "The current was quite rapid and the cable on the east bank had twice broken and the pontoon bridge lay upon the stream nearly in the shape of a half-moon," an officer of the 10th Ohio Cavalry recalled. "It was quite dark when the column commenced moving; the roaring of the waters and swaying of the bridge as we led on by companies made the men nervous and the horses uneasy, and when we reached terra-firma we felt at least safe in taking a full breath." Two men, along with their horses, drowned while crossing the river.[45]

"The country for miles was so covered with water that it was with difficulty, in the darkness, that our horses could keep the road, and fires had to be built here and there by the advance guard in order to find our way. About midnight it commenced raining in torrents, and it was not until near morning that the division, when near Robertsville, found suitable ground to make a halt and get closed up. Here we waited until about noon, when our teams came up, passing through the town, which was burned. That night we camped near Lawtonville. In the morning we came upon Wheeler's rear-guard, driving them through the town, which was mostly burned, nearly all of the inhabitants having fled."[46]

43. Ibid.
44. Gary L. Knepp, ed., *To Crown Myself with Honor: The Wartime Letters of Captain Asbury Gatch* (Milford, OH: Little Miami Publishing Co., 2011), 147.
45. "A 10th Ohio Cavalryman," "Campaign of the Carolinas."
46. Ibid.

"This morning we found ourselves on a fine plantation, plenty of corn for our horses, but the splendid mansion was burned to the ground," a sergeant of the 10th Ohio Cavalry recorded in his diary. The next day he wrote that they left "at 7, marched about 15 miles through a splendid rich country, burned nearly everything on the route, are now encamped on a fine plantation for the night."[47]

"The line of the Salkehatchie being thus broken, the enemy retreated at once behind the Edisto at Branchville, and the whole army was pushed rapidly to the South Carolina Railroad at Midway, Bamberg (or Lowry's Station), and Graham's Station," Sherman stated. Kilpatrick's troopers drove off the Confederate cavalrymen once more. Sherman's army succeeded in cutting the crucial South Carolina Railroad.[48]

Thus, Sherman had accomplished his goal: he had drawn the Right Wing around McLaws's infantry, which remained firmly in place, and cut the railroad. While the Right Wing maneuvered, Sherman kept the Left Wing and Kilpatrick's cavalry uncommitted. It was now time to commit the cavalry. Sherman told Kilpatrick, "Mystify the enemy all you can, but break that road whilst I move straight on it about Lowry's."[49]

On February 6, John M. King of the 92nd Illinois Mounted Infantry recalled that he and his comrades put their cartridge boxes on their heads and held their guns over them while they waded the cold waters of the Salkehatchie, all while under enemy fire. They then "charged up the steep hill opposite and drove them out of their earthworks."[50]

"We first saw the enemy at Salkehatchie Swamp, near Barnwell, February 6," Brig. Gen. Smith D. Atkins, commander of the Union Second Cavalry Brigade, said. "The main force of Wheeler's (rebel) cavalry had here waited our advance."[51] That day, the Union cavalry occupied "an old, though very wealthy and aristocratic town"—as a trooper of the 92nd Illinois Mounted Infantry described it—after driving off a small force of Confederate horsemen.[52] The Union soldiers had a special hatred for the town of Barnwell; it was the

47. George E. Carter, ed., *The Story of Joshua D. Breynfogle, Private, 4th Ohio Infantry (10th Ohio Cavalry) and the Civil War* (Lewiston, NY: Edward Mellen Press, 2001), 320.
48. *OR* 47, 1:19.
49. Ibid., 2:312.
50. Claire E. Swedberg, ed., *Three Years with the 92nd Illinois: The Civil War Diary of John M. King* (Mechanicsburg, PA: Stackpole Books, 1999), 235.
51. *OR* 47, 2:878.
52. Robert E. Berkenes, ed., *Private William Boddy's Civil War Journal: Empty Saddles—Empty Sleeves* (Altoona, IA: TiffCor Publishing House, 1996), 168.

hometown of Senator Robert Woodward Barnwell, an early leader of the secession movement in South Carolina and who was now a member of the Confederate Congress. Robert Barnwell also cast the vote that ensured the election of Jefferson Davis as the president of the Confederacy. Sherman felt that the town should be burned to the ground since it carried the name of one of the Confederacy's leading secessionists.[53]

In addition, Barnwell was the site of a Confederate camp of instruction, Camp Butler, in the opening days of the Civil War. This camp was located at Johnson's Turnout—modern-day Montmorenci—on the railroad and served as a receiving center for Confederate volunteers. Some of the best-known Confederate infantry regiments, including the units that made up Maj. Gen. Joseph Kershaw's brigade that earned fame in the Army of Northern Virginia, were trained at Camp Butler. Sherman and his men were burning to punish the town of Barnwell, and punish it they did.[54]

Kilpatrick established his headquarters at a fine hotel in the town. A controversy developed about what happened next. Kilpatrick claimed that after his cavalry entered Barnwell, his troopers went to work as instructed, destroying government buildings and public property. However, that endeavor soon spun out of control. His division's journal indicated that "in spite of every effort of the general commanding to prevent it, was laid in ashes."[55] Kilpatrick later contended that he had restricted the damage where possible.

Local accounts hold that once Kilpatrick's troopers entered the town, they searched for bales of cotton to burn. The local citizenry pulled the cotton from its bales and scattered it in the woods; the rain-soaked cotton would not burn. Kilpatrick considered this to be a

53. Robert Woodward Barnwell also served in the antebellum United States Senate and was a secessionist firebrand. See, John Barnwell, ed. "Hamlet to Hotspur: Letters of Robert Woodward Barnwell to Robert Barnwell Rhett." *South Carolina Historical Magazine 77* (October 1976): 236-37, 247. Barnwell's father, Robert Gibbes Barnwell, for whom the town was named, served as a lieutenant colonel during the Revolutionary War and then, after the Revolutionary War ended, represented South Carolina in the Confederation Congress and the U.S. House of Representatives.

54. For details on Camp Butler, see Gasper Loren Toole, II, *Ninety Years in Aiken County: Memoirs of Aiken County and Its People* (Aiken, SC: self-published, 1958), 18 and J. Keith Jones, ed., *Boys of Diamond Hill: The Lives and Civil War Letters of the Boyd Family of Abbeville County, South Carolina* (Jefferson, NC: McFarland, 2011), 9-13. See, also, "Historical marker set up for Camp Butler," *Aiken Standard*, November 24, 2012. Toole stated that the property where Camp Butler had stood "fell a victim to General Kilpatrick's forces on his own premises." Ibid.

55. *OR* 47, 1:145-146.

hostile act and decided to burn the town to the ground. "During the night fires broke out all over the city. Kilpatrick was three times burned out, having to move his quarters from place to place," an officer of the 10th Ohio Cavalry recollected. "The fire spread rapidly, from the high wind, and no effort seemed to be made either by the citizens or soldiers to control the spread of the fire. A part of the Second Brigade was camped in and about the park, and it was said that our soldiers were fired upon by the citizens as we came in. How true this may be I cannot say, but doubtless it had the effect to enrage the soldiers, who, in retaliation, burned the houses in the location from whence the firing was received."[56]

Kilpatrick invited the local populace to a grand ball that night. He sent out invitations to local community leaders, who apparently believed that their attendance was required. While these citizens unhappily danced the night away, Kilpatrick's men burned most of their homes while searching for cotton and revenge. "Nero fiddled while Rome was burning," a soldier of the 92nd Illinois Mounted Infantry observed. "It was the bitterest satire on social pleasure ever witnessed."[57] Kilpatrick jokingly told Sherman that the stricken town should be dubbed "Burnwell."[58]

That night, Kilpatrick stabled some of his command's horses in the Episcopal Church of the Holy Apostles and used the church's baptismal font to water the horses, while others were stabled at the local Presbyterian church.[59] "Myself and messmates are in a kitchen very comfortable," trooper Joshua Breyfogle of the 10th Ohio Cavalry observed, "the town is on fire all around us and we may have to get out before morning." The next day, Breyfogle recorded, "Oh what a night has passed, a night the citizens will never forget, the town was on fire in every part and women and children running about crying and begging." He concluded, "the soldiers have sworn vengeance on South Carolina and fearfully they are carrying it out."[60]

Not surprisingly, the burning of the town enraged the locals. When the Federal horse soldiers left, bullet holes pockmarked the entrance to the Episcopal church, fired by angry citizens hoping to kill some of Kilpatrick's horses to avenge the burning of their property. Nineteen of Kilpatrick's troopers mysteriously died during their brief stay in Barnwell; local legends tell that they were either killed in

56. "A 10th Ohio Cavalryman," "Campaign of the Carolinas."
57. *Ninety-Second Illinois Volunteers* (Freeport, IL: Journal Steam Publishing House and Bookbindery, 1875), 212-213.
58. Elmore, *Carnival of Destruction*, 122.
59. Episcopal Church of the Holy Apostles website, history section: http://www.holyapostles-sc.org/about/
60. Carter, *The Story of Joshua D. Breyfogle*, 320.

retribution by the town's men who came out of hiding, or that they were poisoned by a local woman.[61]

Wheeler's cavalry took up positions to defend the South Carolina Railroad. Brigadier General William Allen's division went to Windsor and to Johnson's Turnout, near Aiken. The divisions of Brig. Gen. William Y. C. Humes and Brig. Gen. Alfred Iverson (Iverson would soon be relieved of command in favor of Maj. Gen. Pierce M. B. Young, who had transferred from the Army of Northern Virginia) dispersed along the invasion route between Lowtown and Williston.[62] The small force of cavalrymen represented the only available Confederate troops to resist Sherman's advance in this area; there was little that they could do.

With cutting the railroad accomplished, Sherman's troops then undertook a duty that they relished: destruction. Two possible railroad routes existed between the Deep South and Virginia, both of which came through Branchville, South Carolina. If the railroad was out of commission, there was no way to transport powder to Virginia other than by wagon train. "All hands were at once set to work to destroy the railroad track," Sherman wrote. "From the 7th to the 10th of February this work was thoroughly prosecuted by the Seventeenth Corps, from the Edisto up to Bamberg, and by the Fifteenth Corps from Bamberg up to Blackville."[63] As Sherman later described it, "This was a most important railroad, and I proposed to destroy it completely for fifty miles, partly to prevent a possibility of its restoration and partly to utilize the time necessary for General Slocum

61. Elmore, *Carnival of Destruction*, 122. A local newspaper article commemorating the burning of Barnwell during the sesquicentennial of the Civil War recounted, "A gruesome rumor insinuates that the annihilation of the nineteen was the work of a prominent lady, in whose home they had been billeted. The lady and her family had been subjected to insulting and heartrending torture; so she prepared a tasty supper for them on February 10. The nineteen became sleepy, and, of course, never woke up." There is a portion of Red Hill Cemetery in Barnwell where these men were supposedly buried in unmarked graves. Jerry Morris, "Trail of Fire: The Nineteen," *The People Sentinel*, March 19, 2015.

62. Iverson commanded a brigade of North Carolina infantry in the Army of Northern Virginia's 2nd Corps in 1863, but he performed poorly at the Battle of Gettysburg and was relieved of command under suspicion that he had been intoxicated at Gettysburg. In 1864, he assumed command of a brigade of Georgia cavalry, serving capably in that capacity, and then commanded a division of Wheeler's cavalry for a time. On February 7, 1865, Iverson was relieved of command and returned to Georgia. Iverson's division was merged with Maj. Gen. Pierce M. B. Young's division upon Iverson's reassignment. As will be described in Chapter 3 of this book, Maj. Gen. Wade Hampton, commander of the Army of Northern Virginia's Cavalry Corps, was also transferred to serve in his home state of South Carolina on February 7.

63. *OR* 47, 1:19.

to get up."[64] The men piled the railroad ties up, set them on fire, heated the rails, and twisted them around trees into "Sherman's neckties."

A Union cavalryman recalled, "On the 7th of February Sherman reached the South Carolina Railroad, a line of vital importance to the rebel Government, without much opposition, neither wing meeting, up to this time with very serious resistance. Details of men were set to work to tear up the rails and burn the ties and twist the rails as thoroughly as they did while on the march through Georgia. Thus the army remained strung along the road for at least 50 miles several days, until the road for that distance was completely destroyed."[65] Kilpatrick bragged to Sherman, "At any moment you desire I can drive Wheeler into the Edisto [River]." So far, the results of the campaign suggested that Kilpatrick could do as he promised.[66]

The next day, Kilpatrick's division entered Blacksville, South Carolina, a town of 1,500, after considerable skirmishing. "We charged into the town of Blacksville...[and] drove the Rebs out without any loss of life," a trooper of the 8th Indiana Cavalry boasted.[67] The horsemen burned the depot and freight house, built barricades, and began destroying the railroad. As they went about their work, Wheeler's troopers arrived, and, after a brisk fight, were driven through the town, leaving it to the whims of Kilpatrick's men.[68]

Sherman's army remained strung out along the railroad until February 9, with the 17th Corps on the right and the 15th and 20th corps and the cavalry at Blackville. Major General Slocum reached Blackville that day with Maj. Gen. John Geary's 20th Corps division. Slocum reported that Maj. Gen. Jefferson C. Davis's 14th Corps was approaching by way of Barnwell. On February 10, Sherman rode to Blackville, where he conferred with Slocum and Kilpatrick, learning that the whole army would be ready within a day. Consequently, Sherman gave orders for the next movement north to Columbia, while the right wing struck Orangeburg en route. He ordered Kilpatrick to demonstrate strongly in the direction of Aiken, to maintain the illusion that the army might instead head toward Augusta, Georgia. Kilpatrick's horsemen would be the sole diversion for a potential move on Augusta.[69]

---

64. Sherman, *Memoirs*, 2:274.
65. "A 10th Ohio Cavalryman," "Campaign of the Carolinas."
66. *OR* 47, 1:872.
67. Williamson D. Ward diary, entry for February 7, 1865, Archives, Indiana Historical Society, Indianapolis, Indiana.
68. "A 10th Ohio Cavalryman," "Campaign of the Carolinas."
69. By comparison, Sherman detailed Maj. Gen. John G. Foster's entire Department of the South and the South Atlantic Blockading Squadron to foment the idea that he intended to move on Charleston. Perhaps Sherman

The Confederacy's largest gunpowder factory, the Augusta Powder Works, was located just outside the city of Augusta, between the Savannah River and the Augusta canal, on the grounds of the old U.S. Arsenal. The works produced more than three million pounds of gunpowder throughout the course of the war and were essential to the Southern war effort.[70] The loss of the Augusta Powder Works would deprive the Confederate armies of the ability to resupply gunpowder, but Sherman had decided not to devote the resources to destroying the works.

Sherman wanted to reach Columbia before reinforcements from the Army of Tennessee could arrive. He told Kilpatrick that the state capital was his army's next objective, and that he should guard the army's left flank against Wheeler's men. Reports reached Sherman that elements of the Army of Tennessee had reached Augusta under command of Lt. Gen. Richard Taylor, which provided yet another reason not to attack the town directly.[71]

On February 9, Kilpatrick marched in the direction of Augusta. He was determined to keep up the ruse that his command was headed for the critical Confederate gunpowder factory at Augusta. "February 9, moved to Windsor and thence to Johnson's Station, destroying portions of the railroad," Kilpatrick reported. "Up to that point I had moved from Blackville in such a manner and had so maneuvered my troops as if I was the advance of the main army moving on Augusta." He also informed Sherman that he intended to destroy as much government property and railroad as possible at Aiken.[72]

"We left camp this morning at 9 oclock and marched 12 miles along the Augusta and Charleston railroad and encamped and built barricades and toar (sic) up the railroad and burnt the ties," a trooper of the 9th Pennsylvania Cavalry, of Col. Thomas J. Jordan's First Brigade, noted that night.[73]

Despite Kilpatrick's cavalry feinting toward Augusta, beginning on February 8, Gen. P. G. T. Beauregard tried to gather forces to resist Sherman's advance on the line of the Edisto River. If he could gather sufficient forces there, including Wheeler's cavalry, he might be able to bring Sherman's army to battle and, perhaps, even defeat it. Beauregard

knew and understood that sending Kilpatrick on a feint toward Augusta would draw Wheeler and his cavalry out, much like moths to a flame.

70. Theodore P. Savas, "Heart of the Southern War Machine: The Augusta Powder Works was an Unparalleled Accomplishment of Military Industry." *Civil War Times* 56 (June 2017): 34-43.
71. Sherman, *Memoirs*, 2:274-275.
72. *OR* 47, 1:858 and 2:351.
73. John W. Rowell, *Yankee Cavalrymen: Through the Civil War with the Ninth Pennsylvania Cavalry* (Knoxville: University of Tennessee Press, 1971), 225.

did not want to bring on a general engagement near Augusta, however. Instead, he specifically ordered Maj. Gen. Daniel Harvey Hill, who commanded the Confederate garrison at Augusta, that if it was "evident after reconnaissances that the enemy is in superior force and contemplates an attack on the city, the troops will retire westwardly."[74]

Maj. Gen. Carter L. Stevenson, commander of S. D. Lee's Corps of the Army of Tennessee.

(Alabama Department of Archives and History)

Intent on defending the Edisto River crossings, since he believed that Sherman's true objective was Charleston and not Columbia, Beauregard began gathering troops—including portions of Wheeler's Corps and seven brigades of infantry under command of Maj. Gen. Carter L. Stevenson[75] —along the line of the Edisto, which was the second major barrier river after the Salkehatchie.[76] On February 9, Lt. Gen. William J. Hardee instructed Wheeler to "send a force of 1,000 men to report to General McLaws at Branchville, to cover a retrograde movement of his force, if driven back from the Edisto." Hardee added that Wheeler was to "have a similar force in such position as to cover a retrograde movement (should it become necessary) of Lee's corps, Major-General Stevenson commanding." He noted, "General Stevenson understands that your movement toward Augusta is to meet a movement of the enemy on that place." Hardee ordered Wheeler to stay in constant communication with Stevenson and defend the Edisto River line.[77]

74. *OR* 47, 2:1133.
75. This river is not to be confused with the North and South Edisto Rivers along the coastline of South Carolina. The third line of defense anticipated by Beauregard was the combination of the Congaree, Saluda, and Broad Rivers in front of Columbia.
76. *OR* 47, 2:1123-1124. Stevenson now commanded Lt. Gen. Stephen D. Lee's orps of the Army of Tennessee. Stevenson told one of his subordinates, "It is of the utmost importance that the line of the Edisto should be held as long as possible." Ibid., 1124.
77. Ibid., 1136.

Lt. Gen. William J. Hardee, known as "Old Reliable," commander of the Department of South Carolina, Georgia, and Florida of Johnston's army.

(Alabama Dept. of Archives and History)

The next day, Hardee instructed Stevenson: "Direct Wheeler to bring over the Edisto a large body of cavalry —say 2,000 to protect your movements, and McLaws to hold on to the North Edisto as long as possible."[78] On the afternoon of February 10, in specific orders to Wheeler, Stevenson said, "we have been obliged to abandon the South Edisto, and are now holding the North Edisto. General Deas has been ordered to retire in the direction of Columbia, as far as to where that road crosses the North Edisto. You will order half the cavalry that is to report to General S. to report to General Deas at the point above mentioned, to cover his front and protect his right flank. The other half to report at these headquarters, coming by the nearest practicable route."[79] Nothing in those orders suggested that Wheeler should pursue Kilpatrick. In fact, his orders specifically instructed him not to do so.

However, Kilpatrick's diversion toward Augusta deceived Wheeler. Instead of obeying the order from Stevenson he instead decided to oppose the advance on Augusta; Wheeler believed that the Confederacy simply could not afford to lose the Powder Works, and he was determined to defend his hometown. Instead of obeying orders to defend the North Edisto line, Wheeler marched his entire corps to meet the Union advance, determined to resist it with all of the force available. On February 10, some of his troopers skirmished heavily with elements of the 15th and 17th corps, checking their advance on the town. With two brigades, Wheeler positioned himself between the Union infantry and the town.[80]

78. Ibid., 1144.
79. Ibid., 1147.
80. W. C. Dodson, ed., *Campaigns of Wheeler's Cavalry 1862-1865* (Atlanta, GA: Hudgins Publishing Co., 1899), 320.

However, he then received other orders. Hardee instructed Wheeler, with about 2,000 troopers, to move to Edisto to protect the movements of Maj. Gen. Carter L. Stevenson's infantry garrison from Augusta, consisting of the lead elements of Lt. Gen. S. D. Lee's corps of the Army of Tennessee. Wheeler complied, marching to Aiken with nearly 3,000 men. Aiken is about thirteen miles from Augusta and about five miles from other important factories located at Graniteville, South Carolina. "The consternation in Augusta was extreme," the historian of Wheeler's corps noted, "but few people thought that the salvation of the city was possible." Major General D. H. Hill, in fact, ordered that all cotton be prepared for burning, and even kindled fires to make sure that the bales would ignite quickly. Further, there were thousands of exhausted refugees from the Beaufort and Barnwell districts, with their wagons and property, converging on Aiken. Wheeler also needed to protect these refugees.[81]

Hill instructed Wheeler to concentrate his corps near Aiken. Wheeler pulled his men out of Augusta to create the appearance that the town was empty of Confederate soldiers. In fact, Wheeler intended to set a trap for the reckless Kilpatrick at Aiken.[82] Fortunately for the anxious Augustans, Sherman had no intention of seizing the city—his ruse had worked brilliantly, drawing off the majority of Wheeler's horsemen.

Kilpatrick reported on his progress to Sherman on the night of February 10. "I have advanced as far as this point in the direction of Aiken. Have just driven out a brigade of rebel cavalry, and find that Wheeler has concentrated the majority of his troops at Aiken, and is now in line of battle, barricading his position two miles this side of Aiken," he wrote. "We have had considerable skirmishing, but nothing more. This is a splendid country; plenty of forage and supplies. The enemy now believe that we are marching on Augusta; such, at least, is the impression among the citizens."[83]

While vastly outnumbered and aware that there was little that he and his troopers could do to stop Sherman's advance, Wheeler remained determined to do whatever he could. He was able to meet Kilpatrick's troopers on more or less even terms at Aiken. "From the time we entered the State of South Carolina," a Southern horse artillery officer observed, "we had almost daily skirmishes with General Kilpatrick...up to the City of Columbia."[84] However, these constant actions wore down both horses and men, neither of which

81. Ibid., 321-322.
82. Ibid. 320-321.
83. *OR* 47, 2:382.
84. Andrew M. Sea, "Destruction of the Broad River Bridge," *Confederate Veteran* 21 (November 1913), 542.

Wheeler could afford to lose. "Both our men and horses were exhausted," another trooper wrote on February 6.[85] By February 10, Wheeler had no corn to feed his horses. That afternoon he sent an urgent request to Major General Hill asking to have horse corn sent to him. He repeated this request at 6:45 p.m. and again at 8:15 a.m. the next morning.[86]

The Union cavalry chief was determined to end the ongoing harassment from Wheeler's troopers. Kilpatrick wrote, "No better opportunity ever offered to break Wheeler up; but as he may have supports of infantry I do not consider it prudent to attack. Could he now be driven back and Aiken captured we could secure a large amount of provisions, needed by my command, and I think a wrong impression be produced upon the minds of the enemy which he could not correct until it would be entirely too late. If you will send me a brigade of infantry from the Twentieth Army Corps, which must now be this side of Blackville and consequently less than a day's march from this point, I will render Wheeler powerless to even annoy your wagon trains again during the campaign."[87]

Sherman responded: "I cannot change my plans now, as they are in progress. I don't care about Aiken, unless you can take it by a dash, and as Wheeler's attention is drawn to that quarter you can let it work. To-morrow the Right Wing moves on Orangeburg, and after breaking that railroad good we will proceed as heretofore indicated. [Maj. Gen. Jefferson C.] Davis should be at Williston tonight or early to-morrow; keep in communication with him and conform to his movements. It won't pay to have infantry chasing Wheeler's cavalry; it is always a bad plan, and is injurious to detach infantry, save for a day or a single occasion."[88] As Sherman later stated, "I wanted to reach Columbia before any part of [the Army of Tennessee] could get there. Some of them were reported as having reached Augusta, under the command of General Dick Taylor."[89] Speed, therefore, was of the essence, and it

85. A. D. Kirwan, ed., *Johnny Green of the Orphan Brigade* (Lexington: University of Kentucky Press, 1956), 188.
86. *OR* 53, 408-409. Hill responded on the morning of February 11. He told Wheeler that he had not received the request for supplies until 2:00 a.m. Hill said, "Two efficient staff officers were at once sent to look up the quartermaster and get off the corn. The depot quartermasters, you know, are always lazy except about a personal speculation or a sharp operation versus the Government. The corn has been got off by those staff officers, and not by the other worthy gentlemen." Ibid. 47, 2:1163.
87. Ibid. 47, 2:382.
88. Ibid., 383.
89. Sherman, *Memoirs*, 2:275.

appears that Sherman understood that Wheeler would pursue the Union cavalry and abandon the line of the Edisto River, opening the door to Columbia.

Despite Sherman's lukewarm response to his plan, Kilpatrick remained determined to entice Wheeler into a decisive battle. "Our general thought it would be a good idea to go up and see Aiken," an Ohio cavalryman quipped, "which has since the war become famous as a health resort, but at that time our boys decided that there were other places more healthy than that."[90]

90. J. N. McMaster, "Kilpatrick's Cavalry at Aiken, S. C.," *National Tribune*, July 26, 1888.

CHAPTER 2

JUDSON KILPATRICK AND HIS UNION TROOPERS

Hugh Judson Kilpatrick was born in Deckertown, New Jersey, on January 14, 1836, the second son of Simon and Julia Kilpatrick. The elder Kilpatrick was a colonel in the New Jersey state militia who cut an imposing figure in his fine uniform. The image of his father in his handsome uniform was not lost on little Judson, who, at an early age, decided he wanted to be a soldier. Kilpatrick spent his childhood attending good schools and reading about military history, eagerly learning all he could about great captains and campaigns.[1]

Bvt. Maj. Gen. Judson Kilpatrick, Union commander at the Battle of Aiken.

(Library of Congress)

The boy's dreams came true in 1856 when he received an appointment to the United States Military Academy at West Point, New York. He graduated from West Point in the class of 1861, ranked seventeenth out of 45 cadets. "His ambition was simply boundless," a fellow cadet recalled, "and from his intimates he did not disguise his faith that...he would become governor of New Jersey, and ultimately president of the United States."[2] A few days after graduating, Kilpatrick married his sweetheart, Alice Shealer, the niece of a

1. Samuel J. Martin, *"Kill-Cavalry:" Sherman's Merchant of Terror—The Life of Union General Hugh Judson Kilpatrick* (Cranbury, NJ: Associated University Press, 1996), 15-16.
2. James Harrison Wilson, *Under the Old Flag: Recollections of Military Operations in the War for the Union, the Spanish War, the Boxer Rebellion, Etc.*, 2 vols. (New York: D. Appleton, 1912), 1:370-371.

prominent New York politician. He carried a personal battle flag embroidered with her name into combat throughout the upcoming war, which lasted longer than his marriage to Alice. The young lieutenant and his bride spent only one night together before he began his military career.[3]

A dominant personality trait emerged early in Kilpatrick's career: intense ambition. Recognizing that volunteer service would lead to quicker promotions than service in the Regular Army, the new graduate asked his West Point mathematics professor, Gouverneur K. Warren, to recommend him for a captaincy in the newly-formed 5th New York Infantry. With Warren's help, on May 9, 1861, Kilpatrick received a commission as captain of Company H, 5th New York. One month later, on June 10, 1861, he fought at the Battle of Big Bethel, Virginia, in the Civil War's first battle. The young captain was wounded in combat and earned the distinction of being the first West Pointer on the Union side injured by enemy fire. For someone looking forward to a political career, a glorious combat wound meant that Kilpatrick was off to a good start.[4]

Kilpatrick returned to duty as lieutenant colonel of the 2nd New York (Harris) Cavalry. He was transferred to the newly-formed cavalry regiment. His parting from the 5th New York was not graceful. Kilpatrick took sick leave rather than return to duty with his regiment, all the while angling for higher rank in a cavalry regiment, angering Warren in the process. As the second in command of a regiment of horsemen, Kilpatrick served in Maj. Gen. George B. McClellan's Army of the Potomac. He took part in the 1862 Peninsula Campaign. That summer his regiment left the Virginia Peninsula to serve with Maj. Gen. John Pope's Army of Virginia. The lieutenant colonel eagerly searched for opportunities to gain fame and rapid promotion. As it turned out, Kilpatrick almost never got the chance.

---

3. Martin, *"Kill-Cavalry"*, 17-20. A trooper of the 9th Pennsylvania Cavalry described Kilpatrick's banner: "It is pure red…perfectly red with three white stars denoting the number of brigades in our division. Above the flag float two white streamers about three feet in length, one bearing the inscription in letters of gold—'Kilpatrick's Cavalry,' the other 'Alice.'" This veteran noted, "The rebels hate the flag infernally. They look upon it with horror; and well they may. For wherever it waves, the cavalry make their mark." Diary of William W. Pritchard, entry for June 2, 1865, Civil War Miscellaneous Collection, Archives, U.S. Army Heritage and Education Center, Carlisle, Pennsylvania (hereafter, "USAHEC").
4. For a detailed history of the 5th New York, see Brian C. Pohanka and Patrick A. Schroeder, *History of the 5th New York Volunteer Infantry: Vortex of Hell* (Lynchburg, VA: Schroeder Publications, 2012). For a detailed discussion of the Battle of Big Bethel, see J. Michael Cobb, Edward Hicks, and Wythe Holt, *Battle of Big Bethel: Crucial Clash in Early Civil War Virginia* (El Dorado Hills, CA: Savas-Beatie, 2013).

In the fall of 1862, Kilpatrick was jailed in the Old Capitol Prison, at Washington, D.C., charged with conduct unbecoming of an officer. Specifically, he was accused of taking bribes, stealing and selling horses and tobacco, and impropriety in borrowing money. Such unsavory allegations might have slowed a less resourceful or ambitious man, but not Kilpatrick. In spite of his incarceration, he managed a promotion to colonel of the 2nd New York Cavalry in December 1862. In January 1863, friends in high places and the exigencies of war prevailed, and Kilpatrick returned to his regiment untainted by the scandal of a court-martial.[5] For most young officers, such charges would have been career ending. Kilpatrick, however, survived unscathed and emerged from prison a full colonel.

By the spring of 1863, the New Jersey native commanded a brigade. Brigadier General Alfred Pleasonton, the temporary commander of the Army of the Potomac's Cavalry Corps, had Kilpatrick promoted to brigadier general of volunteers on June 14, 1863, resulting from Kilpatrick's fine performances during Maj. Gen. George Stoneman's spring 1863 raid and the June 9, 1863, Battle of Brandy Station, both in Virginia. On June 28, Maj. Gen. Julius Stahel was relieved of command, and his independent cavalry division was transferred from the defenses of Washington, D.C., to the Army of the Potomac as the newly-designated Third Cavalry Division.[6] On the afternoon of July 3, 1863, while commanding his division at the Battle of Gettysburg, Kilpatrick ordered Brig. Gen. Elon J. Farnsworth's brigade on a foolhardy mounted charge across difficult terrain, an attack that accomplished nothing but the death of Farnsworth and many of his brave troopers.[7]

Thanks in large part to the Union victory at Gettysburg, Kilpatrick was not censured for his poor judgment in ordering the fruitless charge. When bloody draft riots broke out in New York City a few days later, Kilpatrick was sent to assist Maj. Gen. John E. Wool

5. G. Wayne King, "General Judson Kilpatrick," *New Jersey History*, vol. XCI, no. 1 (Spring 1973), 35-38.
6. Stahel outranked Pleasonton, and had his division been assigned to the Army of the Potomac's Cavalry Corps while Stahel still led it, he would have been entitled to assume corps command. There was no way that the ambitious Pleasonton would have allowed that to happen, and he schemed to have Stahel relieved of command before his division was transferred to the Army of the Potomac. Pleasonton's scheming worked, and Stahel was relieved of command and reassigned to command of the cavalry assigned to the Department of the Susquehanna.
7. For a detailed discussion of Farnsworth's charge at Gettysburg, see Eric J. Wittenberg, *Gettysburg's Forgotten Cavalry Actions: Farnsworth's Charge, South Cavalry Field, and the Battle of Fairfield* (El Dorado Hills, CA: Savas-Beatie, 2011).

and assumed command of the Federal cavalry forces sent to help quell the disturbances.[8] After extinguishing the riots, he stayed in New York to visit his wife and newborn son for two weeks. Kilpatrick then returned to duty in Virginia.

The Union and Confederate armies spent a long, bloody fall jockeying for position. Kilpatrick suffered a crushing defeat at the hands of Maj. Gen. James Ewell Brown ("Jeb") Stuart's Confederate cavalry at the Battle of Buckland Mills, Virginia, on October 19, 1863, precipitating a rout known as the "Buckland Races," so named because Stuart's troopers pursued Kilpatrick's beaten horsemen for five miles before finally calling off the pursuit.

When the fall campaigning season ended in a stalemate along the banks of the Rappahannock River, Kilpatrick developed a bold scheme to liberate Union prisoners of war from Libby Prison and Belle Isle in Richmond, Virginia. Glory awaited him if he succeeded. Colonel Ulric Dahlgren, a flamboyant 21-year-old one-legged cavalry officer, commanded one column of the raid while Kilpatrick led the other. Defying Brig. Gen. Pleasonton's vigorous objections, the Union high command approved the risky raid.[9]

Faced with unexpected, heavy Confederate resistance, Kilpatrick was repulsed in front of Richmond, followed by Maj. Gen. Wade Hampton's rebel troopers striking him hard at Atlee's Station later that night. Dahlgren was thrown back at the southwestern defenses of Richmond and killed in an ambush near King and Queen Court House, almost 40 miles from the Confederate capital. Incriminating documents found on Dahlgren's body suggested that the actual purpose of the raid was not the liberation of the prisoners of war, but rather the kidnapping and assassination of President Jefferson Davis and his cabinet, as well as the burning of Richmond.[10] A firestorm of controversy erupted, and Kilpatrick was blamed for the embarrassing debacle. A scathing Detroit newspaper editorial observed that Kilpatrick "cares nothing about the lives of men, sacrificing them with cool indifference, his only object being his own promotion and

8. Martin, *"Kill-Cavalry"*, 127-128.
9. For a detailed discussion of the Kilpatrick-Dahlgren raid, see Bruce M. Venter, *Kill Jeff Davis: The Union Raid on Richmond, 1864* (Norman: University of Oklahoma Press, 2016).
10. Debate has raged for more than 150 years whether the documents found on Dahlgren's body were authentic or whether the Confederates forged them. Admiral John A. Dahlgren, the dead colonel's father, went to his grave denying that the documents were legitimate. For a discussion of their legitimacy, and for a full-length biography of Ulric Dahlgren, see Eric J. Wittenberg, *Like a Meteor Blazing Brightly: The Short but Controversial Life of Colonel Ulric Dahlgren* (Roseville, MN: Edinborough Press, 2009), 238-247.

keeping his name before the public."[11] By this time, he had acquired the unflattering nickname "Kill Cavalry" because of his propensity to use up men and horses in his ongoing pursuit of personal glory.

Meanwhile, General Sherman's Army of the Tennessee needed a new cavalry commander.[12] The Western Theater Federal cavalry had fared poorly during the first three years of the war, and Sherman had been looking for someone to bring aggressiveness to his mounted arm. He had several cavalry commanders to choose from, including Stoneman, Kilpatrick, and Maj. Gen. James H. Wilson, who later became the overall commander of the cavalry assigned to Sherman's theater of operations. Wilson succeeded Kilpatrick in command of the Third Division of the Army of the Potomac's Cavalry Corps. Although Wilson was younger than Kilpatrick, he was a full major general of volunteers in 1865, whereas Kilpatrick was only a brevet major general. Not surprisingly, there was no love lost between the two officers. Sherman resolved this brewing conflict by placing Kilpatrick directly under his own command, thereby removing him from Wilson's authority.

In May, Kilpatrick was badly wounded at the Battle of Resaca during the opening days of the Atlanta Campaign. He did not return to duty until late July 1864. By then, Stoneman was in a Confederate prison after being captured during a failed raid intended to free Union prisoners of war held at the notorious Andersonville prison camp in Georgia. Kilpatrick became the commander of Sherman's cavalry by default—although Wilson outranked him. Kilpatrick then led a division of cavalry during Sherman's March to the Sea.[13] His troopers inspired little confidence in Sherman's infantry. Observing the deployment of Kilpatrick's division near Waynesboro, Georgia, in December 1864, one of Sherman's staff officers observed, "So many cavalry in line in an open plain make a beautiful sight. But it's all show; there's not much fight in them."[14]

Judson Kilpatrick cut an odd figure. He stood only five feet, three inches tall and weighed about 130 pounds. Despite his diminutive size, he was, nevertheless, a memorable character in a war filled with unforgettable personalities. "His face was...marked...showing...individuality in every line," Michigan cavalryman James H. Kidd recalled.

11. *Detroit Free Press*, March 26, 1864.
12. Sherman actually commanded a group of three armies that were functioning together.
13. King, "General Judson Kilpatrick," 43.
14. Paul M. Angle, ed., *Three Years in the Army of the Cumberland: The Letters and Diary of Major James A. Connelly* (Bloomington, IN: University of Indiana Press, 1959), 345.

"[He had] a prominent nose, a wide mouth, a firm jaw, thin cheeks set off by side whiskers rather light in color...the eyes...were cold and lustrous, but searching...a countenance that once seen, was never forgotten." He wore a stylish, tight-fitting blue uniform and "a black hat with the brim turned down on one side, up on the other...which gave to the style of his own name."[15]

Not everyone sang his praises. Others viewed him much less kindly. "He is a very ungraceful rider, looking more like a monkey than a man on horseback," one Federal soldier wrote. The soldier also described Kilpatrick as "the most vain, conceited, egotistical little popinjay I ever saw."[16] That was not the only negative assessment. "It is hard to look at him without laughing," Lt. Col. Theodore Lyman, a staff officer serving with the Army of the Potomac's headquarters, wrote in the spring of 1864.[17]

Though cheerful and approachable, Kilpatrick also possessed a fiery tempter. He was, recalled one man, brave but also "flamboyant, reckless, tempestuous, and ever licentious."[18] Captain Charles Francis Adams of the 1st Massachusetts Cavalry, whose grandfather and great-grandfather were U.S. presidents, possessed the family's notorious acid pen; he observed, "Kilpatrick is a brave, injudicious boy, much given to blowing, and surely will come to grief."[19] Another Federal officer called Kilpatrick "a frothy braggart without brains."[20]

Henry C. Meyer, who had served with Kilpatrick in the 2nd New York Cavalry and as a member of his staff, had many opportunities to observe "Little Kil" during 1862 and 1863. "He had capacity for rallying soldiers and getting them into a charge," Meyer recalled. "His usual method when meeting the enemy was to order a charge. Sometimes this was successful, and at other times it was not so much so and very costly of men. It was because of this that he secured the nickname of 'Kill-Cavalry'."[21]

15. James H. Kidd, *Personal Recollections of a Cavalryman in Custer's Michigan Brigade* (Ionia, MI: Sentinel Publishing Co., 1908), 164-165.
16. Angle, *Three Years in the Army of the Cumberland*, 348.
17. George R. Agassiz, ed., *Meade's Headquarters 1863-1865: Letters of Colonel Theodore Lyman from the Wilderness to Appomattox* (Boston: *The Atlantic Monthly Press*, 1922), 76.
18. Edward G. Longacre, "Judson Kilpatrick," *Civil War Times Illustrated 10* (April 1971), 25.
19. Charles Francis Adams, *A Cycle of Adams Letters, 1861-1865*, Worthington C. Ford, ed., 2 vols. (Boston: Houghton-Mifflin, 1920), 2:44-45.
20. Longacre, "Judson Kilpatrick," 25.
21. Henry C. Meyer, *Civil War Experiences Under Bayard, Gregg, Kilpatrick, Custer, Raulston, and Newbury, 1862, 1863, 1864* (New York: Knickerbocker Press, 1911), 97.

Kilpatrick used language more like a club than a saber, with masterful use of profanity. It was also well known that "a dispatch bearing Kilpatrick's name leads to...doubt of its accuracy," as one Federal artillerist caustically noted.[22] The ever-tactful Maj. Gen. Oliver O. Howard, commander of the Army of the Tennessee during the Carolinas Campaign, wrote, "His memory and imagination were often in conflict."[23]

After Alice Kilpatrick unexpectedly died in November 1863, the newly-widowed general became a notorious womanizer. Several women frequented his bed; two of them dressed in the uniforms of Union privates, while another, known to history only as "Alice"—perhaps a wink and a nod to Kilpatrick's late wife—was reportedly a Northern schoolteacher trapped in the South by the war and earned her passage north by acting as Kilpatrick's lover. She was with him in his tent outside Aiken on the night of February 10, 1865.[24]

William T. Sherman had little faith in the talents of his cavalry commander. Before the New Jersey trooper was assigned to his command, Sherman famously said, "I know that Kilpatrick is a hell of a damned fool, but I want just that sort of man to command my cavalry" during the advance on Atlanta. He understood that Kilpatrick was extremely aggressive, often to the point of being reckless, and Sherman recognized that his complement of cavalry officers lacked aggressiveness prior to Kilpatrick's reassignment.[25] But Kilpatrick was the senior cavalry officer serving with his army group in South Carolina, so Sherman had to make due with what he had. Fortunately, the troopers under his command were experienced fighters and marchers. Kilpatrick commanded a division of approximately 4,400 battle-hardened veterans organized into three brigades. He also had three experienced and capable brigade commanders leading these veteran troopers.

Colonel Thomas Jefferson Jordan commanded the First Brigade. Born in Walnut Hill, Dauphin County, Pennsylvania, on December 2,

22. Charles S. Wainwright, *A Diary of Battle: The Personal Journals of Colonel Charles S. Wainwright, 1861-1865*, Alan Nevins, ed. (New York: Harcourt, Brace & World, 1962), 265.
23. Oliver Otis Howard, *Autobiography of Oliver Otis Howard, Major General, United States Army, 2 vols.* (New York: Baker & Taylor Co., 1907), 2:29.
24. For a detailed discussion of these women, see Eric J. Wittenberg, *The Battle of Monroe's Crossroads and the Civil War's Final Campaign* (El Dorado Hills, CA: Savas-Beatie, 2006), 7-9.
25. Wilson, *Under the Old Flag*, 2:13. Wilson had replaced Kilpatrick in command of the Army of the Potomac's Third Cavalry Division when Kilpatrick requested a transfer to the Western Theater after the debacle of the failed Kilpatrick-Dahlgren raid.

Col. Thomas J. Jordan, commander of Kilpatrick's First Brigade.

(USAHEC)

1821, Jordan was a graduate of Carlisle, Pennsylvania's, venerable Dickinson College, and had served several terms in the Pennsylvania state legislature. His grandfather had been a major and paymaster in the Revolutionary War, and Jordan's wife was the granddaughter of a Revolutionary War general. Jordan was practicing law in Harrisburg when war broke out in 1861. Although he had no formal military training, he had served in the local militia for years and was a friend of Pennsylvania Governor Andrew G. Curtin, who appreciated Jordan's intellectual and administrative abilities.[26]

The day after Fort Sumter fell, Curtin appointed Jordan as an aide to Maj. Gen. William H. Keim, commander of Pennsylvania's military forces. Jordan served Keim well, carrying the first news of the riots in Baltimore, Maryland, to Bvt. Lt. Gen. Winfield Scott. He then accompanied Keim and the Pennsylvania forces into Maryland for their 1861 summer campaign against Brig. Gen. Joseph E. Johnston's Virginia forces. Jordan saw action at Falling Waters and gained invaluable experience there.

When the campaign concluded, Jordan mustered out, received a new commission as a major, and was assigned to assist Col. Edward C. Williams to recruit the 9th Pennsylvania Cavalry. Jordan was captured in June 1862 and spent five months as a prisoner of war, first at Madison, Georgia, and then in Richmond's notorious Libby Prison. He received a promotion to colonel of the 9th Pennsylvania Cavalry, in early 1863, while still a prisoner of war.[27] In March 1863, Jordan was exchanged and led the regiment through September 1864. Major General George H. Thomas was so impressed with him that Thomas asked President Abraham Lincoln to promote Jordan in recognition of

26. Samuel P. Bates, *Martial Deeds of Pennsylvania* (Philadelphia: T. H. Davis & Co., 1875), 704-705.
27. Ibid., 705.

his meritorious service at the Battle of Chickamauga in September 1863.[28] By October 1864, Jordan commanded a veteran brigade of cavalry, which he successfully led during the March to the Sea and then into the Carolinas, defeating Wheeler in combat several times along the way. On February 25, 1865, two weeks after the Battle of Aiken, Jordan received a brevet to brigadier general of volunteers for his praiseworthy service.[29] The 44-year-old thickly-bearded colonel with the receding hairline and sharp countenance was well respected by both his men and his superiors.

Jordan's First Brigade, about 1,500 strong, consisted of a battalion of the 3rd Indiana Cavalry (the remaining companies served in the Army of the Potomac's Cavalry Corps), 8th Indiana Cavalry, 2nd Kentucky Cavalry, 3rd Kentucky Cavalry, and the 9th Pennsylvania Cavalry. These men had fought hard throughout the war, including the 1862 Kentucky Campaign, the 1863 Tullahoma Campaign, the Campaigns of Chickamauga and Knoxville, and all of Sherman's 1864 campaigns. These veterans knew their business and had proved their mettle on battlefields scattered across several states.

Brig. Gen. Smith D. Atkins, commander of Kilpatrick's Second Brigade.

(USAHEC)

Brigadier General Smith D. Atkins commanded Kilpatrick's Second Brigade. Born on June 9, 1835, in Horseheads, New York, Atkins attended the Rock River Seminary in Mt. Morris, Illinois. Before the war, he worked as a newspaper editor and lawyer in Illinois. He was commissioned captain of the 11th Illinois on April 30, 1861, and promoted to major on March 21, 1862. He spent most of the following year serving on the staff of Maj. Gen. Stephen A. Hurlbut. In September of 1862, Atkins was appointed colonel of the 92nd Illinois. By February 1863, he commanded a brigade in the Army of Kentucky. Four months later, in

28. Ibid., 707.
29. Rowell, *Yankee Cavalrymen*, 21; Roger D. Hunt and Jack R. Brown, *Brevet Brigadier Generals in Blue* (Gaithersburg, MD: Olde Soldier Books, 1989), 322; Joseph G. Vale, *Minty and His Cavalry: A History of Cavalry Campaigns in the Western Armies* (Harrisburg, PA: E. K. Meyers, 1886), 543.

June, he was at the head of a brigade in the Reserve Corps of the Army of the Cumberland.

On July 22, Atkins's regiment was converted to mounted infantry and became part of Col. John T. Wilder's legendary Lightning Brigade, an outfit consisting of mounted infantrymen armed with Spencer repeating rifles. The rifle's mobility and firepower made it a prototype for James Wilson's mounted corps in 1865. The Lightning Brigade performed admirably at the September 1863 Battle of Chickamauga, holding off superior enemy forces with their seven-shot Spencer repeating rifles.[30] By the beginning of the 1864 Atlanta Campaign, the Lightning Brigade had been outfitted with sabers and pistols, along with their Spencer rifles, and served as light cavalry, with Atkins in command of the brigade. He received a brevet to brigadier general of volunteers on January 12, 1865, just in time for the commencement of the Carolinas Campaign.[31]

Although one soldier of the 92nd Illinois described him as a "peculiar man," Atkins had many friends and admirers throughout the army. Another noted that he was "a talented lawyer by profession and like many men of that profession had used his talents to save wrong doers from getting justice done them." Although Atkins did not usually imbibe alcohol, his men liked to play tricks on him by spiking his demijohns with whiskey. "He had a slick tongue and was fond of speech making and had a high appreciation of what he said and did," one Union soldier remembered.[32]

Atkins's 1,100-strong Second Brigade consisted of the 92nd Illinois Mounted Infantry, the 9th Michigan Cavalry, the 9th Ohio Cavalry, the 10th Ohio Cavalry, and Maj. William McLaughlin's Squadron of Ohio Cavalry. Like Jordan's troopers, these men were also veterans who had seen extensive service in the Western Theater, including the Atlanta Campaign and the March to the Sea. Several of Atkins's units had served together for some time, but others had joined the brigade only after the fall of Atlanta.

Colonel George Eliphaz Spencer of the 1st Alabama Cavalry, a loyalist unit from the heart of the Confederacy, led Kilpatrick's Third Brigade, which was newly formed for the advance through South Carolina. Born in Champion, Jefferson County, New York, on November 1, 1836, Spencer attended college in Montreal, Canada. He

30. For more detail on the critical role the Lighting Brigade played at Chickamauga, see Richard A. Baumgartner, *Blue Lightning: Wilder's Mounted Infantry Brigade at the Battle of Chickamauga, second ed.* (Huntington, WV: Blue Acorn Press, 1999).
31. Hunt and Long, *Brevet Brigadier Generals in Blue*, 19.
32. Swedberg, *Three Years with the 92nd Illinois*, 8-9.

was a lawyer and also served in the United States Senate. Spencer commissioned as a captain in the U.S. Volunteers on October 24, 1862, serving as an assistant adjutant general and then chief of staff to Brig. Gen. Grenville Dodge. In July 1863, Spencer requested a transfer to the 1st Alabama Cavalry, which did not have a permanent commanding officer. That September, his request was granted, and Spencer was appointed colonel of the Alabama regiment, which was stationed at Corinth, Mississippi.

Col. George E. Spencer, commander of Kilpatrick's Third Brigade.

(USAHEC)

By early 1864, the 1st Alabama engaged in scouting and skirmishing against Wheeler's cavalry around Rome, Georgia. The Alabamians quickly earned the respect of their veteran comrades—though they occasionally behaved badly around Savannah—and were assigned to Kilpatrick's division in the fall, just in time for the March to the Sea. By January 1865, Spencer had assumed command of the Third Brigade. As a competent officer, he received a brevet to brigadier general of volunteers for his meritorious service during the Carolinas Campaign.[33]

Spencer's 1,500 men came from three cavalry regiments: the 1st Alabama, the 5th Kentucky, and the 5th Ohio. The latter were veterans of many campaigns, including the pursuit of Brig. Gen. John Hunt Morgan's raiders across Indiana and Ohio. Spencer's brigade also served throughout the Atlanta Campaign and the March to the Sea. Along the way, these men earned a reputation of sewing terror among the civilian population. Major General Francis P. Blair, commander of Sherman's 17th Corps, scolded Spencer: "The outrages committed by your command during the march are becoming so common, and are of such an aggravated nature, that they call for some severe and instant mode of correction." The men's lack of discipline would haunt Kilpatrick in a most unfortunate manner during the Carolinas Campaign.[34]

33. Hunt and Long, *Brevet Brigadier Generals in Blue*, 575; Glenda McWhirter Todd, *First Alabama Cavalry, USA: Homage to Patriotism* (Bowie, MD: Heritage Books, 1999), 9-13 and 355.
34. *OR* 44, 504-505.

Large mounted forces use and lose many horses, an unfortunate but inevitable consequence of hard campaigning. The difficult marches through the swamps of South Carolina took a heavy toll on Kilpatrick's horses. Because Sherman's army was living off the land as it made its way across South Carolina, no organized system for providing remounts to Kilpatrick's cavalry existed; the only available source of replacement horses came from foraging the local citizenry, which was not an effective means of gathering remounts. By the beginning of March, nearly ten percent of his troopers, or about 400 men, had lost their mounts and were unable to secure replacements. The dismounted men were organized into a provisional brigade consisting of three ad hoc regiments. Assignments to the dismounted regiments corresponded to the soldier's regular brigade. For example, if a trooper in Atkins's Second Brigade lost his mount, then he was assigned to the 2nd Provisional Regiment. As a general rule, the reassigned men continued to carry their cavalry carbines, but to maximize the range of their firepower, some were armed with Springfield rifled muskets rather than the traditional carbines and sabers carried by horse soldiers.

Lt. Col. William B. Way, commander of the Fourth (Provisional) Brigade of dismounted men attached to Kilpatrick's Division.

(Library of Congress)

Lieutenant Colonel William B. Way of the 9th Michigan Cavalry commanded the dismounted Fourth —or Provisional — Brigade, which was an ad hoc organization formed out of necessity. The 30-year-old native of Rochester, New York, was raised in Pontiac, Michigan. When the war broke out, he was mustered in as a first lieutenant in the 1st Michigan Cavalry. By November 1861 he had assumed command of Company C of the 1st Michigan Cavalry, and by October 1862, he was a captain, a promotion earned after hard campaigning in the Shenandoah Valley against Thomas "Stonewall" Jackson and then in Maj. Gen. John Pope's Army of Virginia. The following month, Way mustered out of service with the 1st Michigan Cavalry. On April 30, 1863, he was commissioned major in the newly-formed 9th Michigan Cavalry. Way distinguished himself during Brigadier General Morgan's raid across Indiana and Ohio where he led a contingent of 200 troopers on a wild chase after the Confederate cavalier and his men, capturing 300—including Morgan himself—and killing and wounding many others.[35] On November 30, 1863, Way received a well-deserved promotion to lieutenant colonel, a role he filled until his appointment to command the Provisional Brigade.[36]

Capt. Theodore Northrop, Kilpatrick's chief of scouts.

(Larry Strayer)

Captain Theodore F. Northrop, 20 years old, commanded Kilpatrick's 85-man scout detachment. One of eight children, Northrop was born in southeastern New York on May 31, 1844, to William and Agnes Northrop. In 1861, when the 2nd New York Cavalry regiment was raised in Essex, New Jersey, the young man enlisted as a private in Company G. A short time later he was promoted to sergeant. By the fall of 1862, Northrop found himself a member of Kilpatrick's inner circle when he was made the then-lieutenant colonel's orderly. When Kilpatrick was imprisoned in November of that year, Northrop submitted an affidavit defending his superior from the charges of dishonesty and theft. Kilpatrick rewarded the young man for his loyalty by promoting him. "Capt. Northrop was one of the most steadfast of friends," a comrade noted. "Once he formed a friendship it endured through all the storms of life."[37]

The young man was both tough and courageous. During the cavalry fight at Aldie, Virginia, on June 17, 1863, Northrop was severely wounded in the right shoulder. He carried the bullet for more than 30 years before the troublesome slug was finally cut out. Captured during the Aldie fighting, Northrop was held briefly in Libby Prison before being exchanged to rejoin his command a few days later. As a

35. For more on Morgan's great raid and the Union cavalry's pursuit, see David L. Mowery, *Morgan's Great Raid: The Remarkable Expedition from Kentucky to Ohio* (Charleston, SC: The History Press, 2013).
36. William B. Way service records, RG 94, National Archives and Records Administration, Washington, D.C. ("NARA"); John Robertson, comp., *Michigan in the War* (Lansing, MI: W. S. George & Co., 1882), 705-715.
37. "Death of Civil War Veteran on Sunday," *Wantage Recorder*, February 1, 1918.

reward for his valor, Northrop was commissioned second lieutenant with date of rank made retroactive to June 17, 1863.

On May 2, 1864, Northrop was promoted to first lieutenant, followed by captain in the fall.[38] He was just 20 years old when appointed to command Kilpatrick's scout detachment. It was an important role, for the scouts led the way for Kilpatrick's division.[39] "The duty assigned to me was that of procuring information for headquarters in regard to the enemy's movement, locations, conditions of lines of communications and topography," Northrop recounted in 1917. "It was not my duty to engage in an offensive against the enemy."[40] Although quite young, Northrop proved to be an effective leader in his new role. One of Kilpatrick's staff officers praised Northrop's courage, recalling how he "repeatedly carried out successfully missions involving unusual hazards and requiring great daring."[41]

Northrop proudly claimed that his scouts, who were handpicked from each regiment of Kilpatrick's division, were "as brave and as able a body of rough-riders as ever fought on horseback."[42] Much of their time was spent dressed in enemy uniforms, and most had mastered a convincing Southern drawl. Their boldness allowed them to pass for Confederates and to ride into enemy camps. It was a dangerous assignment; if they were caught, the men would probably be executed as spies.[43] Northrop's scouts fanned out across the Southern countryside, stealing and foraging everything that crossed their path. It did not take long before the people of Georgia, South Carolina, and North Carolina came to hate Northrop and his men and dreaded their approach.[44]

---

38. Interestingly, Northrop's term of service expired in the fall of 1864, and he was ordered to return to his regiment, the 2nd New York Cavalry, in order to be mustered out of service, in part because there were too few men left in his company to keep him in the service., Kilpatrick and army headquarters had to intervene to keep Northrop in the service. See Special Field Orders No. 267, copy in Northrop's service records file, RG 93, National Archives and Records Administration, Washington, D.C. (hereafter, "NARA").
39. "Death of Capt. Northrop," *Sussex Independent*, February 1, 1918, and *The Sussex Register*, January 31, 1918.
40. Theodore F. Northrop to the Adjutant General of the Army, March 12, 1917, RG 94, Records of the Adjutant General's Office 1780-1917, Theodore F. Northrop, Captain of Volunteers File, File No. 1674 vs. 1676, Box 1200, NARA.
41. Meyer, *Civil War Experiences*, 102.
42. Theodore F. Northrop, "Capture of Gen. Rhett," *National Tribune*, January 18, 1906. Northrop was mistaken: Colonel Alfred M. Rhett, captured at the March 16, 1865, Battle of Averasboro, was not a general officer.
43. T. E. Camburn, "Capture of Col. Rhett," *National Tribune*, August 23, 1906.
44. Northrop service records, RG 94, NARA.

Kilpatrick's command also included 94 officers and men of the 10th Battery, Wisconsin Light Artillery, commanded by Capt. Yates V. Beebe, who doubled as Kilpatrick's chief of artillery.[45] Three sections of two guns of horse artillery armed with three-inch ordnance rifles accompanied each brigade of cavalry assigned to Kilpatrick's division. These artillerists were veterans of the Atlanta Campaign and of the March to the Sea, and they had performed good service during their tenure with Sherman's army.

Kilpatrick's command consisted of reliable veteran troopers who had fought, marched, and ridden their way across much of the South. These men were well-armed, well-equipped, and fairly well-mounted. By 1865, the Federal government had become proficient in providing remounts to the cavalry. Virtually all of Kilpatrick's troopers carried seven-shot Spencer carbines, but there were also single-shot breech-loading weapons such as the Smith, Hall, Starr, Sharps, Joslyn, and Burnside carbines, reliable weapons with an effective range of about 300 yards.[46] Most of the men carried sabers and pistols, typically Colt or Remington .44 caliber revolvers. They typically traveled with enough ammunition to keep their cartridge boxes full, and they usually carried several additional cylinders of revolver ammunition so that they could quickly reload their pistols.[47]

---

45. This battery was recruited and organized at New Lisbon, Wisconsin, under Captain Beebe, and left the state on March 18, 1862. The battery initially served with the Army of Mississippi around Corinth, Mississippi, and with that part of the army that later became the Army of the Cumberland. Beebe's battery was not in action at the Battle of Stones River in Tennessee, as they were assigned duty escorting supply trains. That duty continued through May 1864 when they were assigned to Kilpatrick's Cavalry Division and re-equipped with three-inch rifles. The battery served the rest of the war with Kilpatrick. E. B. Quiner, *The Military History of Wisconsin: A Record of the Civil and Military of the Patriotism of the State in the War for the Union* (Chicago: Clarke & Co., 1866), 958-961.
46. These weapons were a variety of calibers, ranging from .52 caliber and .57 caliber in bore. The fact that the Union cavalry wasn't consistent in the armaments they used created logistical problems for maintaining inventories of replacement parts for so many types of weapons. Army doctrine dictated that a cavalry column on the march should carry only forage, provisions, and ammunition See Alonzo Gray, *Cavalry Tactics as Illustrated by the War of the Rebellion Together With Many Interesting Facts Important for Cavalry to Know*, 2 parts (Fort Leavenworth, KS: U.S. Cavalry Assoc., 1910), 1:146. This prompted Kilpatrick to complain on January 3, 1865, about breakage of the Joslyn and Sharps carbines. He said, "My troops are worse armed at present than Wheeler's irregular cavalry." Consequently, he begged to be sent 300 Spencer carbines. OR 44, 361.
47. Douglas D. Scott and William J. Hunt, Jr., *The Civil War Battle of Monroe's Crossroads: A Historical Archaeological Perspective* (Fort Bragg, NC: U.S. Army, 1998), 76-97. The Sharps was the most popular of the single-shot breech-loading carbines utilized by either side during the Civil War. It fired a .52 caliber bullet.

These veteran horse soldiers, confident that the long war was finally winding down, would need all of their experience, courage, and weaponry in the days ahead, and particularly at Aiken. Joe Wheeler had them squarely in his sights.

CHAPTER THREE

JOSEPH WHEELER AND HIS CONFEDERATE CAVALRY

Although attrition wore down the Confederacy armies to shadows of themselves by early 1865, the cavalry corps commanded by 28-year-old Maj. Gen. Joseph Wheeler remained a powerful and effective force. Wheeler and his veteran troopers had seen fighting in scores of battles and skirmishes. Two years ahead of Bvt. Maj. Gen. Judson Kilpatrick at the United States Military Academy at West Point, New York, Wheeler led the cavalry forces attached to the Army of Tennessee for most of the war. Only Maj. Gen. J. E. B. Stuart outranked Wheeler in the Southern mounted arm at that time.

Maj. Gen. Joseph Wheeler, Confederate commander at the Battle of Aiken.

(Library of Congress)

The youngest of four children, Joe Wheeler was born on September 10, 1836. He was the son of a prominent Connecticut businessman who had settled on a large plantation near Augusta, Georgia. Wheeler's paternal grandfather had been an American general in the War of 1812. His diminutive and frail-looking physique earned him the unflattering nickname of "Little Joe." Those who tagged him with that moniker were in for a surprise, because "Little Joe's" size belied his courage; he was utterly fearless.

Wheeler's mother died when he was five years old, and his father suffered a series of financial disasters that left the family bankrupt. A move to Connecticut failed to alleviate the family's plight, so the family returned to Augusta in an effort to regain the father's fortune. When that attempt failed, 13-year-old Joe Wheeler was sent to live with two aunts in Cheshire, Connecticut. When he graduated from Cheshire's Episcopal Academy, Wheeler moved to New York City to work as a clerk and live with a sister and her husband.

In 1854, Wheeler convinced a New York congressman to appoint him to West Point. He proved to be less than a mediocre student, graduating nineteenth out of 22 in the class of 1859. He finished dead last in cavalry tactics. Not to be deterred, though, he was commissioned a second lieutenant and assigned to the 1st U.S. Dragoons. In the spring of 1860, he was transferred to the Regiment of Mounted Rifles, where he saw combat against Indians in the New Mexico Territory. His aggressiveness earned him the nom-de-guerre "Fighting Joe," a moniker he proudly carried for the rest of his life.[1]

Despite his extensive family ties with the North, when Georgia seceded from the Union in 1861, Wheeler resigned his commission and accepted an appointment as a first lieutenant of artillery in the Provisional Confederate Army. He was ordered to report to Pensacola, Florida, where Southern volunteers were trying to level Fort Pickens. It was there that Wheeler met Brig. Gen. Braxton Bragg, whose patronage carried Wheeler to high rank. Within a short time, Wheeler was appointed colonel of the 19th Alabama and received orders to report to Mobile, Alabama. While leading his regiment in Tennessee at the Battle of Shiloh, a spent ball struck him and two horses were shot out from under him.

Late in the summer of 1862, Wheeler assumed command of a cavalry brigade, screening Bragg's advance into Kentucky. At the Battle of Perryville, Wheeler checked an entire Union infantry corps with only five regiments of horse. Impressed by his steely performance and coolness under fire, Bragg appointed the pugnacious little horse soldier as his chief of cavalry. Wheeler's troopers rode and fought night and day covering Bragg's withdrawal from Kentucky, a strong performance that earned him a brigadier general's wreath around his colonel's stars.

Wheeler performed well during the Stones River Campaign that winter, organizing an effective delaying action that hindered the advance of 40,000 Union soldiers for nearly four days. Twice he rode his horsemen around Maj. Gen. William S. Rosecrans's Army of the Cumberland in expeditions reminiscent of Jeb Stuart's more famous "Ride Around McClellan." A week later, Wheeler captured five transports and a gunboat on the Cumberland River, earning nomination for promotion to major general to date from January 20, 1863.[2] Later that year, Wheeler authored a well-regarded cavalry tactics

1. John P. Dyer, *From Shiloh to San Juan: The Life of "Fightin' Joe" Wheeler* (Baton Rouge: Louisiana State University Press, 1961), 1-15. For a good modern full-length biography of Wheeler, see Edward G. Longacre, *A Soldier to the Last: Maj. Gen. Joseph Wheeler in Blue and Gray* (Dulles, VA: Potomac Books, 2006).
2. Ibid., 18-57.

manual for Confederate horse soldiers and mounted infantry that was based on the French cavalry system.[3]

Unfortunately, Wheeler's fellow officers regarded him as the unpopular Bragg's "pet," an association that may have inhibited his career in the Confederate service. After a clash with Wheeler, Brig. Gen. Nathan Bedford Forrest refused to serve again under Wheeler, and other older officers, such as John Hunt Morgan, Earl Van Dorn, and John Wharton, also refused to take orders from "that boy."[4] Wheeler's poor performance during the opening phase of the Chickamauga Campaign permitted Rosecrans to steal a march on Bragg and capture Chattanooga, Tennessee, without bloodshed, a gross lapse that encouraged many to call for Wheeler's removal as Bragg's cavalry commander.[5] However, Wheeler skirted calls for his removal and retained command of the largest Confederate cavalry force in the Western Theater.

By early 1864, Joe Wheeler was one of the most experienced cavalry leaders in the entire Confederate service. Five horses had been shot out from under him, and his saddle, equipment, and uniform were frequently riddled with bullet holes.[6] He also had been wounded three times. One of his staff officers recalled, "No officer, since the commencement of the war, has been more exposed to the missiles of death than General Wheeler."[7] Seven of Wheeler's staff officers had been killed and three wounded. His participation in numerous engagements and close brushes with death earned him the respect of the men under his command, who called him "the War Child."[8]

Joe Wheeler stood only five feet, five inches tall and weighed a mere 120 pounds.[9] "His person is small, and in his manner there is nothing manly and commanding," one of his men observed. Like Braxton Bragg, and possibly a reason for their affinity, Wheeler had a

3. Joseph Wheeler, *A Revised System of Cavalry Tactics, for the Use of the Cavalry and Mounted Infantry, C.S.A.* (Mobile, AL: S. H. Goetzel & Co., 1863).
4. David Evans, *Sherman's Horsemen: Union Cavalry Operations in the Atlanta Campaign* (Bloomington: Indiana University Press, 1996), 242.
5. For a detailed examination of Wheeler's performance during the Chickamauga Campaign, see David A. Powell, *Failure in the Saddle: Nathan Bedford Forrest, Joe Wheeler, and the Confederate Cavalry in the Chickamauga Campaign* (El Dorado Hills, CA: Savas-Beatie, 2010).
6. "A Staff Officer," *Synopsis of the Military Career of Gen. Joseph Wheeler, Commander of the Cavalry Corps, Army of the West* (New York: n.p., 1865), 34.
7. "A Staff Officer," *Synopsis of the Military Career*, 34.
8. J. A. Wyeth, "Gen. Joseph Wheeler," *Confederate Veteran* 6 (1898), 361.
9. T. C. DeLeon, *Joseph Wheeler, the Man, the Statesman, the Soldier, Seen in Semi-Biographical Sketches* (Atlanta: Byrd Printing, 1899), 120 and 131.

rigid and upright demeanor. "The habits and moral character of Gen. Wheeler are of the most circumspect and high-toned nature," a staff officer recollected. "None of the vices of intemperance, or other bad habits common in the country, have been able to allure him from the spotless rectitude which distinguished him from his earliest childhood."[10]

Although possessed of "a spotless rectitude," the horseman was also a humorless martinet and unpopular with his fellow officers. "As a brigadier, he was successful, sober, industrious, and methodical," one critic, who objected to Wheeler's promotion to major general, wrote. "He succeeded well in organizing, but when the field of his operations was enlarged the draft on his intellect, which is one of mediocrity, became too heavy. He has signally failed to give satisfaction...He evidently handles men awkwardly in battle, for he has but few engaged at a time." After an acrimonious debate in the Confederate Senate, a direct appeal from Gen. Joseph E. Johnston finally secured Wheeler's confirmation as a major general in the spring of 1864.[11]

Wheeler performed competently during the Atlanta Campaign, but many problems plaguing his command limited its effectiveness. "We have a brave, gallant corps of Cavalry," a newspaper correspondent remarked, "but there seems to be something lacking."[12] What was lacking was discipline, and Wheeler's men quickly gained the reputation of being little more than hooligans. Some Southerners contended that Wheeler's horsemen inflicted as much damage on the Georgia countryside as did the passage of Sherman's army. Grumbling about Wheeler increased in all quarters. In a letter to the editor of her local newspaper, one woman noted that the people of Georgia were suffering from the "depredations" of Sherman's army and the "shameful" conduct of Wheeler's horsemen. "While the enemy were burning and destroying property on one side...[Wheeler's men] were stealing horses and mules on the other."[13]

A South Carolinian penned an open letter to Confederate Secretary of War James A. Seddon on January 14, 1865, which was published in the *Charleston Mercury*. "I cannot forebear appealing to you on behalf of the producing population of the States of Georgia and South Carolina for protection against the destructive lawlessness of members of General Wheeler's command," he began. "From Augusta

10. "A Staff Officer," *Synopsis of the Military Career*, 35.
11. Thomas L. Connelly, *Autumn of Glory: The Army of Tennessee, 1862-1865* (Baton Rouge: Louisiana State University Press, 1971), 316.
12. *Atlanta Southern Confederacy*, July 5, 1864.
13. Quoted in Jacqueline Glass Campbell, *When Sherman Marched North from the Sea: Resistance on the Confederate Home Front* (Chapel Hill: University of North Carolina Press, 2003), 10.

to Hardeeville the road is now strewn with corn left on the ground unconsumed. Beeves have been shot down in the fields, one quarter taken off and the balance left for buzzards. Horses are stolen out of wagons on the road, and by wholesale out of stables at night." After describing more Confederate cavalry depredations, the correspondent concluded:

> **Are General Wheeler and his brigade commanders not responsible to the country for stealing the stock engaged in the production of food for our army, the falling off in the production of corn alone in the States of Georgia and South Carolina may be counted by the hundred thousand bushels. Make the country one immense camp—let everybody be engaged in working for the support of the whole army, but for the sake of our glorious cause, give the producer the protection necessary to enable him to make bread. If General [Wade] Hampton's cavalry had used Virginia and North Carolina as General Wheeler's men have used Georgia and South Carolina, where would General Lee now be?**[14]

"The enemy care nothing for Wheeler and his seven thousand cavalry in the rear," Georgia politician Robert Toombs wrote to Confederate Vice President Alexander Stephens. "They did not obstruct his trains for more than four days, if that; and Wheeler avoided all depots where there were as much as armed sutlers. He has been gone [to Tennessee] for three weeks. I cannot say he has done no good for he has relieved the poor people of this part of the country temporarily from his plundering marauding bands of cowardly robbers...I hope to God he will never get back to Georgia." Another citizen complained to President Jefferson Davis that the people of Georgia had ceased caring who won the war; Sherman was not making war on them any harder than Wheeler's "robbers." Major General D. H. Hill, commanding at Augusta, wrote in January 1865 that "the whole of Georgia is full of bitter complaints about Wheeler's cavalry."[15]

A South Carolina cavalryman from the Army of Northern Virginia, who arrived a few days after the Battle of Aiken to defend his home state, observed Wheeler's men in the field and came away unimpressed. "While General Wheeler and his command possessed many good fighting qualities, yet neither he nor his men were immune to many bad ones," he recalled. "It is a well-known fact that they as a

14. "Outrages of Wheeler's Command," *Charleston Mercury*, January 14, 1865.
15. Dyer, *From Shiloh to San Juan*, 165.

whole or in part were badly disciplined, and were greatly dreaded by their friends at times."[16] This strong condemnation suggested that something had to be done quickly about Wheeler and his undisciplined horde, particularly given the nature of the crisis facing the Confederacy.

Wheeler's troopers were under orders to "drive off all cattle, sheep, and hogs not necessary for [their] consumption, and impress and send to Charleston" in an effort to deprive Sherman's army of forage as it advanced. Further, "all mills, boats, [or] buildings that may be used by the enemy for military purposes, and all rice, corn, and other provisions not necessary for the subsistence of the cavalry, and not absolutely needed for the consumption of owners, their families, and slaves" should be destroyed. "All wagons and teams (with drivers) on plantations about to fall into the hands of the enemy, and which are not required by the owners for the removal of their own property, will be impressed for the use of the army."[17]

During the winter of 1864-1865, Col. Alfred Roman, the inspector general of the Military Division of the West and a nephew of Gen. P. G. T. Beauregard, conducted a lengthy inspection of Wheeler's command. He did not like what he saw. Roman determined that Wheeler's cavalry corps was poorly organized and poorly armed, with no uniformity in its weaponry. More importantly, Roman noted, "Too much familiarity exists between officers and men. Discipline is thereby impaired. It has become loose, uncertain, wavering. Orders are not promptly obeyed. The military appearance is bad."

Roman continued:

> **Much has been said and is still being said of the gross misconduct of Gen. Wheeler's men. Their alleged depredations and straggling propensities and their reported brutal interference with private property have become common by-words in every county where it has been their misfortune to pass. Public opinion condemns them everywhere; and not a few do we find in Georgia as well as in South Carolina who look upon them more as a band of highway robbers than as an organized military body.**

Colonel Roman saved his strongest criticism for Joseph Wheeler himself. "No one admires General Wheeler more than I do," he began.

16. Charles M. Calhoun, "Credit to Wheeler Claimed by Others," *Confederate Veteran* 20 (1912), 82.
17. Quoted in Elmore, *Carnival of Destruction*, 108.

"He is a modest, conscientious, industrious officer. His activity is proverbial, and is equaled only by his gallantry. But he is wanting in firmness. His mind and his will are not in proper relation to one another. He is too gentle, too lenient, and we know how easily leniency can be made to degenerate into weakness." Roman also remarked, "General Wheeler's men like him, but do not appear to be proud of him. They know that he will always fight well, but seem to feel he cannot make them fight as well. The proposition that all who are able are not fit to be cavalry commanders," Roman concluded, "is assuming more and more the proportions of a self evident proposition."

Roman ended his eye-popping report with both a stunning and damning condemnation of the Augusta native:

> **My honest conviction is that General Wheeler would be a most excellent brigade or division commander, but I do not consider him the proper man to be placed at the head of a large independent cavalry corps. Under him and in spite of his good discipline and soldierly qualities, no true discipline will ever be perfect in his command nor with the whole efficiency of his corps, the entire fighting capabilities of his men, their dash, their intrepidity, be ever fairly and fully developed.**
>
> **Had I the power to act in the matter, I would relieve General Wheeler from his command, not as a rebuke, not as a punishment, for he surely deserves neither, but on higher grounds, that is, for the good of the cause and for his own reputation. We have no time to lose at this juncture of our affairs. If we wanted to resist we must do it gloriously, promptly and fear no personal dissatisfaction in the performance of our duties. We have too much at stake to hesitate a moment.**[18]

18. Alfred Roman to Col. G. W. Brent, January 22, 1865, Papers of Alfred Roman, Manuscripts Division, Library of Congress, Washington, D.C. Lieutenant General William J. Hardee, the department commander, disagreed with Roman's assessment. On January 8, 1865, he wrote to Jefferson Davis: "Wheeler's cavalry has been reorganized under my direct supervision, and now consists of three divisions and eight brigades. It is a well-organized and efficient body. The reports of its disorganization and demoralization are without foundation, and the depredations ascribed to his command can generally be traced to bands of marauders claiming to belong to it. I know of nothing at present to add to its effectiveness except the promotion of Brigadier-General Allen to major-general, and of Colonel Dibrell to brigadier-general, for which recommendations have been sent on." *OR* 47, 2:1000.

General Pierre G. T. Beauregard, commander of the Military Division of the West and Roman's uncle, agreed with his nephew's assessment. A few days after receiving the damning report, Beauregard sent a letter to Gen. Robert E. Lee, who by this time was the general-in-chief of the Confederate armies. Beauregard wrote, "I earnestly recommend, for the good of the service and cause, that General Hampton be promoted temporarily to command all the cavalry of this department, which cannot be rendered otherwise as effective as present emergencies demand. Major-General Wheeler, who ranks only a few days, is a modest, zealous, gallant, and indefatigable officer, but he cannot properly control and direct successfully so large a corps of cavalry."[19] Lee, who had never overseen any of Wheeler's operations, reluctantly agreed; Hampton was the capable commander of the Army of Northern Virginia's cavalry corps, the successor of Major General Stuart, and served as Lee's eyes and ears in Virginia.[20] Hampton's promotion, and its implications, is addressed in Chapter Seven of this book. Despite the pleas for Wheeler's removal, he retained command of his corps for the rest of the war, finally relinquishing it to Sherman's army as part of the mass surrender of Confederate forces negotiated on April 26, 1865.

A post-war photograph of Brig. Gen. William Y. C. Humes, commander of Humes' Division of Wheeler's Corps.

(Miller, Photographic History of the War)

Wheeler had about half of his corps with him at the Battle of Aiken. Specifically, he had the divisions of Brig. Gens. William Wirt Allen and William Y. C. Humes, numbering approximately 2,100 troopers organized into six brigades, forming a powerful force of veteran cavalrymen.

Brigadier General William Young Conn Humes commanded one of Wheeler's three divisions. Although he is known for his cavalry career, Humes spent the first half of the war as an artillerist. He was born in Abingdon, Virginia, on May 1, 1830, and later ranked

19. *OR* 47, 2:1165.
20. For the best full-length biography of Hampton, see Rod Andrew, Jr., *Wade Hampton: Confederate Warrior to Southern Redeemer* (Chapel Hill: University of North Carolina Press, 2008).

second in the class of 1851 at the Virginia Military Institute. After a year in Knoxville, Tennessee, he moved to the western end of the state and settled in Memphis where he studied law, was admitted to the bar, and opened a law office. In 1861, Humes received a commission as a lieutenant of artillery in the Confederate service, and soon after he made captain. He was captured in Tennessee when Island Number 10 fell on April 8, 1862. A short prison stint on Johnson's Island, in Lake Erie's Sandusky Bay, followed before he was exchanged on September 20.

For a time Humes commanded what was known as a "consolidated battalion" of exchanged prisoners slated to join Maj. Gen. Sterling Price's Army of the West. Little is known about this outfit, but it probably served as infantry. At Mobile, in the early weeks of 1863, Humes oversaw artillery and earthworks until Joe Wheeler asked that he be assigned to serve as his chief of artillery in March. Humes was wounded in a fight at Farmington on October 7, 1863, during Wheeler's Middle Tennessee Campaign. His actions won the plaudits of his superior, who praised Humes for his "great gallantry." Humes received a promotion to brigadier general to date from November 16, and assumed command of a brigade of Tennessee cavalry in Wheeler's corps. Difficult service followed under Lt. Gen. James Longstreet's command in eastern Tennessee. By the spring of 1864, Humes was back with the Army of Tennessee in northern Georgia. His duties significantly increased when he was given a division of cavalry shortly before the Atlanta Campaign began.

Humes participated in nearly every engagement of the Atlanta Campaign. "Throughout the whole campaign from Dalton to Atlanta the cavalry were kept busy, sometimes guarding the flank of the army, at times making raids to the rear of the enemy, and at other times meeting Federal raiders and defeating them," a biographer noted. Humes's command accompanied Wheeler on his disastrous raid into North Georgia, Tennessee, and northern Alabama in the late summer of 1864. His troopers harassed Sherman's men on the March to the Sea, earning the division commander a recommendation for promotion to major general. According to one writer, like many citizen-soldiers, Humes "learned to look upon danger and death as matters that could not be helped. Just as men strive to win the war in business by diligent application to duty, so men strove to win their way to promotion by proving themselves efficient and bold in battle."[21]

21. Ezra J. Warner, *Generals in Gray: Lives of the Confederate Commanders* (Baton Rouge: Louisiana State University Press, 1959), 144-145; Clement A. Evans, ed., *Confederate Military History: A Library of Confederate States History, Written by Distinguished Men of the South,* 12 vols. (Atlanta: Confederate Publishing Co., 1899), 8:313-314 (hereafter referred to as

A post-war photograph of Brig. Gen. Thomas Harrison, who commanded a brigade in Humes' Division.

(Museum of the Confederacy)

Humes's division consisted of three brigades. Brigadier General Thomas Harrison commanded one of them. His brigade was comprised of Texans and Arkansans. Harrison was born in Jefferson County, Alabama, on May 1, 1823, but he was raised in Monroe County, Mississippi. In 1843, he moved to Texas where he studied law before returning to Mississippi to serve in Jefferson Davis's 1st Mississippi Rifles during the Mexican-American War. At the end of that war Harrison returned to Texas, settling first in Houston and later in Waco, where he practiced law and took up politics. Because he had been the captain of a volunteer militia company, he was quickly commissioned a captain in the 8th Texas Cavalry—the renowned Terry's Texas Rangers. By April 1862, Harrison was a major and assumed command of his regiment during the second day at the Battle of Shiloh, in Tennessee, where the regimental commander was wounded. Harrison was appointed colonel just before the Battle of Stones River in December 1862. By July 1863, he was in charge of a cavalry brigade, which he capably led under Wheeler at Chickamauga and during the campaigns in Georgia and the Carolinas. "On January 14, 1865, he was commissioned a brigadier-general, an honor that he had long merited, having been in command of a brigade for more than a year."[22] Harrison's hard-fighting brigade, which Wheeler's men called the "charging Brigade," consisted of the 8th Texas, 11th Texas, 3rd Arkansas, and the consolidated 4th/8th Tennessee.[23]

"CMH"); Richard M. McMurry, *Virginia Military Institute Alumni in the Civil War: In Bello Praesidium* (Lynchburg, VA: H. E. Howard Co., 1999), 149. Humes was a VMI classmate of Brig. Gen. Alfred Vaughan, who commanded a brigade of Tennessee infantry in the Army of Tennessee. Humes was apparently nominated for a commission as a major general in late 1864 or early 1865, but the Confederate Senate likely never confirmed the promotion. If he received the promotion, word did not reach Humes before the Battle of Aiken.

22. Ibid., 126-127; *CMH* 11:239-240.

23. Roman to Brent, January 22, 1865. There were actually two different regiments designated as the 4th Tennessee. General Nathan Bedford Forrest

Colonel Henry M. Ashby commanded Humes's Tennessee brigade. Only 24 years old, Ashby hailed from Knox County, Tennessee. In the spring of 1861, he raised a company of cavalry in Knox County and was given a captain's commission for his efforts. The company became part of the 3rd Battalion Tennessee Cavalry, later consolidated into the 2nd Tennessee Cavalry Regiment. Ashby was appointed colonel of the 2nd Tennessee in May 1862. Serving in Wheeler's command, Ashby led his regiment in eastern Tennessee and Kentucky and in the Battles of Stones River and Chickamauga. While participating in a raid deep into Kentucky, the bone of Ashby's right heel was shot off, a painful wound that crippled him for life.

Col. Henry Ashby, commander of the Tennessee brigade of Humes' Division, Wheeler's Corps.

(Library of Congress)

When Wheeler reorganized his corps in the spring of 1864, Ashby assumed command of a brigade in Humes's division that May. "With this brigade Col. Ashby rendered conspicuous service under Gen. Wheeler, hovering on Sherman's flanks and rear down through Georgia and up through the Carolinas." Ashby earned the respect of all who served under him. "From the first to the last of his service Col. Ashby was on the front, always in the face of the enemy; and his ability, vigilance, and efficiency are attested by the fact that at no time during the four years of service was any body of troops, large or small, under his command surprised by the enemy," one of Ashby's staff officers remembered. "Personally he was one of the most genial of gentlemen, and no officer of any rank was more devotedly loved or implicitly trusted by his troops. Few officers were better known in the Army of Tennessee, and his superb horsemanship...was the admiration of all who knew him. Whether in camp, on the march, or in combat,

raised one regiment, and it was part of Col. William S. McLemore's brigade. The other 4th Tennessee fell under Wheeler's command and was the regiment that served in Harrison's brigade, which was consolidated with the small remnant of the 8th Tennessee Cavalry. The reader should be careful not to confuse these two regiments.

Col. William S. McLemore, commander of Dibbrell's Brigade of Humes' Division.

(Kevin McLemore)

Henry M. Ashby was a born soldier."[24] In the Carolinas, Ashby led the consolidated 1st/6th Tennessee, the 2nd Tennessee, and the 5th Tennessee cavalry regiments.

Humes's third brigade still carried the name of its original commander, Brig. Gen. George G. Dibrell, who now commanded Wheeler's third division. Colonel William L. S. McLemore, 33 years old, commanded Dibrell's brigade in February 1865. McLemore was tall with fair skin, and had dark hair and blue eyes. He would become a successful attorney from Williamson County, Tennessee. At seventeen, he enrolled at Transylvania University in Lexington, Kentucky, followed by the Cumberland Law School in Lebanon, Tennessee, in 1849. After completing his legal studies in 1851, McLemore opened a practice in Franklin, Tennessee. Three years later he unsuccessfully ran for attorney general for a three-county district. In 1856 he was elected county court clerk, a position he held until 1860 when he declined re-election and resumed practicing law. The following year McLemore became editor of a local newspaper, and he was sworn in as an assistant attorney general for the Confederate States of America.

In 1861, McLemore enlisted in Company F, 4th Tennessee Cavalry, serving under both Forrest and Wheeler. His unit was one of two designated as the 4th Tennessee Cavalry and was known as a "crack regiment." To distinguish these units, they were usually referred to by the names of their respective commanders. Thus, McLemore's command was known as the "Starnes-McLemore Regiment." In 1862, he received a promotion to captain and assumed command of Company F, although he also led the regiment when the regimental commander was wounded. While serving under Forrest, McLemore's 4th Tennessee helped capture Col. Abel D. Streight's mounted

24. James P. Coffin, "Col. Henry M. Ashby," *Confederate Veteran* 14 (1906), 121; "Henry Ashby's 2nd Tennessee Cavalry in the Confederate Heartland," by James L. Mohon in *Civil War Regiments: A Journal of the American Civil War, vol. 4, no. 1* (1994), 1-43.

command in northern Alabama. Since Col. J. W. Starnes was killed in battle on June 30, 1863, during the Tullahoma Campaign in Tennessee, McLemore received promotion to colonel on February 25, 1864, upon Forrest's written recommendation. "He has proved himself in every respect worthy and capable to fill the position," Forrest declared.[25] McLemore assumed command of Dibrell's brigade after Dibrell's promotion to division commander. McLemore had three horses shot out from under him in battle, but he was never wounded.[26] McLemore's brigade of Tennessee horse soldiers included Shaw's battalion, the 4th Tennessee Cavalry, and the 11th Tennessee Cavalry.[27]

Brigadier General William Wirt Allen commanded Wheeler's second division. On September 11, 1835, Allen was born in New York City into a family that was among the earliest settlers of Montgomery, Alabama. He graduated from Princeton in 1854 and read law after leaving college, although he chose not to practice. Instead, Allen took up planting, engaging in that pursuit when war found him in 1861. He entered the Confederate service as a lieutenant in the Montgomery Mounted Rifles in April 1861, reporting to Brig. Gen. Bragg in Pensacola, Florida. Allen remained with Bragg until the next fall, when he was elected major of the 1st Alabama Cavalry. He had a horse shot out from under him at the Battle of Shiloh in April 1862, and six months later on October 8, while he was in Kentucky, he was slightly wounded at the Battle of Perryville. When he returned to duty, Allen took command of the mounted forces attached to the left wing of

Brig. Gen. William W. Allen, commander of Allen's Division of Wheeler's Corps.

(Alabama Department of Archives and History)

25. Nathan Bedford Forrest to James A. Seddon, August 30, 1863, Kevin D. McLemore Collection, Fort Campbell, Kentucky.
26. At the 1863 Battle of Thompson's Station, McLemore's canteen was shot through, and he mistook the warm water dribbling down his side for blood. See Diary of Bethenia McLemore, Kevin D. McLemore Collection, at 106-107.
27. B. L. Ridley, "Chat with Col. W. S. McLemore," *Confederate Veteran* 8 (1900), 262-263; John E. Fisher, *They Rode with Forrest and Wheeler: A Chronicle of Five Tennessee Brothers' Service in the Confederate Western Cavalry* (Jefferson, NC: McFarland, 1995), 51.

Bragg's army. Allen was badly wounded at Stones River. "As a soldier he was cool and fearless in danger and tireless in the performance of duty. As a citizen he was cordial in manner and of ardent public spirit," a biographer observed.[28]

On February 26, 1864, Allen received an appointment as brigadier general and led a brigade during the Atlanta Campaign. Later that summer he assumed command of a division and led it throughout the March to the Sea and into the Carolinas. On March 4, 1865, Allen was appointed major general with temporary rank, but the Confederate Senate failed to confirm the promotion. "I would add that I was in active service and on duty in the field from the beginning to the close of the war, except when disabled by wounds received in action," an aged Allen wrote in 1894. "I was shot three times and had horses shot [from] under me ten times."[29]

Colonel James Hagan commanded one of Allen's brigades. Born in Ireland in 1821, Hagan and his parents immigrated to the United States when the boy was an infant. The family settled in Pennsylvania, where his father took up farming. Upon reaching adulthood, James joined his uncle's business in New Orleans and eventually settled in Mobile, Alabama. After gallant service in the Mexican-American War, Hagan took up planting, and in 1854 he married the beautiful and socially prominent daughter of Alabama's attorney general. With the outbreak of war, Hagan enlisted as a captain of a cavalry company raised in Mobile County, Alabama, and was later elected major when the 1st Alabama Cavalry was formed under Allen's command.

Col. James Hagan, commander of a brigade of Alabamans in Allen's Division, Wheeler's Corps.

(Library of Congress)

Not long after the Battle of Shiloh in 1862, Hagan was appointed colonel of a new regiment, the 3rd Alabama Cavalry. From that point forward he served with Wheeler's cavalry in all its campaigns, taking charge of a brigade of Alabama horse soldiers in 1863.

28. *CMH* 7:385-386.
29. William B. Jones, "The Late Maj. Gen. William Wirt Allen," *Confederate Veteran* 2 (1894), 324.

Hagan was wounded during battle twice in Tennessee (and would be a third time at the March 10, 1865, Battle of Monroe's Crossroads in North Carolina). "Being a man of generous nature and manly impulses, he was greatly admired and loved by his soldiers," Joe Wheeler remembered, long after the war. "He knew how to obey as well as command, and set before his men an example of the implicit obedience due by a subordinate to a superior officer."[30]

Hagan's veteran brigade consisted of the 1st, 3rd, 9th, 12th, 51st, and 53rd Alabama Cavalry regiments and the Alabama and Georgia companies of the 10th Confederate Cavalry regiment.

Brigadier General Robert H. Anderson commanded a brigade of Georgia horsemen in Allen's division. He was born in Savannah, Georgia, on October 1, 1835. After attending local schools, Anderson received an appointment to West Point. Graduating in 1857, he spent his Regular Army career in the infantry in the Pacific Northwest before resigning his commission in 1861 to enlist in the army of the new Confederacy. He was appointed a lieutenant of artillery, but soon thereafter, in September 1861, he received a promotion to major. Anderson served as Maj. Gen. W. H. T. "Shot Pouch" Walker's adjutant before transferring to a line regiment, the 5th Georgia Cavalry, in January 1863. The 5th Georgia joined Wheeler's corps and became part of Allen's brigade. When Allen assumed division command, Anderson succeeded him in command of the brigade. On July 26, 1864, he was promoted to brigadier general and served well throughout the Atlanta Campaign and the March to the Sea. Anderson was a competent officer with a solid command consisting of the 3rd, 5th, and 6th Georgia Cavalry and

Brig. Gen. Robert Anderson, commander of a brigade in Allen's Division.

(Museum of the Confederacy)

30. Bruce S. Allardice, *More Generals in Gray* (Baton Rouge: Louisiana State University Press, 1995), 111-113; CMH 7:415-416. There is some dispute whether Hagan received a promotion to brigadier general in the waning days of the war, and there is some evidence to indicate that he did. For the purposes of this work, Hagan will be considered a colonel.

Col. Charles C. Crews, commander of Crews' Brigade of Allen's Division, Wheeler's Corps.

(USAHEC)

the Alabama and Mississippi companies of the 8th Confederate Cavalry.[31]

Allen's third brigade consisted entirely of Georgians that Col. Charles C. Crews led. Thirty-five-year-old Crews was born in Harris County, Georgia, and raised in Ellerslie, where he studied law and medicine. He graduated in 1853 from Carleton Medical College and established a practice in Cuthbert, Georgia. In January 1861, he was elected ensign in a cavalry militia company before being commissioned a captain in the 2nd Georgia Cavalry in March 1862. He was captured during a raid in Kentucky that fall. After being exchanged in November, Crews was promoted to colonel of the regiment. He was severely wounded in the hip on January 3, 1863. After a painful convalescence, he resumed command of a brigade consisting of the 1st, 2nd, 4th, and 12th Georgia Cavalry regiments in 1864. Crews led the brigade for an extended period of time and received several citations for gallantry from Wheeler. Crews had a habit of attracting enemy metal and found himself wounded yet again while in South Carolina in 1865. His command was known to be a particularly unruly unit, perhaps the worst of all of Wheeler's undisciplined corps.[32]

The gray-clad troopers riding with Wheeler carried a hodgepodge of weapons. Colonel Alfred Roman's inspection report of January 1865 indicates that Wheeler's troopers carried "arms of eight or nine different calibers, but mostly calibers .57 and .54," including a large number of captured Federal weapons. Most of the arms were Enfield, Springfield, and Austrian rifle-muskets rather than cavalry carbines. In January the corps numbered 6,607 weapons in serviceable condition, which included 3,896 rifles, 500 carbines, and 1,978 pistols. "When the

31. Warner, *Generals in Gray*, 9-10; *CMH* 6:392-394.
32. Allardice, *More Generals in Gray*, 66-67; John Randolph Poole, *Cracker Cavaliers: The 2nd Georgia Cavalry Under Wheeler and Forrest* (Macon, GA: Mercer University Press, 2000), 13 and 182.

war closed in 1865," one of Wheeler's Alabamans recalled, "more than fifty per cent of the arms, accouterments and equipment generally of the Confederate cavalry, bore the imprint of the United States."[33] A deficiency resulted of about 1,447 rifles and carbines and 3,747 pistols, meaning that most of Wheeler's command did not have a full complement of weapons during the final phase of the war. In addition, only 50 to 60 members of Anderson's brigade carried sabers. Wheeler's command would have to fight with only firearms.[34]

The Southern horsemen were very short on ammunition too. They carried an average of 35 to 40 rounds per man, and Wheeler's reserve train hauled approximately 40 rounds per man. This meant that extensive resupply, during or after a severe firefight, would have been a difficult proposition.[35] Because the Confederate government dictated that cavalrymen were responsible for their own mounts, replacing killed, wounded, or crippled horses was a daunting task—especially in 1865. "When a soldier owns the horse he rides, when experience teaches him that though bound to pay for its loss in action, the Government is never ready to do so, that soldier will invariably take so much care of his horse so as to feel at least disinclined to risk him in a battle," Colonel Roman astutely observed. "That soldier therefore cannot do as good service as if he knew that as many horses might be shot under him just as many more would the Government give him."[36] Men who lost their mounts had two choices: struggle along with their command as a dismounted trooper or obtain leave and try to find a replacement. Either way, the government remount policy hampered the effectiveness of the Confederate cavalry.[37]

33. "Unveiling of Confederate Monument at Montgomery, AL: Major Falkner's Words," *Charleston Sunday News*, November 20, 1898. For a detailed description of the weaponry Wheeler's corps carried, see Wayne R. Austerman, "C. S. Cavalry Arms—1865," *North South Trader*, vol. XII, no. 2 (Jan.-Feb. 1985), 22-27.
34. Roman to Brent, January 22, 1865. In fact, the Confederates tended to prefer captured Yankee ordnance to their own weapons. This made supplying ammunition for the captured weapons difficult, at best.
35. Dodson, *Campaigns of Wheeler and His Cavalry*, 408-420.
36. Roman to Brent, January 22, 1865. Colonel Roman speculated that this was part of the reason for the poor discipline in Wheeler's command.
37. By contrast, in 1863, the Union established a Cavalry Bureau. The primary task of the Cavalry Bureau was to provide remounts for Union cavalry regiments. While the Cavalry Bureau was plagued by corruption charges, it nevertheless provided an efficient means of replacing cavalry horses lost in the field. Government purchasing agents bought the horses, and the United States government supplied them to its soldiers. The system was not perfect, but it was far more efficient than what the Confederacy employed. For more detail, see Stephen Z. Starr, *The Union Cavalry in the Civil War, 3 vols.* (Baton Rouge: Louisiana State University Press, 1981), 2:4-6.

At the beginning of February 1865, when it was announced that cavalry forces from the Army of Northern Virginia were transferring to South Carolina, calls for 1,500 horses went out across the countryside. Local newspapers published patriotic appeals for the local populace to provide remounts for the Confederate cavalry. "Will not every man who has a horse he can do without—not that he can conveniently spare—sell him to the government at a moderate price, rather than to keep him to consume grain needed by the army, or to sell him for a fancy price, and thus risk all." The newspaper announcements indicated that Wheeler's chief of scouts, Capt. Alexander Shannon of the 8th Texas Cavalry, was authorized to receive the horses and forward requests for payment.[38]

However, only department commanders had authority to impress horses into service, and the local citizenry was in no mood to give up its horses. In South Carolina, General Beauregard was the department commander, and he did not issue impressment orders. Three weeks after the initial patriotic appeals went out, a newspaper from Edgefield, South Carolina, declared that "when such urgent appeals and such strenuous efforts were being made to procure horses...Gen. Hardee, then in command of the department, gave no order for impressment—though the need was so great and pressing. Our people will remember this. Therefore, all these orders from Gen. Wheeler...ought to be sternly and stubbornly resisted. They have no authority whatever to issue such orders."[39] Fed up with the depredations of Wheeler and his troopers, civilians were in no hurry to provide desperately needed remounts for the Confederate cavalry.

Though it was hampered, the Southern cavalry prepared to vigorously engage its Northern counterpart. Most of these commands had fought many times across several states in a wide variety of battles. They knew each other well, having tangled many times, and they were about to clash again.

38. *The Tri-Weekly Journal*, February 1, 1865.
39. "Unlawful Impressments," *Edgefield Advertiser*, February 22, 1865.

CHAPTER FOUR

FEBRUARY 10, 1865: THE DAY BEFORE

Aiken was a a strategic spot. It sits thirteen miles from Augusta, Georgia, and five miles from the important mill town of Graniteville, South Carolina. Incorporated on December 19, 1835, Aiken was developed around the terminus of the South Carolina Canal and Railroad Company, which connected Charleston to the Savannah River. It was named for William Aiken, the first president of the railroad. As the terminus of the railroad, Aiken was critical to maintaining operations on the rail line, and, consequently, the town sprang up around it. Because of the railroad's importance, Aiken was a logical place for the Confederate cavalry to defend, and, likewise, it was a logical target for the Union army, which was determined to deprive the Southern armies access to the railroad. By the 1860s, the town became a major health resort that boasted several hundred permanent residents. Aiken was laid out on a grid that featured 150-feet-wide tree-lined avenues.[1]

The Union troopers took out their long-awaited revenge against the local countryside. A year after the Battle of Aiken, a former Union officer noted, "From Branchville to Aiken the railroad had been completely destroyed." He continued, "Rail fences were destroyed. Half burned sleepers and bent rails were everywhere in sight and piles of ashes indicated where the bivouacs had been. Unsightly chimneys not yet overgrown with foliage showed the sadder features of war."[2]

"The 1 Brigade left camp at 7 AM and marched 4 miles," trooper Cornelius Baker, 9th Pennsylvania Cavalry, wrote in his diary on February 10. "Found the rebels in foarce [sic] in our front and right and the balance of our forse [sic] were immediately brot [sic] up for protection." He noted that his brigade commander, Col. Thomas J. Jordan, was nearly captured.[3]

Brevet Major General Judson Kilpatrick's men made three different attempts to burn James Courtney's house. Determined to

1. Toole, *Ninety Years in Aiken County*, 9-12.
2. Suzanne Stone Johnson and Robert Allison Johnson, eds., *Bitter Freedom—William Stone's Record of Service in the Freedmen's Bureau* (Columbia: University of South Carolina Press, 2008), 4.
3. Rowell, *Yankee Cavalrymen*. 226.

defend his home, Courtney somehow managed to extinguish the flames each time until a Union horse soldier finally shot him in the leg, keeping him from interfering with their efforts. As Courtney bled to death, he begged for a doctor, but his pleas fell on deaf ears. He died watching the flames take hold of his home for the final time.[4]

"The following day we reached Windsor without much opposition, where we drew three days' rations from the wagons, and on the 10th we camped at night within five miles of Aiken, where we found Wheeler gathering his forces to give battle, the scouts reporting him only two miles ahead in our front and in force," a captain of the 10th Ohio Cavalry recalled. "The division was placed in position and at once began throwing up works, and by morning we had strong barricades which extended along our entire front and on both flanks, with artillery in position."[5] Another Buckeye horse soldier claimed that the barricades covered half a mile and were situated in a semicircle around the train station. "We have not been disturbed today but Expect to have a pretty smart one tomorrow," he concluded.[6] The men spent the day tearing up nearly five miles of track. Each of Kilpatrick's regiments was responsible for destroying a length of the railroad equal to the ground the regiment covered standing dismounted in a single rank, or about 1,000 feet.[7]

Lieutenant Colonel William B. Way and his dismounted Provisional Brigade, marching as infantry, arrived about 3:00 p.m. at Johnson's Turnout (also known as Johnson's Station, located at the modern village of Montmorenci, South Carolina). Along the way his men burned several culverts, four flatcars, and five boxcars and destroyed one mile of railroad track. They then took a position covering both the dirt road and railroad to Aiken.[8]

At Johnson's Turnout on the railroad, Kilpatrick established his camp at Pascalina, the handsome plantation belonging to John and Theodosia Wade. The sound of sharp skirmishing signaled the presence of the enemy, so the Union troopers threw up barricades for protection.[9] His men fanned out across the countryside, foraging. The DeCaradeuc and Heyward families lived at the Montmorenci

4. Pete Peters, *The Battle of Aiken Commemorative Program, 131st Anniversary of the Battle of Aiken* (Aiken, SC: Brig. Gen. Barnard E. Bee Camp, Sons of Confederate Veterans, 1996). For additional similar stories about how Kilpatrick's men treated civilians that day, see Elmore, *Carnival of Destruction*, at 136.
5. "A 10th Ohio Cavalryman," "Campaign of the Carolinas."
6. Carter, *The Story of Joshua D. Breyfogle*, 321.
7. Berkenes, *Private William Buddy's Civil War Journal*, 169.
8. *OR* 47, 1:903.
9. Hinman, *The Story of the Sherman Brigade*, 911.

Pascalina plantation house, the home of John and Theodosia Wade, served as Kilpatrick's headquarters while in the Aiken area.

(Author's photo)

plantation in Johnson's Turnout. Northern troopers showed up at Elizabeth Heyward's gate shouting, "Here come the Yankees, look out now you d----d rebels." Before Heyward knew what was going on, the Federals were inside her house. They forced Heyward and her grandmother to turn over keys to the house and demanded the women bring their liquor, gold, and silver, while ordering that the "old women, hurry yourselves!"[10]

Heyward later wrote that "there were hundreds of them in the house, upstairs, in the garret, in every chamber, under the house, in the yard, garden, &c., &c., some singing, shouting, whistling, and Oh, my God, such cursing." The Yankee troopers destroyed furniture, including a piano, threw clothing everywhere, and stole almost everything of value, including the silver, jewelry, and even some paintings. They also looted the quarters of the family slaves.[11]

10. Mary D. Robertson, ed., *A Confederate Lady Comes of Age: The Journal of Pauline DeCaradeuc Heyward, 1863-1888* (Columbia: University of South Carolina Press, 1992), 65-66.
11. Ibid., 66.

After the main raiding party left, little of value remained in the house. "A horrid looking ruffian came into the parlor, seeing only women there, he entered shut both doors, & said in an undertone, 'You cursed rebels, now empty your pockets.'" Heyward had a bag of ammunition in her pocket, which she hid while another woman distracted the Northerner. He found Heyward's watch in her pocket. "Ah," the Yankee said, "This is a pretty little watch, now where is the key, & does it go good?" He took everyone's money and watches, and then looked at Heyward's mother, Elizabeth Ann DeCaradeuc, in the eye and growled, "Now you've just got to tell me where your gold & silver is buried, I know you've got it, and if you know what's good for yourself & all in this room, you'll tell me where it is."

"I have no gold, and my silver you have all taken with every other valuable in the house," DeCaradeuc calmly replied.

"That's a d----d lie, now I'll burn your house this minute, if you don't tell me."

"I have nothing more to tell, do you think I'd tell a lie," she responded.

"I don't know," said the Northerner. He walked up and down the room swearing, threatening, and spitting, searching for the treasure he knew had to be hidden there. He even took a slave outside, held a gun to the man's head, and threatened to blow his brains out if the slave didn't disclose the location of the treasure. Frustrated, the Union trooper finally left, leaving the distraught women to clean up the mess and take stock of their losses.[12]

The Toole family also lived near Johnson's Turnout. Loren Toole, who was a boy in 1865, recalled that Kilpatrick's troopers "took my father's horses, corn, and all supplies they could find. What they could not carry away they burned in the field. My mother often told me my father had tried to save the horses. Too old to go to war, he was at home at the time and was hiding the horses in the swamp. My brothers, Harrison and Frank, were with him but Ransey and Kelly had been left at home because my parents thought them too young for the Yankees to molest."

He noted that the Federals, hoping to scare the boys into telling them where their father was hiding, put ropes around their necks, placed them on horses, and carried them into the woods, implying that they were going to hang the boys. Although terrified, the boys "kept their mouths steadfastly closed, refused to tell, and the Yankees let them go."

12. Ibid., 66-67.

A Union officer, "a little more human than the rest, told my mother that, if her husband and other men folks were hiding, she had better inform them that they would be shot like dogs if the raiders and hunters came across them. She took his advice and sent for my father and brothers who turned the horses loose, all of which were caught and stolen by the Yankees except one colt." Toole's father was promptly arrested and carried away with the Union army, but he and a captured neighbor escaped and returned home a few days later, none the worse for the ordeal.

After her husband was marched away, a distraught Mrs. Toole was forced to cook for the Union officers while they camped at her home. Some of them smashed the family's dishes against a tree after they finished eating, just to be spiteful. Before leaving, the troopers tried to set the house on fire, but the enterprising Mrs. Toole snuffed the flames and saved the family homestead.[13]

While his men plundered, Kilpatrick met with Maj. Gens. William T. Sherman and Henry W. Slocum at Blackville, South Carolina. This was the first time that Sherman had spoken with his subordinates since departing from Savannah. He told them that the Left Wing would march directly to the state capital at Columbia, while the Right Wing would march to Columbia via Orangeburg, South Carolina.[14] The stage was now set for the drama that would play out in Aiken the next day.

Judson Kilpatrick and Joe Wheeler were old adversaries, having met many times during the Atlanta Campaign and again during the March to the Sea. The streets in Aiken would be their next meeting ground. Would Wheeler or Kilpatrick prevail?

---

13. Toole, *Ninety Years in Aiken County*, 16.
14. Sherman, *Memoirs*, 2:274.

Maj. Gen. Daniel Harvey Hill, division commander in Hardee's Department.

(Museum of the Confederacy)

The house that served as Wheeler's headquarters during the Battle of Aiken.

(Author's photo)

CHAPTER FIVE

WHEELER SPRINGS HIS TRAP

Major General D. H. Hill, commanding the Confederate garrison at Augusta, encouragingly said to Maj. Gen. Joseph Wheeler on the morning of February 11, "I regret very much the delay about the corn. I want to help you all I can. I do trust that you may be able to concentrate and beat that marauding rascal, Kilpatrick."[1] Fighting Joe was working on a plan to do just that when Hill's note arrived. Wheeler had established his headquarters in druggist W. H. Harbors's modest yellow frame house, located at 204 Park Avenue in the center of Aiken.[2]

Hill also transferred the local Aiken Mounted Infantry to serve as guides for Wheeler and his men. The Mounted Infantry was a militia unit "composed of old and young men exempted from regular fighting" who enlisted in the Barnwell, Aiken, and Lexington districts. The company consisted of about 60 men armed with rapid-firing breech-loading carbines. The men had originally planned to patrol the Savannah River in order to keep an eye on Sherman's movements, but when the Federals turned toward Aiken, Hill ordered the Mounted Infantry to return to their hometown. They established their camp outside town and awaited further orders. On the morning of February 11, Wheeler ordered the Mounted Infantry's commander, Capt. William F. Percival, to send guides to accompany the general toward town, where Wheeler planned on laying out his defensive position. The rest of the Mounted Infantry fell in with Wheeler's main body.[3]

Wheeler knew that his mounts and men were near the limits of their endurance, particularly the starving horses. Consequently, he realized that any plan requiring his men to chase after Bvt. Maj. Gen. Judson Kilpatrick's troopers would not work; his horses lacked the necessary stamina to engage in a protracted chase. Instead, Fighting Joe

---

1. *OR* 47, 2:1163.
2. R. Wayne Jones and Thomas D. Perry, *The Battle of Aiken South Carolina. Kilpatrick vs. Wheeler February 11, 1865* (Ararat, VA: Laurel Hill Publishing, 2011), 55.
3. "A Member of the Aiken Mounted Infantry," "For the Advertiser," *Edgefield Advertiser*, January 25, 1865. An article published more than 50 years later referred to these men as the Aiken Home Guard and not as the Aiken Mounted Infantry. See "Anniversary Aiken Fight. Fifty-Two Years Ago Wheeler and Kilpatrick Fought Here," *The Journal and Review*, February 14, 1917.

decided to set an ambush for the unwary Federals as they marched into Aiken. Knowing his former West Point chum Kilpatrick tended to be rash and impulsive, Wheeler intended to make maximum use of the grid-like layout and wide avenues of the town. He planned to draw the Yankees into his ambush by placing pickets outside the town who would then retreat into Aiken with the Federals pursuing. Once Kilpatrick's entire force had entered the town, the rest of Wheeler's command would pounce on it. Woods and farm fields surrounding Aiken would hide Wheeler's men from the unwitting Northerners as they marched into the trap.[4]

"The country was level with timber and cornfield alternating," a Union colonel recalled.[5] The terrain lent itself well to camouflaging the Confederate troopers. Wheeler hid his men in columns in the avenues of the town, with each column prepared to charge. He placed Brig. Gen. William Y. C. Humes's entire division in line, while Brig. Gen. William Allen's dismounted men deployed in the nearby streets.[6] The wide streets gave the Confederate cavalrymen a distinct advantage. The large number of trees provided camouflage and cover for the Southerners. Wheeler also scattered his men at irregular intervals to try to hide their numbers. "We were formed into a hollow square, leaving one side open, through which Kilpatrick would have to march," trooper D. B. Morgan, 5th Georgia Cavalry, described. "The Alabama regiment guarding the entrance on both sides was ordered not

St. Thaddeus Church, Aiken, South Carolina.

(Aiken Historical Society)

4. Posey Hamilton, "Incidents of the Fighting at Aiken, S.C.," *Confederate Veteran* 32 (February 1924), 58.
5. William Douglas Hamilton, *Recollections of a Cavalryman of the Civil War After Fifty Years, 1861-1865* (Columbus, OH: The F. J. Heer Printing Co., 1915), 183.
6. Collier, *The War Child's Children*, 128.

to fire a gun until the entire force passed through, as the first shot would be a signal for a general engagement."[7]

"I was a boy then," Alabama trooper John C. Baird of Wheeler's command remembered, "but I don't think I ever felt as large before or since as I did when we rode down that street among the cheers of [the] beautiful women" of Aiken. The women made sure that the Confederate troopers had food and water while they waited for the arrival of Kilpatrick's command, and some even helped to bring ammunition to the Confederate troopers.[8] Eight-year-old H. A. Busch carried water to Wheeler's waiting men, drawn up in line of battle in front of his family's house. He dipped the water out in a gourd, which he kept as a souvenir.[9]

Rev. John H. Cornish, rector of St. Thaddeus Church.

(St. Thaddeus Church)

Reverend John H. Cornish was the rector of the local Episcopal church, St. Thaddeus. Reverend Cornish, known for "his zealous, faithful work, and held the love and esteem of all who came in contact with him as a true friend and earnest Christian," was having breakfast in his house with a captain from Humes's division when a breathless courier arrived to inform the officer that it was time to join his command.[10] Reverend Cornish's son Willie had been stationed at a

7. D. B. Morgan, "Incidents of the Fighting at Aiken, S. C.," *Confederate Veteran* 22 (1924), 300.
8. Isabel Vandervelde, *The Battle of Aiken* (Aiken, SC: Art Studio Press, n.d.), 14; "Anniversary Aiken Fight."
9. Elizabeth C. Teague, "The Battle of Aiken," copy in files, Aiken County Historical Museum, Aiken, South Carolina, 1. Young Busch witnessed the death of two soldiers in front of him at the height of the battle.
10. Joseph E. Cornish, *The History and Genealogy of the Cornish Families in America* (Boston: Geo. H. Ellis Co., 1907), 85. John Hamilton Cornish was born in Ypsilanti, Michigan Territory, in 1815. He left home in 1833 and enrolled in Washington College in Hartford, Connecticut, graduating in 1839. Cornish then studied at the General Theological Seminary in New York City for a few months, but did not graduate. He relocated to Edisto Island, South Carolina, where he became a tutor on a plantation and later ran an academy there. In 1843 he was ordained. Cornish married Martha Jenkins of Edisto

fence post to serve as a lookout and spotted the approach of Kilpatrick's vanguard in the distance. Willie then spread the alarm that the enemy was approaching.[11]

Wheeler concentrated the largest portion of his command to the south of the town where they could pounce on Kilpatrick's rear and cut off his escape route. James Lambright, who rode with the 5th Georgia Cavalry, recalled that the Confederates had formed a large "V" "extending with top towards the approach; side lines on each side of the road, and bottom of [the V] at Aiken."[12] Orlando Chester, who also rode with the 5th Georgia, recalled that Wheeler "placed a small force at the opening of the V with orders to fight them a little while and I think to stampede and draw them in and they charged them on both flanks."[13] Park Avenue and the railroad split the "V." Wheeler designed a brilliant plan that played to his foe's well-known weaknesses and propensity for rashness. He had five brigades—23 regiments of cavalry—and one battalion of horse artillery. If all went as planned, Kilpatrick's command would be drawn into the ambush and then crushed.[14] However, it is a maxim of war that "no plan of operations extends with any certainty beyond the first contact with the main hostile force," as the great nineteenth century strategist and chief of the Prussian General Staff, Field Marshal Helmuth von Moltke, famously declared.[15] Aiken proved to be no exception to Moltke's rule.

Captain James Brazier commanded a company of the 10th Confederate Cavalry Regiment. A Confederate cavalryman recalled that Brazier "was a very quiet man, kind to his men, but a brave

---

Island, and they had six children. He became the rector of St. Thaddeus Church in August 1846. He was 50 years old in February 1865, and had been the rector of the church for nearly 20 years. Cornish resigned his position in 1868, performing missionary work in various parts of South Carolina. On May 24, 1878, at the age of 63, Cornish died. He was buried in the St. Thaddeus Church graveyard. Ibid.

11. H. Addison McClaren, *St. Thaddeus of Aiken: A Church and Its City* (Spartanburg, SC: The Reprint Co., 1994), 35
12. Timothy Daiss, ed., *In the Saddle: Exploits of the Fifth Georgia Cavalry* (Atglen, PA: Schiffer, 1999), 28.
13. Ibid., 115.
14. Dyer, *From Shiloh to San Juan*, 170 and Peters, *Battle of Aiken*. Most accounts of the Battle of Aiken suggest that Wheeler had 2,100 men present that day, but if he had six brigades, as Dyer and other sources claim, then all but a single brigade of his corps was present. Since the strength of his corps was approximately 4,000 men, and all but one brigade was present at Aiken, then he had more than 2,100 troopers with him. For purposes of this study, I have assumed that Wheeler's effective strength at Aiken on February 11, 1865, was closer to 3,000 troopers.
15. Daniel J. Hughes, ed., *Moltke on the Art of War: Selected Writings* (New York: Presidio Press, 1993), 92. Moltke's iconic statement is sometimes paraphrased as "no battle plan survives contact with the enemy."

officer." The captain would need his courage that day. Brazier and about 15 of his troopers were out on picket duty that morning. While he made his way back to his command, Brazier entered a farmhouse to get breakfast, leaving some of his men on watch at the gate. Soon, his men sent up the alarm, and Brazier was back in the saddle before even getting his breakfast. One of Kilpatrick's troopers dashed up and slashed Brazier from his saddle with a saber. The rest of Brazier's men escaped and reported that Brazier and two or three of his men had been captured. A few minutes later, and to the surprise of the Confederates, Captain Brazier and his bedraggled men arrived on foot, receiving a hearty greeting and congratulations on their escape. Brazier was furious about his humiliation and anxious to get revenge. Someone gave him a horse, and he took his position in Wheeler's line to await the arrival of the Yankee cavalry, eagerly anticipating his chance to return the favor to Kilpatrick's horsemen.[16]

A local 14-year-old boy named James A. Jones carried Confederate mail to Aiken for delivery that morning. As he approached the town from the direction of Johnson's Turnout, he heard rapid firing and saw large numbers of gray-clad horse soldiers just marking time. He passed through the group of mounted soldiers and headed into town when he ran into a group of officers. "A fine looking officer approached me and said, 'Hello, young man. Where are you going?'" Jones told him that he was carrying the mail to Aiken. "He then said he was General Wheeler and asked me if I heard the shooting in Aiken and if I was not afraid to go into town. I replied I was not afraid. He told me not to go into town and he would report that he turned me back with the mail."[17]

Kilpatrick expected Wheeler to attack him on the morning of February 11, so he decided to preempt Wheeler and take the fight to his adversary. At 3:00 a.m., Capt. Harvey M. Timms led out a detachment of scouts from the 92nd Illinois Mounted Infantry to surprise and attack Wheeler's pickets.[18] "We were dismounted, leaving our horses at the Reserve Picket Post, by going over the fields and through the timber," Pvt. William Boddy, 92nd Illinois, recalled. "We managed to surprise them, capturing one man and killing one and skedaddling the rest to their camp and capturing four horses with no

16. Hamilton, "Incidents of the Fighting at Aiken, S. C.," 58-59.
17. James A. Jones, "A Reminiscence of the Aiken Skirmish," *Aiken County Historical Society Journal* Vol. 3, No. 3 (October 1988), 1-2.
18. *OR* 47, 1:882-883.

loss to our side." The Illini then attacked the main Confederate vidette reserve, driving them back to their main force.[19]

Kilpatrick still expected Wheeler to attack and was surprised when it never came. The Union general divided his command, leaving three of his four brigades in camp at Johnson's Turnout. He elected to use Smith Atkins's Second Brigade to advance on Aiken. "This morning at seven o'clock our whole Brigade was ordered out on a scouting party," Sgt. Joshua D. Breyfogle, 10th Ohio Cavalry, wrote in his diary that night. "It is a beautiful day for the business."[20] The Second Brigade's order of march that morning placed the 92nd Illinois in advance, followed by the section of artillery, and then the 9th Michigan, 10th Ohio, and 9th Ohio Cavalry bringing up the rear.[21] General Kilpatrick, riding his favorite horse, a paint named Spot, led the Second Brigade on its scout while the rest of the division remained at Johnson's Turnout.[22]

Capt. John M. Schermerhorn, 92nd Illinois Mounted Infantry.

(Abraham Lincoln Presidential Library & Museum)

"Not receiving an attack, Kilpatrick early the next morning, after taking a fresh supply of ammunition, with the Second Brigade moved out to develop the strength and position of the enemy, also taking with him four guns of Capt. Beebe's 10th Wis. battery, leaving the other three brigades behind their works," an officer of the 10th Ohio Cavalry reported.[23] Captain John M. Schermerhorn

19. Berkenes, *Private William Boddy's Civil War Journal*, 170. Vidette is a French term meaning "a mounted sentry placed in front of a body of troops." Their job was to provide an early warning system for the main body by detecting the advance of the enemy and resisting their advance. Vidette posts were placed every 30 to 40 feet apart, and typically consisted of three or four men commanded by a non-commissioned officer. The vidette reserve, otherwise known as the grand guard, were the body of soldiers available to reinforce the videttes on duty at the front.
20. Carter, *The Story of Joshua D. Breyfogle*, 321.
21. *OR* 47, 1:887. A section of artillery is two guns.
22. Ibid., 879; McMaster, "Kilpatrick's Cavalry at Aiken, S. C."
23. "A 10th Ohio Cavalryman," "Campaign Through the Carolinas."

and a battalion of the 92nd Illinois Mounted infantry led the way on the left, while Capt. Theodore F. Northrop and his scouts had the vanguard on the right; all set out hoping to locate Wheeler's horsemen.[24]

"Wheeler during the night had withdrawn his division then in our front, to the west and just beyond the town, leaving only a light picket-line in our front, which as we advanced was easily driven back," an Ohioan recollected. "Coming in sight of the town the four regiments were massed by regimental front in a peach orchard just east of the place, while Kilpatrick with his staff and escort rode rapidly up into the town to make observation and destroy the depot. As we sat upon our horses we could see his colors as we entered the main street, not a half mile away."[25] Not long after they moved out, a local woman told Atkins and Kilpatrick that Wheeler and Maj. Gen. Benjamin F. Cheatham, who commanded a corps of the Army of Tennessee, had been at her house that morning, which motivated the Federals to continue their advance toward Aiken.[26] Kilpatrick took Wheeler's bait.

Wheeler's bait, a detachment of 25 mounted troopers, waited for Kilpatrick's arrival near a pond about half a mile east of the town. When Schermerhorn's troopers spotted the 25 mounted Confederates about 10:30 a.m., they abruptly halted and opened fire. Trooper Posey Hamilton was one of the Confederates assigned to decoy duty. His comrade Buck Busby "was an arm's length on my right and received a shot in his right side which passed through his body and only a few inches in front of me," Hamilton recalled. "The poor fellow cried, 'I am shot' and insisted on my getting down to help him off his horse while we were in front of that company of soldiers and them shooting at us with pistols as rapidly as they could fire." Hamilton wheeled his horse around and told his wounded comrade to follow. They found a place where Busby would be sheltered from the continual gunfire. Hamilton helped the severely wounded Busby dismount. Hamilton spread his blanket on the ground and made Busby as comfortable as possible, but the 21 year old died that night in a field hospital. Another Confederate trooper, named Motes, was briefly captured. Motes had hidden a gun under his saddle blanket, which he pulled out and used to kill his captor, and then escaped.[27]

24. *OR* 47, 1:882; Pepper, *Personal Recollections*, 363.
25. "A 10th Ohio Cavalryman," "Campaign Through the Carolinas."
26. *OR* 47, 1:879. It seems very unlikely that Cheatham had breakfast with Wheeler that morning. While Cheatham wasn't far away, the likelihood is that he did not arrive in time to have breakfast with Wheeler before the fighting broke out at Aiken.
27. Hamilton, "Incidents of the Fighting at Aiken, S.C.," 58.

Lieutenant Henry C. Cooling of Company B of the 92nd Illinois, "as cool and brave an officer as there was in the regiment," reported to Atkins that he had located long lines of Rebel cavalry on the right of the road in the fields and woods, dismounted, holding the reins of their horses. Atkins immediately called a halt. "It was evident that a trap had been laid," the historian of the 92nd Illinois recalled, "and into the jaws of that carefully planned Rebel trap the Brigade Commander did not dare to go." The firing on their left plainly said that the Union troopers had found the enemy.[28]

Puzzled by the column's unexpected halt at the sound of gunfire, Kilpatrick came up to investigate. Just then a train came chuffing down the railroad tracks. Kilpatrick ordered his artillery to deploy and fire on the train, but the terrified engineer retreated out of harm's way, reversing the locomotive five miles all the way to Graniteville to escape capture.[29] After the train escaped, Little Kil ordered the 92nd Illinois's Silver Cornet Band to play "Yankee Doodle." Finally, at about 11:00 a.m., after half an hour of unnecessary pomp and circumstance, Kilpatrick ordered a charge on the town.[30] He intended to ride through the town to reconnoiter, and he ordered his troopers "to hold up their heads and go through the town in style."[31] That wasted half hour gave Wheeler plenty of time to prepare for the coming assault.

Kilpatrick led the advance, his colorful headquarters flag fluttering over the column as it marched. It "felt like we were going into a trap," Sgt. John Reed of the 92nd Illinois presciently stated.[32] Atkins's brigade "pushed on, our advance easily driving the enemy to the east side of Aiken. The town apparently being in the process of being vacated, General Kilpatrick directed me to send the Ninety-second Illinois to charge into the town, which they did handsomely, but found it held in force by the enemy," Atkins reported. "A division of the enemy, posted in the woods on their left (our right), charged in rear of the Ninety-second Illinois and formed in line."[33]

The local citizens, aware that Wheeler had set a trap for the Federals, did what they could to further the deception. As the Illinois men advanced, "The ladies of the town waved their handkerchiefs in welcome and smilingly invited the men and officers into their houses. But that kind of welcome was unusual in South Carolina," trooper

28. *92nd Illinois Mounted Infantry*, 214.
29. Toole, *Ninety Years in Aiken County*, 14.
30. *OR* 47, 2:450; William S. Brockington, Jr. and Judith T. Van Steenburg, eds., *Historical Sketches on Aiken* (Aiken, SC: The Sesquicentennial Committee of Aiken, 1985), 40.
31. McMaster, "Kilpatrick's Cavalry at Aiken, S. C."
32. John Reed, "The Battle at Aiken, S.C.," *National Tribune*, August 30, 1888.
33. *OR* 47, 1:879.

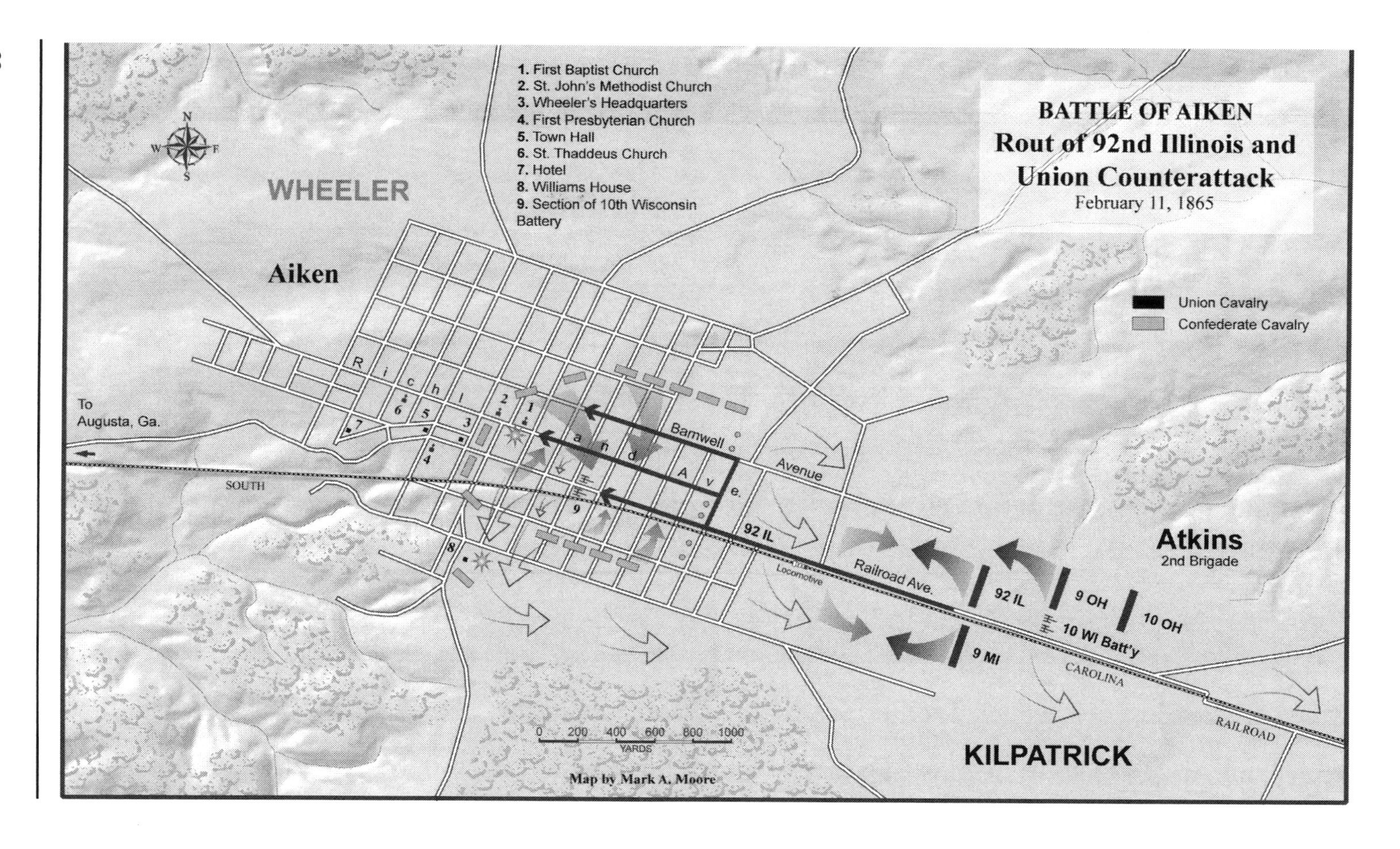
BATTLE OF AIKEN
Rout of 92nd Illinois and
Union Counterattack
February 11, 1865
1. First Baptist Church
2. St. John's Methodist Church
3. Wheeler's Headquarters
4. First Presbyterian Church
5. Town Hall
6. St. Thaddeus Church
7. Hotel
8. Williams House
9. Section of 10th Wisconsin Battery
Union Cavalry
Confederate Cavalry
WHEELER
Aiken
To Augusta, Ga.
Richland Ave.
Barnwell Avenue
SOUTH CAROLINA RAILROAD
92 IL
Locomotive
Railroad Ave.
Atkins
2nd Brigade
92 IL
9 OH
10 OH
10 WI Batt'y
9 MI
KILPATRICK
0 200 400 600 800 1000
YARDS
Map by Mark A. Moore

Reed observed. "Not an officer or soldier accepted the seductive invitation. It was an additional evidence of danger."[34] Kilpatrick still did not believe that anything unusual was going on and blithely advanced, utterly oblivious to the threat.

Captain Schermerhorn and his battalion "found the enemy's pickets and attacked them, driving them from successive lines of barricades into the town of Aiken upon their main force...posted in strong position in the town," Lt. Col. Matthew Van Buskirk, commander of the 92nd Illinois, reported. Van Buskirk placed two companies in front of him facing Laurens Street and turned the rest of his regiment around, only to find a Confederate line of battle deployed along Chesterfield Street, the second street to his rear. "There's a regiment gone to Hell," Kilpatrick declared as he watched Van Buskirk's deployment.[35]

Some of Wheeler's Alabamans got excited and opened fire too soon, spoiling the well-planned surprise and, once again, reinforcing von Moltke's observation. "When not more than half of Kilpatrick's troops had passed, some part of the Alabama boys opened fire and thus precipitated a general engagement," Pvt. D. B. Morgan of the 5th Georgia Cavalry recalled, "subjecting Wheeler's men to firing from both front and rear, instead of letting us close in on all four sides."[36] Reacting quickly, Wheeler turned to Humes and said, "General Humes, have at 'em!"

Humes did not need to be told twice. Rising in his stirrups, he pointed his saber at the enemy and roared, "CHARGE!"[37] Wheeler placed himself at the head of one of his leading squadrons and led the charge himself.[38] The troopers of the 8th Texas Cavalry dashed forward, crashing into the Federals in their front. The 3rd Arkansas Cavalry swept around the Aiken First Baptist Church and rode down the confused Northerners. Colonel Henry M. Ashby's troopers, who had taken a different street to reach the fighting, joined the fray, crashing into Kilpatrick's exposed flank.[39] A Confederate called out for the 92nd Illinois to surrender, but the Illinois men responded with a withering volley from their Spencer rifles.[40]

Sergeant Charles Waters served in the 1st Ohio Independent Cavalry Squadron and was part of Atkins's Second Brigade. "All the

34. Reed, "The Battle at Aiken, S.C."
35. *92nd Illinois Volunteers*, 84.
36. Morgan, "Incidents of the Fighting at Aiken, S. C.," 300.
37. Collier, *The War Child's Children*, 128.
38. Dodson, *Campaigns of Wheeler and His Cavalry*, 322.
39. Collier, *The War Child's Children*, 128.
40. *92nd Illinois Volunteers*, 216.

time the Johnnies were getting ready for a scrimmage," Waters described. "As soon as they were ready, a body of them charged furiously upon the Ninety-second Illinois Mounted Infantry. The shock was so great that the Shuckers were obliged to fall back upon our right, in some confusion. The rebels swarmed around upon their flanks and rear, and they [sic] was some close hand-to-hand fighting, the Illinois men clubbing their guns and pounding the heads of their adversaries."[41]

Captain George Knox Miller commanded Company A of the 8th Confederate Cavalry. Writing to his wife a few days after the battle, Miller proudly declared that "we gave Kilpatrick a good drubbing" at Aiken. In Wheeler's original formation, the 8th Confederate was located on the left of four columns facing the main street of town. After the decoys fell back, Miller "ordered a charge and every squadron dashed at the federal column in column of platoons using pistols only at close quarters."

The captain continued, "The federals bunch up then began to give way with us in pursuit." As the Confederates shoved Kilpatrick's troopers back, Miller received orders to join his regiment on a parallel street to the left of the main street. Colonel John S. Prather, commander of the 8th Confederate Cavalry, said, "Captain, you are harder to pull off than a bull dog. I had to send three couriers before I could get you." Miller replied that only one had reached him, and he thanked Prather for the compliment.

"The other parts of our cavalry were now closing in on the enemy and [the Federals] began to give way rapidly," Miller remembered. "Our whole regiment soon charged and took the lead in hot pursuit. A federal solder [sic] dropped his hat and I ran my sabre [sic] in it [to pick it up] and put it on. The hat came down nearly to my shoulders." In a letter to his wife a few days after the battle, Miller declared, "I had four men and six horses wounded out of thirteen that I carried into the fight—no men killed. I escaped without a scratch," although he lost his hat in the melee.[42] Miller's company numbering only 14 men, including him, demonstrates the attrition of the Confederate forces at such a late date in the war.

Things quickly became chaotic in the streets of Aiken. "The bugles sounded a charge," Reverend Cornish stated. "It is marvelous what a different aspect was thrown over the scene in an instant. The horses

41. Hinman, *The Story of the Sherman Brigade*, 911.
42. Richard M. McMurry, ed., *An Uncompromising Secessionist: The Civil War of George Knox Miller, Eighth (Wade's) Confederate Cavalry* (Tuscaloosa: University of Alabama Press, 2007), 269 and 328.

started and came tearing down by Richland Street, the men rising in their stirrups, with their pistols in their hands, yelling and screaming, each one looking as if he could devour a dozen Yankees." Reverend Cornish had a problem: not only were his children not scared by the chaos raging in the streets, "it was difficult to keep them out of the street during the fight."[43] Young P. F. Henderson responded to the battle raging in the streets of his town with "an odd mixture of pride and fear." Years later, he recalled seeing three bullet holes high up on the steeple of the Presbyterian church in downtown Aiken. "We were proud that our church had stopped those otherwise lethal bullets which might have killed friendly Confederates."[44]

Katherine Dow Ligon, daughter of Rev. John Dow, the pastor of Aiken Presbyterian Church, witnessed the battle as a young girl. Like young Henderson, Katherine and her friends could not resist the excitement of the conflict. "We children were placed in a back kitchen behind a large chimney to protect us from flying shots," she recalled. "We escaped from the nurse, ran around to the front yard where we saw our mother washing away the blood from the wound on the head of a young boy soldier."[45]

A Union sergeant captured the chaos of the clash perfectly. He described "a crash of horses, a flashing of sword blades, five or ten minutes of blind confusion and then those who have not been knocked out of their saddles by their neighbors' horses, and have not cut off their own horses' heads instead of the enemy, find themselves they know not how, either running away or being run away from. And so it was in this affair, Wheeler being driven into Aiken. Our trophy was a battle flag captured by Sergeant Charles Waters of Co. B of the 1st Ohio Independent Cavalry Squadron."[46]

Reacting quickly, 30-year-old Lt. Col. Matthew Van Buskirk, commander of the 92nd Illinois, described as "a man of fine personality" who "was...admired and respected by all who met him," put his regiment into line of battle and attacked the center of Wheeler's line. "Their line being much longer and force greatly superior they turned

---

43. McClaren, *St. Thaddeus of Aiken*, 35; *Diary of Rev. John Cornish*, entry for February 11, 1865, Archives, Aiken County Historical Society, Aiken, South Carolina.
44. P. F. Henderson, *A Short History of Aiken and Aiken County* (Columbia, SC: The R. L. Bryan Co., 1951), 19.
45. Brockington and Van Steenburg, *Historical Sketches on Aiken*, 40. Katherine also recalled that the Presbyterian church's silver "was hidden in a cistern in our yard" upon learning of Kilpatrick's approach. It stayed buried there until after the end of the Civil War. Ibid.
46. Hinman, *The Story of the Sherman Brigade*, 911.

both my right and left flank," Van Buskirk reported, "charging in and forming line in my rear."[47]

Lt. Col. Matthew Van Buskirk, the brave commander of the 92nd Illinois Mounted Infantry, who was the hero of the Battle of Aiken for the Union. *(Abraham Lincoln Presidential Library and Museum).*

"We rode forward to the charge," trooper John Reed of the 92nd Illinois said. "The rebel line of battle stretched far off to the right and left, and the rebels, confident of taking us in, very coolly awaited our approach until close range, when they demand a halt and surrender, and were answered by every man in the regiment pumping into them the eight Spencer bullets in his trusty repeating rifle. Several of the boys shoved their guns up against the rebels and shot them off their horses." He continued, "It was a desperate charge, and the 92nd Ill. men fought face to face and hand to hand. So mixed up were the gray and the blue in a confused, helter-skelter, jumbled crowd, pressing on to the brigade, each

47. *OR* 47, 1:882; William J. Moir, ed., *Past and Present of Hardin County Iowa* (Indianapolis: B. F. Bowen & Co., 1911), 520. Matthew Van Buskirk was born in Buckmantown, Clinton County, New York, on January 1, 1835. He was the son of Lorenzo Dow and Louisa Van Buskirk, and had one brother, Albert, born March 20, 1841 (Albert Van Buskirk was killed in action at the Battle of Drury's Bluff near Petersburg, Virginia, on May 16, 1864). After completing his education, the young man relocated to Illinois in 1851, where he remained until the war kicked off in 1861. He enlisted in the 92nd Illinois Volunteer Infantry, and he was elected captain of Company E. He served with distinction in that role until October 1864 when he was promoted to lieutenant colonel of the regiment. In 1863, the regiment was mounted, and it later converted to light cavalry in 1864. "He was popular with his soldiers and trusted by his superior officers," one biographer noted. With the end of the war, he settled in Iowa Falls, Iowa, where he successfully operated a store selling boots, shoes, and crockery, as well as dry goods and other items, growing the shop into a general merchandising business. Later, he became a gentleman farmer. He married Nellie C. McGiven in 1866, and they had seven children together. Van Buskirk died on January 10, 1901, and was buried in Iowa City's Union Cemetery. "He was a clear-brained, noble-minded man of action and his life record is worthy of emulation by the youth of this locality whose careers are yet matters for the future to determine," his biographer declared. Moir, *Past and Present of Hardin County Iowa*, 520-521; *History of Hardin County, Iowa* (Springfield, IL: Union Publishing Co., 1883), 767; and Lt. Col. Matthew Van Buskirk listing. *https://www.findagrave.com/memorial/37645239/matthew-van_buskirk.*

claiming the other as prisoner, not a shot could be fired by the brigade."[48] The Illinois men fought ferociously. They feared that Wheeler's men would execute any prisoners as retribution for destroying the countryside. They had good reason to fear the Confederate troopers: "The fear of no quarter for barn burners made heroes out of cowards."[49]

"We had hardly lost sight of the flag before we heard Wheeler's carbines in the distance over the hill, to which the scouts replied, and in less than 10 minutes we saw them coming back at full speed," a captain of the 10th Ohio Cavalry recalled. He continued, "Kilpatrick at once sent the artillery to the rear and ordered the brigade to hold their fire until the enemy came within short range. Our skirmishers were soon engaged. Wheeler's entire force seemed to be in our front with double skirmish-line, followed closely by the reserve. We had no works before us for protection."[50]

Reacting quickly, General Atkins ordered the rest of his brigade to deploy into line of battle. The 9th Michigan deployed on the left of the road and on the railroad, while the 9th Ohio Cavalry deployed on the right of the road along the edge of a wood fronting a cornfield about 300 yards wide, beyond which was another woodlot. The 10th Ohio remained in reserve. Atkins ordered the 10th Ohio to erect a crude barricade in front of its position.[51] "It was evident we were before Wheeler's center, as his lines extended to the right and left as far as the eye could reach," an officer of the 10th Ohio observed.[52] Atkins also deployed the two guns of the 10th Wisconsin Battery near the freight depot, located on the railroad about half a mile away, where they could support Kilpatrick's troopers. Within minutes, "fights took place all over town."[53]

"The Ninety-second was completely enveloped by overwhelming numbers, and came up to our line of battle so mixed up with the enemy we did not dare to fire," Atkins recounted, "each was claiming the other prisoners and pulling one another off their horses, neither being armed with sabers."[54] Wheeler's determined men "fought stubbornly." Confederate troopers seized Van Buskirk and demanded his surrender.[55] Fighting for his life, Van Buskirk killed two

48. Reed, "The Action at Aiken, S.C."
49. Collier, *The War Child's Children*, 130.
50. "A 10th Ohio Cavalryman," "Campaign Through the Carolinas."
51. *OR* 47, 1:879.
52. "A 10th Ohio Cavalryman," "Campaign Through the Carolinas."
53. Toole, *Ninety Years in Aiken County*, 15.
54. *OR* 47, 1:879.
55. Hinman, *The Story of the Sherman Brigade*, 911.

Confederate troopers on his own and knocked a third off his horse with his empty pistol while making his escape.[56] "The Rebs had a hand-to-hand fight over the Ninety-second Illinois flag but did not get it," an Ohio trooper recalled.[57]

"Now the brigade bugle sounded the charge, and with a yell the 9th Ohio and the 9th Michigan charged, the 92nd wheeling and charging with them into the town of Aiken and back to their former position, recapturing a great many of the boys that had been taken prisoners," John Reed of the 92nd Illinois recalled. He concluded, "We were five miles from camp, where the balance of the division lay behind their rail barricades."[58]

The men of the 92nd Illinois had heard the horror stories about the Confederate prisoner of war camp at Andersonville, Georgia. They had seen some of their comrades slaughtered after surrendering. The Northerners were determined to stand firm and avoid such a horrific fate. "There was now no hope for us but to cut our way out or be captured, a fate worse than death, so out we came, some shooting the enemy with their pistols and others knocking them down with the butts of our guns," Pvt. William Boddy of the 92nd Illinois declared. "A good many rebs were unsaddled and a few brought out prisoners, while some few of our boys were captured."[59]

"Enveloped by the huge mass of Rebel cavalry surrounding them, and mixed up helter-skelter, gray-coats and blue-coats in a confused and jumbled crowd, they pressed on to the Brigade, and soon saw the Stars and Stripes floating over the immovable line of battle formed by the Ninth Ohio and Ninth Michigan Cavalry, that gave new courage to the men of the Ninety-second." However, the men of both sides were so hopelessly jumbled that the carbineers of the 9th Ohio and 9th Michigan were unable to open fire for fear of hitting their friends.[60]

An unidentified captain of the 10th Ohio Cavalry described the scene: "When [Wheeler] had advanced midway between us and the town they came down to a walk and at once threw a strong force forward on both flanks. The 10th Ohio Cav. was in front, supported by the 92d Ill. Mounted Inf., armed with the Spencer rifles. I think I never saw a more perfect line of rebel cavalry than was before us. They steadily advanced, keeping up a sharp fire, with their lines well closed."

56. Ibid.
57. Frank Smith, "A Maine Boy in the Tenth Ohio Cavalry," *First Maine Bugle* Vol. 4, No. 1 (January 1897), 20.
58. Reed, "The Action at Aiken, S.C."
59. Berkenes, *Private William Boddy's Civil War Journal*, 170.
60. *92nd Illinois Mounted Infantry*, 215-216.

The Ohioan continued, "When within speaking distance we opened a well-directed fire at short range. This for a moment threw their first line into some confusion and broke their ranks, which at once closed up; but they still advanced, pouring in our faces a deadly fire." The heavy Confederate fire forced the Union front line back until it withdrew to the rear, giving the men of the 92nd Illinois the opportunity to employ the firepower of their Spencer rifles. "This regiment, with their seven shooters, was as good as a brigade in a tight place, and they succeeded in checking their advance, breaking their center, and for a full half hour held their positions, when, the enemy bringing up reinforcements, they were in like manner obliged to fall back and form in the rear. Thus one regiment after another would fall back after taking the brunt of battle and hastily throwing up works as best they could."[61]

Captain James Brazier of the 10th Confederate Cavalry had been impatiently awaiting his chance to avenge his humiliation at the hands of Kilpatrick's troopers that morning. He soon found his opportunity, crossing sabers with a Federal officer and killing him. By the end of the day, Captain Brazier "had the marks of five bullets in his clothing, but was unhurt."[62]

Thirty-two-year-old Col. William Douglas Hamilton was in command of the 9th Ohio Cavalry.[63] The popular Hamilton was

61. "A 10th Ohio Cavalryman," "Campaign Through the Carolinas."
62. Hamilton, "Incidents of the Fighting at Aiken, S. C.," 59.
63. William Douglas Hamilton was born in Lanarkshire, Scotland, on May 24, 1832. He immigrated to the United States with his parents six years later, and the family settled near Zanesville in Muskingum County, Ohio. He graduated from Ohio Wesleyan College in Delaware, Ohio, and from the Cincinnati Law School in 1859. He then established a law office in Zanesville and practiced law until the outbreak of the Civil War in 1861. Abandoning his law practice, he raised the first company for three years' service in that part of Ohio, and he was assigned to the 32nd Ohio Volunteer Infantry as a captain. He served in the West Virginia and Shenandoah Valley campaigns of 1861 and 1862. Fortunately, he was at home in Zanesville when his regiment surrendered at Harpers Ferry in September 1862, so he avoided that disgrace. In December 1862, Governor David Tod directed Hamilton to recruit the 9th Ohio Cavalry, and appointed him colonel of the new regiment. Hamilton served in the Atlanta Campaign, the March to the Sea, and the Carolinas Campaign. He was brevetted to brigadier general of volunteers for his meritorious service in the Carolinas Campaign. After the Civil War, Hamilton abandoned the practice of law and became an industrialist in the coal and iron business. He published a well-regarded memoir of his wartime service in 1915. Hamilton died in Columbus, Ohio, on January 22, 1916, and was buried in Greenlawn Cemetery. Whitelaw Reid, *Ohio in the War: Her Statesmen Generals and Soldiers*, 2 vols. (Cincinnati: The Robert Clarke Co., 1865), 1:967-968; Obituary, *Ohio State Journal*, January 23, 1916; Hunt and Brown, *Brevet Brigadier Generals in Blue*, 257.

Col. William D. Hamilton, commander of the 9th Ohio Cavalry, Atkins' Brigade.

(USAHEC)

known as an officer who "takes great care of his soldiers" and who "does not let them suffer." He ordered his men to tear down all fences in front of their position, located near the Aiken First Baptist Church on Richland Street, toward the center of town, in order to clear his fields of fire and to facilitate the movement of his mounted men.[64] Atkins ordered Hamilton to extend his right to protect against the Confederates' attempted flanking movement. Hamilton shifted his Third Battalion, commanded by Capt. James S. Irvine, to the right, moving its left flank forward to be ready to meet any threat that might come from that direction. Hamilton also advanced a company to observe the movements of the enemy.[65]

"Kilpatrick had got into the town and he and his body guard were almost surrounded before he was aware of this fact," the Buckeye colonel noted. "They escaped capture only by a hasty retreat with a close chase in the cornfield. A rebel officer at the head of his company was seen so close to Kilpatrick that he had his saber drawn in an effort to reach him when Captain William Henderson...who was commanding Company 'D' on the left flank, ordered his men to fire on the rushing crowd and turned them back." A trooper of the 92nd Illinois said, "As he came within sight of the line of battle of the Ninth

64. Hamilton, *Recollections of a Cavalryman*, 184; George W. Pepper, *Personal Recollections of Sherman's Campaigns in Georgia and the Carolinas* (Zanesville, OH: Hugh Dunne, 1866), 366. Writing 50 years after the battle, Hamilton incorrectly claimed, "It developed that General Beauregard had reached Aiken by trains in the night with his entire command on his way to join Johnston, but as we could go no further, he had unloaded his force to help Wheeler." This error may be attributed to the passage of so many years; Hamilton was 82 or 83 years old when he wrote it, with only a few months left to live. Ibid.

65. *OR* 47, 1:888. A battalion is two squadrons, or four companies, of cavalry. Each full-strength regiment has three battalions.

Ohio and Ninth Michigan, the Rebels were actually grabbing for him, as he hugged his horse's neck, and roweled his horse's flanks with his spurs. It was laughable in the extreme; but the Ninth Ohio and Ninth Michigan could not fire a gun at the enemy, so mixed up were the General and his staff officers and orderlies with the pursuing Rebels."[66] Kilpatrick lost his hat while escaping, leaving behind an important souvenir for his chum Wheeler. As the jaws of Wheeler's well-laid trap snapped shut, and having only narrowly escaped capture, Little Kil finally recognized the peril for what it was and ordered Hamilton to immediately fall back.[67]

"Just as Kilpatrick and his staff had entered the town here came our scouts and skirmishers pell-mell, closely followed by the rebel cavalry, and before there was time to find out what was the matter Kilpatrick was almost surrounded," trooper James N. McMaster, 9th Ohio Cavalry, noted. "The order was given to fall back, which a great many proceeded to carry out in a very irregular manner."[68]

Hamilton watched as some of Wheeler's troopers followed Kilpatrick and his escort almost all the way to the position of the artillery. When Kilpatrick and his staff came to the right end of the line, the general stopped to observe the situation. "While he was taking observations, the bearer of the headquarters flag was shot, and fell from his horse," a trooper of the 1st Ohio Independent Cavalry Squadron stated. "The rebels made a dash to secure the flag, but were met by the flashing sabers of the Squadron. The rebels found it too hot, and retreated without the prize."[69]

The regimental surgeon of the 9th Ohio sent an orderly to Hamilton, begging him to hold on until the surgeon could gather up the wounded. At the same time, the officer in command of the artillery sent word to wait long enough to save the guns. Things were desperate.[70] When Hamilton arrived at the spot that his other two battalions occupied, they had just begun slowly retreating. The colonel asked the officer in charge why they were retreating, and the officer replied that one of Kilpatrick's staff officers had ordered them to fall back. "Feeling sure, as I did, that there must have been some mistake about the order, as such a movement at that time would endanger our artillery, and also expose a large number of our men of the Ninety-

66. *92nd Illinois Mounted Infantry*, 215. The regimental historian of the 92nd continued, "Let no one think that this reflects upon Kilpatrick's courage; it does not; he was the bravest man in all his brave Division." Ibid.
67. Hamilton, *Recollections of a Cavalryman*, 184.
68. McMaster, "Kilpatrick's Cavalry at Aiken, S. C."
69. Hinman, *The Story of the Sherman Brigade*, 912.
70. Hamilton, *Personal Recollections of a Cavalryman*, 185.

second Illinois and Ninth Michigan Regiments to capture," Hamilton reported, "I ordered the battalion about and charged back upon the enemy, driving them back across the field into the edge of the town, the charge being led against the heaviest force of the enemy by my adjutant, Lieut. A. T. Hamilton, who, at the head of the left flank of the regiment, most gallantly dashed into the town, driving the enemy before him in confusion."[71]

Hamilton colorfully described this action years after the war. "My young bugler Bob Rownd was in his glory as he sounded the charge," the colonel wrote. "The enemies' bullets rattled among the dry cornstalks as we drove the surprised enemy back into the roads. They evidently thought reinforcements had arrived."[72] Another Buckeye noted, "This stayed the tide for a while, until the road was clear."[73] According to Col. George S. Acker, 9th Michigan Cavalry, fighting in the streets of Aiken lasted for nearly an hour.[74]

Some questions remain as to precisely how many of Atkins's troopers participated in the charge. Hamilton's report suggests that only his left flank made the charge, whereas Atkins's report implies that the entire brigade charged. It seems clear that the Federals did not charge until the rear guard of the 92nd Illinois had successfully retreated to the safety of the main body of Atkins's command. Atkins claimed that the charge drove Wheeler's troopers off the field, but that seems unlikely.[75] Van Buskirk wrote, "With the Ninth Michigan on my left and Ninth Ohio on my right we charged the enemy and relieved my skirmishers. He fled before the combined charge, and we drove him nearly through the town, when orders came to withdraw, which was done in good order. The fighting was determined and desperate, and each officer and man of my regiment proved himself a hero."[76]

"Wheeler met and repulsed two charges of the enemy," a Confederate reported. "The charges were beautifully made and handsomely repulsed."[77] Wheeler later claimed that because his

71. *OR* 47, 1:888. Lieutenant Arthur T. Hamilton, the regimental adjutant, was Colonel Hamilton's cousin.
72. Hamilton, *Recollections of a Cavalryman*, 185.
73. McMaster, "Kilpatrick's Cavalry at Aiken, S. C."
74. *OR* 47, 1:885. An unidentified captain of the 10th Ohio Cavalry claimed that the battle lasted for four hours, but there is no corroboration for this claim. "A 10th Ohio Cavalryman," "Campaign Through the Carolinas."
75. Ibid., 879.
76. Ibid., 884.
77. "South Carolina," *Daily Confederate*, February 17, 1865.

command lacked sabers and had to fight with pistols, the need to stop to reload guns delayed his men's advance, giving the Federals an opportunity to escape the trap and make their countercharge.[78]

Lieutenant Henry Morrison, described by Hamilton as "one of my best young officers," who commanded Company A of the 9th Ohio, dashed up to Hamilton and breathlessly declared, "Colonel the enemy is moving in force around our right flank. Hadn't we better fall back?" Hamilton agreed, ordering the command to reform behind the 9th Michigan's position. The Buckeye troopers withdrew to an orchard and reformed their command; they held the Confederate advance in check on the right side of the road while the 9th Michigan did the same on the left side of the road.[79]

Private Simon Poland of Lexington, Ohio, who served in Company L of the 10th Ohio Cavalry, was on the 10th Ohio's skirmish line that morning. He, along with about 75 of his comrades, was captured. These unfortunates were soon on their way to a prison camp in Andersonville, Georgia. Wheeler enraged the captured men by asking them to renounce their fealty to the Union and to take up arms for the Confederacy. "But not a man would bring himself the curse of God and the obloquy of those whose hearts the flag is enshrined in as a sacred emblem by complying with his request," a newspaper later reported. Fortunately, Poland survived his short stay at Andersonville and lived a long life.[80]

"I admit that we left Aiken in a hurry," William H. Morris, Company B, 10th Ohio Cavalry, said years later. "Two of my company were killed there and three captured." He quipped, "For Heaven's sake,

78. Morgan, "Incidents of the Fighting at Aiken, S. C.," 300; Hamilton, "Incidents of the Fighting at Aiken, S. C.," 59.
79. Hamilton, *Recollections of a Cavalryman*, 185.
80. "Neighborhood News. Lexington," *Mansfield News*, May 8, 1900. An account of Poland's life states: "The prisoners were about a week in reaching their prison at Andersonville, Georgia. They were placed in the stockade and for three months endured all of the miseries of that famous prison. Their rations were not a pint of coarse ground corn meal, a few inches of meat, and twice a week they received a gill of black molasses. They were all more or less afflicted with the scurvy, Mr. Poland losing his teeth by that disease. He had in his possession on entering the prison three hundred dollars in Confederate money. He paid thirty dollars of it for a skillet to bake his corn bread on and three dollars for a spoon with which to eat his soup. He now owns a cane made from pine wood taken from the 'dead line' at Andersonville, and has also a piece of pine out of the stockade of the same prison." *Richland County, Ohio Civil War Veterans* Extracted from *Hardesty's Historical and Genealogical Encyclopedia* (Mansfield, OH: Richland County Historical Society, 1998), 95.

do not give me the Rebel yell, for it used to give me the cold chills."[81]

The 10th Wisconsin Battery's two guns remained busy while the fighting raged. "By order of General Kilpatrick I opened fire upon the enemy's charging line of cavalry as they emerged from the woods in front with both guns, while Second Brigade was forming in the barricades on the right, and fired slowly till the enemy opened fire on my left, when I, by order of Captain [Yates] Beebe, chief of artillery, cavalry division, moved quickly to the left to the rail barricade, 600 yards distant and had time to fire two rounds of canister before the enemy, already whipped by the Eighth Indiana Cavalry (my support on the left), got out of range," Lt. Elbert Fowler of the 10th Wisconsin reported.[82]

The reproduction of the 1890's depot for the South Carolina Railroad in Aiken, which is now a visitor center. This was the site where the Union horse artillery deployed.

(Author's photo)

The Wisconsin gunners worked their weapons effectively that day. "Several shells came whizzing by us from a battery on Railroad Avenue," Reverend Cornish of St. Thaddeus Church remembered. "Two shells went through the house at the corner of Railroad Avenue and Laurens Street; one struck in the yard of the old parsonage." He continued, "Mr. Sander's family put out and came to my house. One struck the corner of Mr. Ladson's house on the molding and lodged in the attic. One went through the kitchen over his servants' heads, one fell in front of his house among the soldiers and was afterwards picked up and brought to me—a six pound Parrott shell—nobody hurt by them."[83] An errant Union artillery shell slammed into and damaged a saloon located across the street from the First Baptist Church.

81. William H. Morris, "Ohio Veteran Doesn't Like the Rebel Yell," *Confederate Veteran* 18 (1910), 61-62.
82. *OR* 47, 1:906.
83. McClaren, *St. Thaddeus of Aiken*, 35; Cornish Diary, entry for February 11, 1865.

"Fired this day from the two guns fifty-nine rounds, of which two were canister, the rest fuse-shells," Lieutenant Fowler reported. "What execution my fire did I was unable to learn, as I had no opportunity to visit the field after the fight."[84] The effectiveness of Fowler's guns is somewhat suspect since friendly fire casualties occurred as a result of the lieutenant's artillery fire. Nonetheless, the presence of those guns supported Kilpatrick and unquestionably blunted Wheeler's troopers' pursuit of the Union commander.[85]

Both sides paid a heavy price fighting in the streets of Aiken. The 92nd Illinois alone lost 26 killed and wounded.[86] The Confederates also had relatively heavy casualties in the brief but bitter fighting. Wheeler captured colors, prisoners, horses, and arms, and Union casualties lay strewn throughout the town. One of Kilpatrick's staff officers was captured and another wounded in the melee.[87] The stout stand by the 92nd Illinois bought sufficient time for the Federals to rescue most of their wounded.[88]

However, the day's contest was not yet over.

84. *OR* 47, 1:906.
85. Henderson, *A Short History of Aiken and Aiken County*, 18.
86. *92nd Illinois Mounted Infantry*, 217. The regimental historian of the 92nd Illinois claimed that Wheeler lost 80 men killed in the Battle of Aiken, but these claims cannot be corroborated.
87. Dodson, *Campaigns of Wheeler and His Cavalry*, 322-323.
88. *OR* 47, 1:879.

CHAPTER SIX

PURSUIT TO JOHNSON'S TURNOUT

While Bvt. Maj. Gen. Judson Kilpatrick and the Second Brigade sortied to Aiken, the rest of Kilpatrick's division built breastworks near Pole Cat Pond, located close to Johnson's Turnout (also known as Johnson's Station).[1] The works were "somewhat concealed in the woods, with open fields in front, and [the men of the other two brigades] hearing of our repulse were prepared to receive the enemy."[2] The blue-clad horse soldiers clearly heard gunfire—distantly at first—coming from the fighting in the streets of Aiken. As Brig. Gen. Smith Atkins and his brigade retreated to Johnson's Turnout, the gunfire echoes grew louder.[3] The rest of Kilpatrick's division awaited the arrival of Atkins's men and Maj. Gen. Joseph Wheeler's pursuing Confederate troopers.

That morning, while the Second Brigade made its foray into Aiken, some of Kilpatrick's troopers visited the DeCaradeuc and Heyward families' Montmorenci plantation at Johnson's Turnout, as some Federals had done the day before. "One of our villainous neighbors told them our boys fired the first gun on Sumter, so they said this house was the root of the rebellion & burn it they would, but our good servants & Mother and [Grandmother] entreated in such a way that they desisted," recalled young Pauline DeCaradeuc Heyward recalled, "They then said they had to arrest and shoot every influential citizen in S. C., every mover of secession, & from the accumulation of wealth, the quantities of food, books & clothes in this house, the finest they had seen in these parts, that they knew Father was wealthy, literary & influential, & they had heard enough of him, to make an example of him & catch him they would. We have no less than five large libraries of refugees, here, besides our own, & the accumulated clothing and valuables of four separate families, no wonder they found us so rich, & came here so often."[4] Fortunately, the house survived.

As the men of Atkins's Second Brigade retreated slowly toward the main body of Kilpatrick's division at Johnson's Turnout, the 92nd

1. Pole Cat Pond evidently was a man-made pond located near the Montmorenci mansion, but it no longer exists.
2. "A 10th Ohio Cavalryman," "Campaign Through the Carolinas."
3. Carter, *The Story of Joshua D. Breyfogle*, 321.
4. Robertson, *A Confederate Lady Comes of Age*, 67.

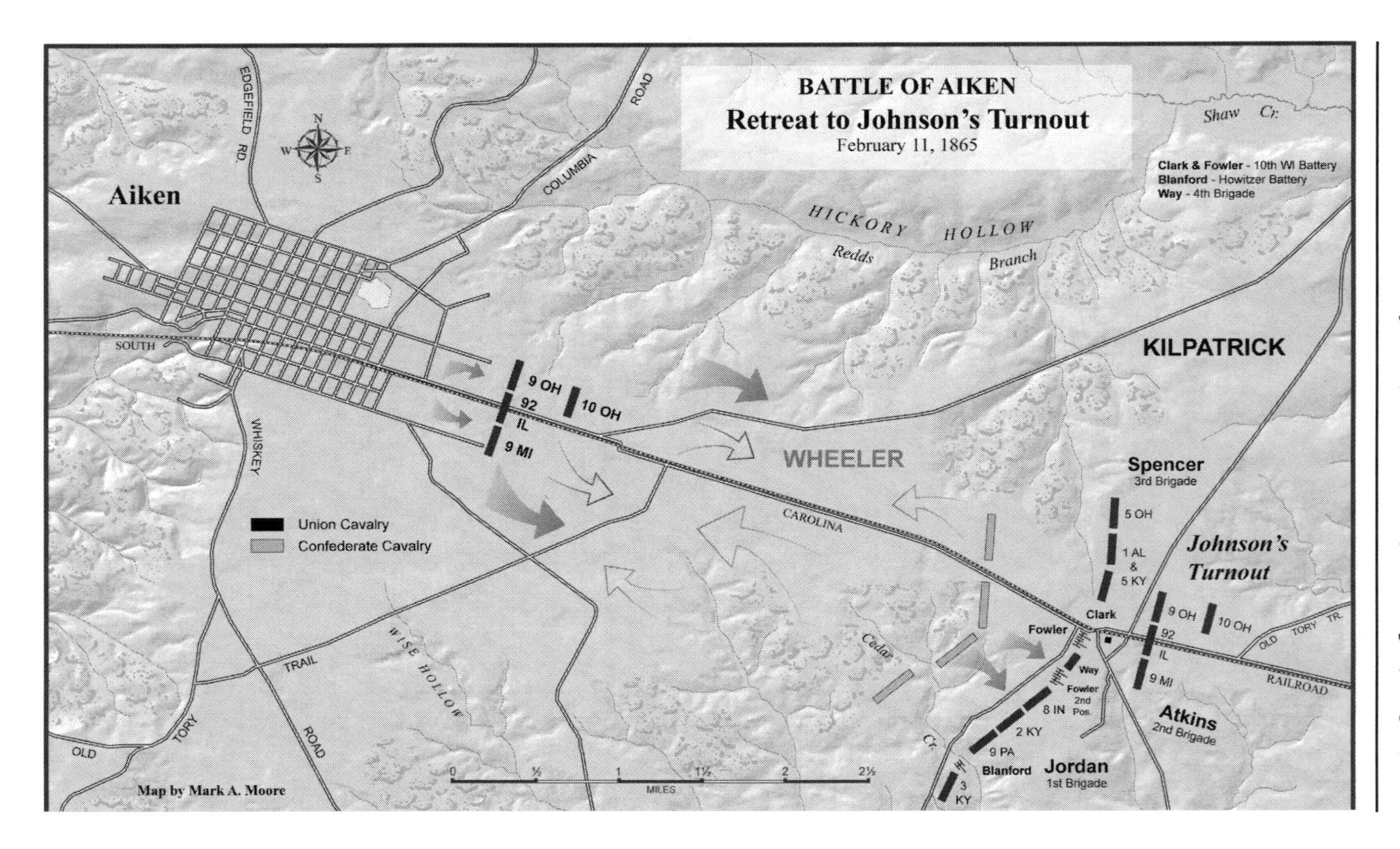
BATTLE OF AIKEN
Retreat to Johnson's Turnout
February 11, 1865
Clark & Fowler - 10th WI Battery
Blanford - Howitzer Battery
Way - 4th Brigade
Aiken
KILPATRICK
WHEELER
Spencer
3rd Brigade
5 OH
1 AL & 5 KY
Johnson's Turnout
Clark
Fowler
Way
Fowler 2nd Pos.
8 IN
2 KY
9 PA
3 KY
Blanford
Jordan
1st Brigade
Atkins
2nd Brigade
9 OH
10 OH
92 IL
9 MI
Shaw Cr.
HICKORY HOLLOW
Redds Branch
Cedar Cr.
WISE HOLLOW
EDGEFIELD RD.
COLUMBIA ROAD
WHISKEY ROAD
OLD TORY TRAIL
OLD TORY TR.
SOUTH CAROLINA RAILROAD
Union Cavalry
Confederate Cavalry
0 ½ 1 1½ 2 2½
MILES
Map by Mark A. Moore

Illinois Mounted Infantry and the 9th Michigan Cavalry, armed with either Spencer carbines or rifles, took turns making stands. In this manner they covered the retreat of Atkins's remaining Second Brigade. "Orders then came to fall back to the barricade at the pond, the enemy following us all the way, firing into our rear guard," Pvt. William Boddy, 92nd Illinois, remembered.[5]

"Thus one regiment after another would fall back after taking the brunt of battle and hastily throwing up works as best they could," a 10th Ohio Cavalry officer said. "Thus for four hours the brigade covered its front, steadily falling back, contesting every foot of ground, being outnumbered four to one."[6] After effectively delaying Wheeler's troopers, Atkins's brigade conducted a fighting retreat for nearly five miles back to the main body's position, with Wheeler's troopers tailing closely the whole way. Atkins estimated that the five-mile retreat to Johnson's Turnout spanned three hours.[7]

"General Atkins fell back, fighting gallantly, disputing every foot of ground, to my position at Johnson's Station," Kilpatrick reported, "giving me sufficient time to make all necessary dispositions to check the enemy's farther advance."[8] Atkins echoed a similar sentiment when he wrote that "the brigade leisurely fell back, the enemy following in force. We fell back over open ground, splendid for a cavalry fight, the enemy seeking our flanks, but not daring to attack strongly our line of battle, which we continually presented him. His charges were always broken by a few volleys coolly given, and a single regiment charging would always drive him."[9]

"Seven [brigades] of Rebel cavalry, baffled and defeated at Aiken, came thundering down upon the four little regiments, and the [five] miles back to camp was a battlefield all the way," a trooper of the 92nd Illinois claimed. The trooper overestimated the Confederate pursuers' strength and greatly exaggerated the results from the combat in town. "Time and time again, the Rebels in overwhelming force, charged the two regiments, who always met them coolly, with murderous volleys from their Spencer Rifles (92nd Illinois) and Spencer Carbines (9th Michigan), the two regiments together, many times, not only repulsing the enemy's charge, but charging and routing them in turn," he continued.[10]

5. Berkenes, *Private William Boddy's Civil War Journal*, 170.
6. "A 10th Ohio Cavalryman," "Campaign Through the Carolinas."
7. *OR* 47, 1:879.
8. Ibid., 857-858.
9. Ibid., 879.
10. *92nd Illinois Mounted Infantry*, 217-218.

Private James N. McMaster, Company C, 9th Ohio Cavalry, said, "The regiment then fell back in pretty good order, closely followed by the enemy, until the barricade was reached, the rebels charging furiously on the rear-guard whenever they had a good chance, capturing quite a number of our men who became unhorsed."[11]

Not everyone remembered the retreat being quite so orderly. According to one of Wheeler's troopers, "we continued a running hand-to-hand fighting, driving the dispersed fugitives back upon their infantry supports, all of which retreated rapidly to an entrenched position five miles from Aiken." He continued, "During the running fight, General Wheeler captured colors, prisoners, horses and arms, besides strewing the ground with their killed and wounded." The Confederates claimed they captured Fourteenth Corps infantrymen. However, no Union infantry was in the vicinity of Johnson's Turnout that day.[12]

"We had a splendid time chasing Kilpatrick the other day at Aiken," trooper Orlando D. Chester, 5th Georgia Cavalry, bragged. "We had a right sharp fight with them before they understood we were whipping them and in it I got struck for the first time with a minnie ball. It struck a tree first and glanced and hit me on the leg just above the knee. It bruised me a little and caused a slight swelling but did not hurt me much. Henry Russell of our company was shot in the head about the same time but injured so little that he was ready for duty the next day."[13]

Private Othnel P. Hargis served in Company I, 1st Georgia Cavalry of Col. Charles Crews's brigade and as a special scout. "We routed [Kilpatrick] and ran him about four miles as fast as their horses could carry them," Hargis declared. "I asked an old lady if the Yankees were going much fast as they passed her house and she said yes, 'they were going as the old scratch could take them.' They had torn up her feather bed and she was good and mad, and I don't blame her."[14]

---

11. McMaster, "Kilpatrick's Cavalry at Aiken, S. C."
12. Dodson, *Campaigns of Wheeler and His Cavalry*, 322-323. Dodson was not the only Confederate to assert that Kilpatrick had infantry reinforcements at Johnson's Turnout. Alabama trooper J. B. Ulmer made a similar claim. Perhaps the Springfield rifles that some men of Lt. Col. William B. Way's dismounted Provisional Brigade carried suggested that Kilpatrick had received infantry reinforcements. See J. B. Ulmer, "Ruffin Dragoons with A. S. Johnston," *Confederate Veteran* 17 (1909), 597.
13. Daiss, *In the Saddle: Exploits of the 5th Georgia Cavalry*, 115.
14. O. P. Hargis Reminiscences, Southern Historical Collection, Wilson Library, University of North Carolina, Chapel Hill, North Carolina.

Colonel William D. Hamilton of the 9th Ohio Cavalry recalled that the regiments of Atkins's brigade fell back by forming their companies to the rear of the regiments in their front, and then the regiments in the front fell back, alternating by regiment until they reached the support of the other brigades at Johnson's Turnout. "I would so notify the Tenth Ohio and the Ninth Michigan and we would fall back in as good order as possible as we had learned by this time that Wheeler had been reinforced," Hamilton wrote. "I would not try to give the impression that the retreat was carried out as methodically as this plan would indicate, but it was better than a stampede, which it prevented."[15]

Unbeknownst to Hamilton, however, he offered a conspicuous target to Wheeler's pursuing troopers. Years after the war, a Georgian of Wheeler's corps told Hamilton that his fine black horse, which became all white with sweat from the extreme exertion of the retreat, had stood out, and that Wheeler had told him to get the horse out of the way. Luckily, Hamilton escaped danger.[16]

Corporal Elliott B. McKeever, Company L, 9th Ohio Cavalry, wrote, "My horse was not a good runner...so I was about the last to wheel into line formed just back of another piece of woods. Just as I got into place a reckless Johnnie on a mule rode up quite close and stopped behind a little pine tree. His was a daring piece of work. I could see the mule's breast but not the rider but guessing at his location I fired at him before he got a shot at any of us. He got out of there in a hurry and I hope I did not wound him seriously."[17]

Frank Smith of the 10th Ohio Cavalry was pressed into service as Atkins's orderly on that chaotic day. "The staff and orderlies having all been dispatched on errands, I found myself following General Atkins alone, who had a fine horse, called 'Old Blue,' that could go like the wind," Smith recalled. "I had a little mare, lately captured, high-spirited, and with a mouth too tender for a curb-bit, and during this melee, I had as much as I could do to manage her, hold the flag, keep up with and follow the general, who rode at the top of 'Old Blue's' speed." Smith had his hands full keeping up with Atkins while Wheeler's troopers followed in close pursuit.[18]

"There was a stream to cross," a member of the 1st Ohio Independent Cavalry Squadron remembered, "and part of the Squadron, with two pieces of artillery, was stationed to guard the

15. Hamilton, *Recollections of a Cavalryman*, 185-186.
16. Ibid., 186.
17. McKeever, *He Rode with Sherman*, 24.
18. Smith, "A Maine Boy in the Tenth Ohio Cavalry," 20.

Lt. Arthur Hamilton, 9th Ohio Cavalry, mortally wounded at the Battle of Aiken.

(William D. Hamilton, Personal Recollections of a Cavalryman After Fifty Years)

bridge. As soon as the troops had passed over the bridge, the detachment withdrew to the barricade."[19]

Within 200 yards of the remaining division's barricades at Johnson's Turnout and while forming the last line before reaching the barricades, Lt. Arthur T. Hamilton, the cousin and adjutant of Col. William D. Hamilton of the 9th Ohio Cavalry, helped lead the 9th Ohio Cavalry's charge. The lieutenant suffered a shot to the right knee, which killed his horse and mortally wounded the popular adjutant. However, the charge succeeded in driving the Confederates back across the field. "This stayed the tide for a while, until the road was clear."[20]

Lieutenant Hamilton lingered until March 6 when he finally expired, "making the third son of the family who has fallen in their country's service," Colonel Hamilton, who had lost two brothers earlier in the war, sadly noted. "He was regarded by all as one of the most valuable officers in the regiment, noble, generous, and brave; he died the highest and truest type of an American soldier, and I would respectfully ask that he receive from the commanding general an honorable mention among the dead who have fallen during our memorable campaign."[21]

19. Hinman, *The Story of the Sherman Brigade*, 912.
20. McMaster, "Kilpatrick's Cavalry at Aiken, S. C."
21. *OR* 47, 1:888. When he penned his memoir 50 years after the war, Hamilton went into further detail about his cousin's wounding and death. "My cousin, Adjutant Arthur T. Hamilton, while riding his horse on the railroad bed, directing some of the men, was struck by a ball that went through his leg near the knee joint, killing his horse. He was taken up with his saddle and bridle, by hospital steward Robert H. Moffitt. I found him among the other wounded in an old cabin. He smiled and said he was not much hurt. I told him the war would soon be over and he would be safe and out of danger till the close, and we would go home together. The wounded were placed in ambulances and sent to the infantry. Two days later I learned from the surgeon that his wound was not doing well, as signs of blood poisoning had appeared. I turned over the command to Lieutenant-Colonel [William] Stough, who commanded the regiment through South Carolina, and devoted myself to his care. I saw that

Captain George Knox Miller, who served in the 8th Confederate Cavalry of Anderson's brigade, recalled, "After a pursuit of some three miles we came to a small sedge field on the far side of which there were entrenchments thrown up and where the enemy had encamped the previous night. I waved a halt to my squadron now moving as skirmishers. The last regiment of the enemy was entering those entrenchments." One of Miller's troopers named John Cullen Duncan asked permission to dash forward for a last shot at the retreating Federals. "I told him he would do no good and more than likely get killed by sharpshooters behind the breastworks. He insisted, and I told him to go ahead."

Duncan dug his spurs into his horse, charging forward to within a few yards of the last of Atkins's men as they filed into position behind the breastworks. "He discharged his pistol and about that moment his horse fell to his knees, but arose at once, and trooper and horse came back at an uncertain gait," Captain Miller revealed. Turning to Miller, Duncan declared, "Well, Captain, they got me." The bullet had passed between the horse's ears, splitting the animal's scalp and causing it to drop to its knees. The bullet then struck Duncan in the shoulder, disabling him. Miller directed Duncan to go to the rear and try to find a surgeon. Miller did not see Duncan again until long after the Civil War ended.[22]

Private D. B. Morgan, who served in the 5th Georgia Cavalry of Anderson's brigade, wrote, "We charged the enemy through scrub oak forest and open peach orchard, driving them back whence they came. As we halted in one of the charges, my mule was shot from under me, the ball passing immediately under my left leg and entering the poor creature's heart. With an unearthly yell, such as animals make when

his wound was carefully cared for and I held him in my arms for hours as the ambulance jolted over corduroy roads made by the pioneer corps through the swamp lands of South Carolina. During this time blood poisoning had fully developed and the adjutant was plainly growing weaker. After traveling in this way for one hundred and seventy-five miles with the infantry we reached the town of Cheraw where the army was crossing the Pedee river on a pontoon into North Carolina. This took most of a day. During this time I held the adjutant in my arms. In the afternoon he looked up at me and smiled faintly and I saw he was dying. I had a box made and a grave dug in the town cemetery, and when all was over I washed his face and hands and wrapped him in his blanket like a soldier. We buried him at midnight by the fierce light of a burning town." Arthur Hamilton's body was later disinterred and moved to the National Cemetery at Florence, South Carolina. Colonel Hamilton did not resume command of his regiment until March 5. Hamilton, *Recollections of a Cavalryman*, 186-188.

22. McMurry, *An Uncompromising Secessionist*, 328-329. Miller reported, "John Cullen's horse remained with the command I think and was delivered to him after the surrender, of this I am not certain. John was furloughed home from the hospital." Ibid., 329.

shot, she bounded into the air, and, in falling, caught me half-dismounted, with my left leg under my body. The soft plowed ground on which I fell prevented it from being broken."

Morgan gingerly got to his feet, jumped on the back of a passing lieutenant's horse, and went into the fight. Since he had no horse of his own, he was ordered back to the rear to get another mount and rejoin the fighting as quickly as possible. Near the carcass of his expired mule he spotted a dead Yankee trooper and decided that the Yankee's shoes would be more valuable to himself than to a dead man, but he was unable to wrestle them from the corpse. Instead Morgan helped himself to the deceased trooper's overcoat and cape, while allowing a comrade to take the man's pocket watch. Morgan continued on and found Sgt. Maj. James Bird, of his own regiment, seated on a porch with an arm wound. Bird called Morgan over, telling him that the ladies of the house would be happy to feed him. Hungry, Morgan enjoyed a quick bite to eat before finding a horse. He "set off at a lively gallop to overtake my command."[23]

"When within a mile of the division's works our ammunition and that of the enemy gave out, and they charged upon us with the saber, and from that time until we reached our reserve-line of works we had it hand to hand, and such of the enemy as had no sabers clubbed us with the butts of their guns," a captain of the 10th Ohio Cavalry recollected. "I had six of my men thus struck down while using their [revolvers]."[24]

The Union used their artillery to great effect. "I had hardly reached the position specified when I received an order to return to the position occupied during the night, as the enemy were moving on our left flank," Lt. Charles Blanford, commander of the Union battery, reported. "Having again taken up my position I had not long to wait, as the enemy were engaging our skirmishers, driving them slowly back across an open field. As the enemy's line emerged from the woods about 1,000 yards in my front, I opened on them with shell, with apparent good effect, several of my shells bursting in their ranks causing considerable confusion. They soon fell back out of range of my guns, when I ceased firing and was not engaged again during the day."[25]

Colonel Thomas J. Jordan, commander of the First Brigade, reported that the retreating Federals were "closely pursued by the enemy till our guns, in position at the barricades, stopped their

23. D. B. Morgan, "Incidents of the Fighting at Aiken, S. C.," 300.
24. "A 10th Ohio Cavalryman," "Campaign Through the Carolinas."
25. *OR* 47, 1:877-878.

pursuit, and the Second Brigade formed behind our defenses. The enemy finding the right of our position so strongly defended, formed in the thick woods on our left, and in a few minutes made a most determined assault upon our works."[26]

"The rebels forced them up to our barricades and they made several charges but were handsomely repulsed," Cornelius Baker of the 9th Pennsylvania Cavalry of Jordan's brigade observed. "They didn't even drive in our skirmishers."[27] Colonel Jordan stated, "The Eighth Indiana, Second Kentucky, and Ninth Pennsylvania Cavalry of my command, most gallantly met the charge and hurled back the foe, killing and wounding a large number. The artillery and howitzer batteries did good service in this action, sending shell and canister into their exposed ranks, adding greatly to the enemy's discomfiture."[28]

"The rebels immediately charged the works with great spirit," a trooper of the 1st Ohio Independent Squadron recalled. "They made a gallant attempt to dislodge us but were repulsed with severe loss in killed and wounded."[29] The pursuing Confederates "pressed forward nearly up to our works, and as we passed around to the right the artillery opened with canister, while the roar of small-arms extended along the entire line," a 10th Ohio Cavalry captain noted. "At the first fire their lines were broken and driven back in great confusion, after which for a half hour they replied at intervals upon the flanks. Their lines were drawn back in our front, and the Second Brigade at once formed on our left in open ground, and we filled our cartridge boxes."[30] "They got a good drubbing," a 92nd Illinois trooper declared, "being handsomely repulsed with considerable loss, leaving their dead behind them."[31]

Lieutenant Colonel William B. Way and his dismounted Provisional Brigade threw out a strong skirmish line that Capt. John B. Riggs commanded; Riggs led Way's 3rd Regiment. His men made good use of their longer-range muzzle-loading infantry weapons. "The enemy made his appearance along the whole line and opened a brisk skirmish fire," Way reported. "Two guns of the Tenth Wisconsin Battery were in position, covering both the dirt and railroad, and opening upon the enemy, he did not press forward in our front, but moved around to our left and made a desperate charge, striking the right of the First Brigade, Colonel Jordan commanding, and the First

26. Ibid., 866.
27. Rowell, *Yankee Cavalrymen*, 226.
28. *OR* 47, 1:866.
29. Hinman, *The Story of the Sherman Brigade*, 912.
30. "A 10th Ohio Cavalryman," "Campaign Through the Carolinas."
31. Berkenes, *Private William Boddy's Civil War Journal*, 170.

Regiment of my command, which was upon my left, Major [Charles A.] Appel commanding. The enemy was handsomely repulsed. Skirmishing was kept up all the afternoon."[32]

During the lull, Atkins's men rested, briefly stacking their weapons behind the barricades. Judson Kilpatrick rode out to inspect his lines; the general wanted to know why the men were not deployed in line of battle. Kilpatrick received a reply that there was no need of it—the men lay resting near their guns, and if an assault was made, they could spring for the weapons quickly. The Federals were confident that General Wheeler would never attack the barricades after Kilpatrick's troopers repulsed the Southerners with heavy losses in a similar attack during the Atlanta Campaign. They guessed wrong, however—Wheeler was not finished yet.[33]

About 1:00 p.m., Wheeler received a note from Maj. Gen. D. H. Hill, who commanded the Confederate garrison at Augusta, Georgia. "A strong infantry force will be here by 2 o'clock. I congratulate you on your success. Many stragglers from your command."[34] The telling note proved that Wheeler had accomplished his goal; by bringing the fight to Kilpatrick at Aiken, Wheeler had bought sufficient time for infantry from the remnant of the Army of Tennessee to reinforce Hill's little garrison, thus saving the Confederacy's powder works. Now Wheeler could safely retire if he desired. However, Wheeler craved a decisive victory against his schoolmate and wished to continue the battle.

Col. George S. Acker, commander of the 9th Michigan Cavalry, Atkins' brigade.

(USAHEC)

Wheeler brought up his horse artillery and shelled the Union works for an hour, hoping to soften Kilpatrick's stout defensive position for one final attack. Just as the sun was setting, the Confederates "made a final charge on our left, which was repulsed," a captain of the 10th Ohio Cavalry remembered.[35] "During the engagement the regiment occupying

32. *OR* 47, 1:903.
33. *92nd Illinois Mounted Infantry*, 218.
34. *OR* 47, 2:1164.
35. "A 10th Ohio Cavalryman," "Campaign Through the Carolinas."

the extreme left of our line made a saber charge upon the rebel right as they were advancing upon us and repulsed them handsomely," Col. George S. Acker, commander of the 9th Michigan Cavalry, reported.[36] A Yankee described Wheeler's assaults on the quickly constructed breastworks as "several ineffectual attempts to carry our works."[37]

Nineteen-year-old Pvt. D. B. Morgan, 5th Georgia Cavalry, had galloped back from Aiken to rejoin his command after his mule was shot out from under him that morning, arriving just in time to participate in the unsuccessful final assault. "About dark I charged up to what I thought was Confederate soldiers, as the two commands were engaged in a hand-to-hand combat, but I discovered that I was in the midst of the enemy's lines," he recalled. "They did not immediate *[sic]* realize that I was not one of them, and when they did, I was well under way making my exit. They said, 'Halt! Surrender!' and fired on me at a lively rate, but I did not stop, and in the darkness made my escape and reached my own men." Morgan survived the war and paroled with the rest of his regiment in April 1865.[38]

"The engagement lasted until long after darkness covered our movements, when details were sent out on the flanks to build fires and beat the infantry tattoo, indicating that infantry reinforcements had come up," an Ohio cavalryman recounted. "Sky-rockets were sent up, giving out the impression to the enemy that we had received support;

36. *OR* 47, 1:885. George S. Acker was born near Rochester, New York, on December 25, 1835. In 1839, his family relocated to Kalamazoo, Michigan, where he lived the rest of his life. "He was a bright and chivalrous young man," a local resident remembered. He worked in a Kalamazoo hotel before the outbreak of the Civil War, enlisting when it kicked off. He helped recruit a company of the 1st Michigan Cavalry and commissioned as a captain. In September 1862, he was promoted to major for his gallantry. When the 9th Michigan Cavalry formed that fall, Acker was assigned as its lieutenant colonel. He was wounded in combat in the spring of 1863, and in November he was commissioned colonel of the 9th Michigan. "He was very prominent in the pursuit and capture of the notorious rebel Gen. John H. Morgan in Ohio in July and August 1863," his obituary noted. It also stated, "He said to his command, 'Come,' and led them wherever the enemy opposed or danger threatened." He briefly commanded a brigade during the March to the Sea, and retained command of his regiment for the rest of the war. A soldier of the 92nd Illinois remembered him as "a cool and brave cavalry soldier." He was brevetted to brigadier general of volunteers at the end of the war and mustered out in June 1865. After the Civil War he led a quiet life, working as a hotelkeeper and milkman. Acker died on September 6, 1879, and was buried in Riverside Cemetery in Union City, Michigan. Hunt and Brown, *Brevet Brigadier Generals in Blue*, 3; "The Late General Acker," *Kalamazoo Daily Telegraph*, September 8, 1879; Reed, "The Action at Aiken, S. C."
37. *OR* 47, 1:146.
38. Morgan, "Incidents of the Fighting at Aiken, S. C.," 300.

but the fact was we were at least 25 miles from Slocum's left wing."[39] The Federals' deception convinced Wheeler that Union infantry reinforcements had arrived, meaning he thought his forces would be outnumbered. "There is a little skirmishing going on in front but the fighting I think is over for today," Sgt. Joshua D. Breyfogle of the 10th Ohio Cavalry penned in his diary that afternoon. "Our infantry will be here tonight and they will take them in hand."[40] The short winter day rapidly drew to a close, and the combination of repulsing his final attack and believing Kilpatrick had received reinforcements, forced Wheeler to break off and withdraw to Aiken, where he and his victorious command spent the night.

"They did not try us again, but we laid still behind our barricades ready to give them a good reception if they had the impudence to try us," Pvt. William Boddy, 92nd Illinois, wrote in his diary that night. "Tonight we are in line behind the barricades, each company having its own videttes in front."[41] Those not on picket duty spent the night standing, sitting, or lying at the heads of their horses, prepared to mount up if necessary. The horses remained saddled in case the Northern troopers had to beat a hasty retreat. "Signal rockets were sent up as soon as it got dark for we were in great danger of capture by a much larger command," weary Cpl. Elliott B. McKeever, 9th Ohio Cavalry, recalled.[42] Kilpatrick's exhausted, beaten troopers spent a long, chilly night waiting and watching for Wheeler and his men to resume the attack.

"One of the funny things after all was over was to hear John Timmons cuss because Serg't. [James M.] McCune had lost all our cooking utensils," Pvt. James N. McMaster, Company C, 9th Ohio Cavalry, reminisced. "He had them all tied in a sack on his saddle, and in the retreat, when closely pressed by the enemy, his horse ran against a tree and brushed it off. McCune was so impressed by the sulphurous [sic] nature of the cussing that he went straightaway and drew a frying-pan, tins and a camp kettle from the 92nd Illinois while they slumbered and slept."[43] At least the spent Buckeyes would eat that night after their long day of tangling with Wheeler and his still-feisty troopers.

---

39. "A 10th Ohio Cavalryman," "Campaign Through the Carolinas."
40. Carter, *The Story of Joshua D. Breyfogle*, 321.
41. Berkenes, *Private William Boddy's Civil War Journal*, 170. Videttes were mounted sentries lined up in front of the main position to provide an early warning system for the main body.
42. McKeever, *He Rode with Sherman*, 24.
43. McMaster, "Kilpatrick's Cavalry at Aiken, S. C."

"Having destroyed during the day in rear of our works what railroad they could, Kilpatrick decided to fall back. After feeding our horses and taking a fresh supply of ammunition, the barricades were set on fire and our teams sent to the rear under guard," a 10th Ohio Cavalry captain recalled. "Our horses remained saddled, as we anticipated a night attack. The Second Brigade had received a hard blow. "He continued, "There was a good deal of firing during the night along the whole line. About midnight our pickets were quietly with drawn [sic] and the division moved out in the direction of Blackville."[44]

"General Wheeler did not think it wise to follow Kilpatrick farther that night, so camping on the battlefield, he awaited the morning to see that he had thwarted the attempt to reach Augusta," Private Morgan noted.[45] Actually, Wheeler had other plans. After blunting Kilpatrick's advance on Aiken, Augusta, and Graniteville, and protecting the refugees, Wheeler returned to his headquarters in Aiken, the home of W. J. Williams. Williams opened his home to the tired Confederate officers. His daughter Eloise enjoyed telling how she climbed out her bedroom window and obtained the "best dresses" for all the girls in the house without waking a single slumbering soldier in the process. That way, each of the girls was arrayed in her finest when the handsome

The graves of two Confederate soldiers killed during the Battle of Aiken and personally buried by Reverend Cornish in the graveyard at St. Thaddeus Church.

(Author's photo)

44. "A 10th Ohio Cavalryman," "Campaign Through the Carolinas."
45. D. B. Morgan, "Incidents of the Fighting at Aiken, S. C.," 300.

young officers came to dinner that night, before claiming all of the home's available beds. The next day, Wheeler gifted the Williams's children a horse that the family owned for the rest of the animal's life.[46]

That night, five wounded Confederate troopers were brought to Rev. John H. Cornish's house to recuperate. Surgeons attended to them, and the men received the best care possible under the circumstances. Reverend Cornish also officiated at the burial of two Confederates who died in the day's fighting. Their bodies were placed in wooden coffins and buried in the St. Thaddeus Church graveyard. The two deceased Southerners were 21-year-old Louis Deadman of Company D, 1st Tennessee Cavalry and 24-year-old Ensign Jesse Morris of the 2nd Tennessee Cavalry, both of whom had served in Ashby's brigade of Humes's division.[47]

War had come to the sleepy town of Aiken; structures were damaged and carried the scars of urban combat. Dead and wounded men and horses were strewn everywhere. The wounded needed care and the dead needed to be buried. These unpleasant and thankless tasks largely fell upon the town's civilians. However, because of Wheeler's inspired battle plan, Aiken was spared the fate of Barnwell and so many other South Carolina towns that Sherman's soldiers visited. The residents of Aiken remained grateful to Wheeler for the rest of their lives.

46. Teague, "The Battle of Aiken."
47. McClearen, *St. Thaddeus of Aiken*, 35. Ensign was the equivalent of a second lieutenant in the archaic terminology of the day.

CHAPTER SEVEN

AFTERMATH

A captain of the 10th Ohio Cavalry gave an honest assessment about the fighting at the Battle of Aiken. "While the Second Brigade was advancing on and returning from Aiken," he wrote in his diary, "we got most beautifully whipped by Wheeler with overwhelming numbers, in a direct attack and flank movement." Later he recalled, "Our boys would often tantalize the Johnnies, when prisoners, while referring to places where they were defeated; as, for instance, Jonesboro, Lovejoy Station, Waynesboro, etc. They would at once retaliate by inquiring: 'How about Macon, Briar Creek, and Aiken?' Whenever they referred to Aiken we generally changed the subject, for we conceded they had the best of it there.'"[1]

Unlike the unidentified captain of his 10th Ohio Cavalry, Brig. Gen. Smith Atkins claimed victory at Aiken. "This spirited little engagement has done much to convince me of the superiority of our cavalry over the enemy's. For upward of three hours, with four small regiments--the Ninety-second Illinois, Ninth Michigan, Ninth and Tenth Ohio--I successfully fought Wheeler's entire command." While Atkins's brigade undoubtedly held its own against Maj. Gen. Joseph Wheeler's corps, and considering that not all of Wheeler's corps was present, the Confederate cavalry bested the reckless Bvt. Maj. Gen. Judson Kilpatrick that day.[2]

"A fine morning after a very cold sleepless night," Pvt. William Boddy, 92nd Illinois, noted in his diary. "The expected attack did not come."[3] Sergeant Joshua D. Breyfogle of the 10th Ohio Cavalry wrote, "Our pickets are firing occasionally and I think will bring on a general fight during the day." He also remarked that "a great many of our men have gone foraging."[4]

On February 12, Kilpatrick's troopers spent the day at Johnson's Turnout "destroying track as usual, and constantly demonstrating in

---

1. "A 10th Ohio Cavalryman," "Campaign Through the Carolinas." "Waynesboro" refers to the December 4, 1864, Battle of Waynesboro, Georgia, during Sherman's March to the Sea. At Waynesboro, Kilpatrick and Wheeler tangled in a very similar battle to Aiken. The comparison between the Battles of Waynesboro and Aiken is set forth in Appendix C.
2. *OR* 47, 1:879.
3. Berkenes, *Private William Boddy's Civil War Journal*, 170.
4. Carter, *The Story of Joshua D. Breyfogle*, 321.

the direction of Augusta, till the night of the 12th, when I left Wheeler's front, crossed the Edisto at Guignard's Bridge, and encamped four miles beyond, picketing the Edisto as high up as Pine Log Bridge against Wheeler's cavalry."[5] Later that day, infantry of Bvt. Maj. Gen. Absalom Baird's Third Division of the 14th Corps arrived and completed the work of destroying the railroad that the Union cavalrymen had begun, which had been deemed inadequate. A few days later, a Southern newspaper reported, "The Carolina [railroad] as far as the enemy has progressed has been completely destroyed," depriving the South of yet another crucial supply line.[6]

An Ohioan recalled that on February 12 he and his comrades "did not unsaddle, as it was necessary to be prepared for any emergency."[7] "The enemy appeared in some force in front of our picket-line, but without making an attack," Col. George S. Acker of the 9th Michigan Cavalry stated.[8] Lieutenant Colonel Matthew Van Buskirk, the 92nd Illinois commander, sent out scouts to his right to try to find Wheeler's troopers, but they failed to locate the Rebels and returned to camp. However, about six miles from camp at Johnson's Turnout, the Federals found two of Kilpatrick's dead troopers with their throats cut, their clothes stolen, and their bodies only partly buried. Infuriated, and assuming that local bushwhackers were responsible, the Illinoisans burned all nearby houses to the ground.[9] On the evening of February 12, Kilpatrick requested and received from Wheeler a truce for both sides to gather their wounded and bury their dead.

Some troopers of the 10th Ohio Cavalry went out scouting that day. They came across an old black man who told them where they could find 25 to 30 horses to impress into service if they would not disclose that he had told the Yankee troopers where to find the horses. The troopers hesitantly followed him down a narrow, quiet cow path, worried that he was leading them into an ambush. About two miles into the trek, the Northerners made the man swear that he was not leading them into an ambush and that he was telling the truth. The

5. *OR* 47, 1:859.
6. "South Carolina," *The Daily Confederate*, February 17, 1865. The same newspaper article included two different accounts by residents of the Aiken area who reported about Wheeler's battlefield victory.
7. Hinman, *The Story of the Sherman Brigade*, 913.
8. *OR* 47, 1:885.
9. Berkenes, *Private William Boddy's Civil War Journal*, 171. The execution of prisoners of war became a major issue throughout the following weeks, leading to unpleasant accusations between Wheeler and Kilpatrick. Eventually, Maj. Gen. William T. Sherman and Lt. Gen. Wade Hampton had to intervene, and they exchanged letters under flags of truce regarding the issue.

Buckeyes kept their carbines unslung the whole time, in case they needed to rapidly fire their weapons.

One of them, James Shoemaker, dismounted and went ahead to scout. Shoemaker returned a few minutes later, telling the black man he could go; the troopers began planning their approach on the sleeping Confederate camp. The men decided to split up and approach from three sides. "Never was a company of men more surprised or astonished as, at a given signal, we rode, yelling and firing our guns in the air, right into their midst, Shoemaker in a loud voice commanding an imaginary troop to halt and remain on the hill out of sight." The terrified Confederates surrendered as the Buckeyes gathered up their arms. The ambushers ordered that the horses be saddled up and prepared to move out. Some prisoners were required to help lead the 25 captured horses and mules. "As we came in the army was just going into camp along the railroad. And such cheers we received as we marched our prize to headquarters," one of the troopers exclaimed.[10]

In the meantime, some of Maj. Gen. William T. Sherman's infantry approached within five miles of Johnson's Turnout, spending the day destroying the railroad. The plan paid off to draw Wheeler's troopers away from the Edisto River line. Sherman advanced so rapidly that by February 13 only Kilpatrick's cavalry and the 14th Corps were south of the North Branch of the Edisto River.[11] The 15th, 17th, and 20th corps made bridgeheads across the North Branch of the Edisto on February 12, which only elements of Major General Carter L. Stevenson's command opposed. Only the 17th Corps met serious opposition as it advanced Orangeburg, South Carolina. By that night, at least six Union divisions had crossed the North Fork of the Edisto, and Major General Francis P. Blair's 17th Corp had cut the Columbia Branch Railroad at Orangeburg. Just the Congaree River remained between Sherman and Columbia, with Stevenson's infantry scattered to resist their advance; however, Stevenson fell back from Orangeburg that night.[12] Had the Confederate cavalry been present and in its

10. J. N. McMaster, "How They Surprised a Rebel Camp," *The National Tribune*, February 23, 1888.
11. *92nd Illinois Mounted Infantry*, 218.
12. *OR* 47, 1:196, 225, 406, and 684-685. Also on February 13, the 9th Illinois Mounted Infantry led a column that had returned from Pocotaligo, South Carolina. This was an important event for several reasons. First, it was the last communication or resupply Sherman had with the coast until his army reached Fayetteville, North Carolina, on March 11. Second, it underscored a missed opportunity for Wheeler to operate against Sherman's supply lines, as he had done successfully in Tennessee a year before.

assigned position along the Edisto, the Union infantry's passage across the barrier would have been much more difficult. Sherman's army was closing in on Columbia—no thanks to Wheeler.

Leaving Johnson's Turnout on February 13, Kilpatrick's division marched to Lexington, South Carolina, which was 10 miles from Columbia.[13] "We gave the Rebels the slip by turning to the left, marched about 12 miles and camp on the Edisto and I don't think Wheeler knows we are gone yet," a 10th Ohio Cavalry trooper claimed.[14] After passing near Aiken, an Illinois trooper said. "The Ninety-second men were disappointed in not visiting Aiken again. They would have liked to have occupied the town for a few hours; they would have gone into the houses without any smiling invitations from the Secesh ladies; and when they had marched out of the town, no houses would have been left."[15] Sherman ordered Kilpatrick to continue screening to the left (or west) of his main body, and the Union cavalry headed north toward the North Carolina state line on February 17.

Both sides had prisoners of war to contend with. The two main prisoner of war camps for Union captives in South Carolina were the Florence Stockade, used for enlisted men and almost as terrible as the camp in Andersonville, Georgia, and Camp Asylum for officers, otherwise known as Camp Lunacy for its location inside the state lunatic asylum in Columbia. Undoubtedly, some of Kilpatrick's men were sent to the camps. Others remained with the main body of Wheeler's column. On February 27, Wheeler and Kilpatrick met in person under a flag of truce, working out a partial prisoner exchange that likely included Aiken captives.[16]

On Sunday, February 12, between 20 and 30 Confederate horse soldiers attended services at Reverend John H. Cornish's church, St. Thaddeus. The rest of Wheeler's command sat drawn up in line of

---

13. Ibid., 882.
14. Carter, *The Story of Joshua D. Breyfogle*, 322.
15. *92nd Illinois Mounted Infantry*, 218-219.
16. *OR* 47, 2:615. This is what Kilpatrick reported to Sherman: "I received this morning twenty of my prisoners in exchange for an equal number sent General Wheeler yesterday; in all, he has taken from me but one officer and thirty men since entering upon the present campaign. I have, over and above that number, seventy of his men and four commissioned officers. As I feel confident that I can keep even with him or Hampton in prisoners, if you will give permission, and any of the corps commanders desire it, for infantry officers and soldiers now in Wheeler's hands I will exchange the prisoners I now have on hand. Three infantry soldiers belonging to the Twentieth Army Corps represented themselves as belonging to my cavalry, and were exchanged last evening." Ibid.

Maj. Gen. Matthew C. Butler, commander of Hampton's Division.

(Library of Congress)

Gen. Robert E. Lee, general-in-chief of the Confederate military forces.

(Library of Congress)

battle on Richland Avenue and also to the right and left of town, but Kilpatrick did not sortie in that direction. That night, Wheeler and his staff dined with the Cornish family before moving on.[17]

Wheeler rested his weary command for a few days. They were worn down from hard campaigning, and his horses were in bad shape. Their absence from the front made Sherman's advance easier. When Wheeler did march, his cavalry led the way for the Army of Tennessee out of Augusta. With the railroad down, though, the Confederate Cavalry had to march, and they needed Wheeler's cavalry to screen their advance. While Wheeler and his men rested, significant changes in the Confederate cavalry's structure were occurring.

Shortly after the new year in 1865, Maj. Gen. Matthew C. Butler, who commanded a division of the Army of Northern Virginia's Cavalry Corps, which included a brigade of South Carolinians, approached Confederate general-in-chief Robert E. Lee about returning home to South Carolina to recruit new men and try to find fresh mounts.[18] Lee decided to send Maj. Gen. Wade Hampton to Columbia with Butler. "I think Hampton will be of service," Lee told

17. McClearen, *St. Thaddeus of Aiken*, 35.

18. Butler was also a South Carolinian and one of Wade Hampton's protégés. After the war, he served alongside Hampton in the U.S. Senate. He became one of four former Confederate generals to be commissioned major general

Lt. Gen. Wade Hampton, commander of all Confederate cavalry forces in the Carolinas after February 15, 1865.

(Library of Congress)

Confederate president Jefferson Davis, "in mounting his men and arousing the spirit and strength of the State and otherwise do good." Lee also worried that Wheeler would absorb Butler's division into his command, and Lee wanted Butler and his cavalrymen back in time for the spring campaigning season.[19] The necessary orders issued on January 15, 1865, arrived in Columbia on January 29, along with Hampton and the other men.[20]

Hampton received no specific orders other than to report to Lt. Gen. William J. Hardee in Charleston. After doing so, Hampton returned to Columbia and became Gen. P. G. T. Beauregard's de facto second in command. Hampton assumed responsibility for overseeing the construction of Columbia's defenses. Thus, a few days after receiving Col. Alfred Roman's inspection report for Wheeler's corps, Beauregard, the department commander, wrote to Lee. "I earnestly recommend, for the good of the service and cause, that General [Wade] Hampton be promoted temporarily to command all the cavalry of this department, which cannot be rendered otherwise as effective as present emergencies demand," he said. "Major-General Wheeler, who ranks only a few days, is a modest, zealous, gallant, and indefatigable officer, but he cannot properly control and direct successfully so large a corps of cavalry."[21] Lee reluctantly agreed to release the commander of the Army of Northern Virginia's Cavalry Corps.

---

of volunteers during the Spanish-American War, even though Butler had only one leg as a result of a combat wound sustained at the June 9, 1863, Battle of Brandy Station, in Virginia. For a full-length biography of Butler, see Samuel L. Martin, *Southern Hero: Matthew Calbraith Butler: Confederate General, Hampton Red Shirt, and U.S. Senator* (Mechanicsburg, PA: Stackpole Books, 2001).

19. Douglas Southall Freeman, ed., *Lee's Dispatches: Unpublished Letters of General Robert E. Lee to Jefferson Davis and the War Department of the Confederate States of America 1862-65* (New York: G. P. Putnam's Sons, 1915), 315 and 317.

20. Douglas Southall Freeman, *Lee's Lieutenants: A Study in Command*, 3 vols. (New York: Charles Scribner's Sons, 1942-1944), 3:639.

21. *OR* 47, 2:1165.

"I am going to go out to see if I can do anything for my state, as Genl. Lee thinks that I can do good there," Hampton told his sister.[22] Hampton was determined to "fight as long as I can wield my saber;" however, he refused to serve under Joe Wheeler.[23] Hampton's forthright rebellion threatened to cause a serious command problem since Wheeler outranked Hampton.[24] On February 16, Hampton received a telegram from President Davis informing him that he had been commissioned a lieutenant general, to rank from February 14.[25] "The best events may be expected from [Hampton's] appointment," a New Orleans newspaper declared. "Hampton's presence will not fail to inspire confidence and enthusiasm."[26]

Although Hampton's promotion was deserved, and perhaps overdue, it was politically motivated in its timing—until then, no

22. Charles E. Cauthen, ed., *Family Letters of the Three Wade Hamptons, 1782-1901* (Columbia: University of South Carolina Press, 1953), 113. Forty-six-year-old Wade Hampton III was one of the wealthiest men in the South. Tall, amiable, and handsome, Hampton had no formal military training, although he was the grandson of an American general of dragoons. He graduated from South Carolina College (now the University of South Carolina) and took up the life of a planter and politician. He was modest and unpretentious with refined manners. Although he initially opposed secession, when South Carolina seceded, Hampton cast his lot with the Confederacy. He raised the Hampton Legion—a combined force of infantry, cavalry, and artillery—out of his own pocket, leading it at the July 1861 First Battle of Bull Run, where he was wounded on Henry House Hill. On May 31, 1862, he was promoted to brigadier general and assumed command of a brigade of cavalry. He was badly wounded at the Battle of Seven Pines during the 1862 Peninsula Campaign, but he returned to duty. Hampton commanded a brigade until receiving serious wounds at the Battle of Gettysburg. When he returned to duty in September 1863, he was promoted to major general and assumed command of a division. After J. E. B. Stuart's death in May 1864, he became commander of the Army of Northern Virginia's cavalry, which he led until his transfer to South Carolina. The Civil War left him destitute, but Hampton remained active in public service. He was elected as South Carolina's first post-war Democratic governor in 1876, seeing the end of Reconstruction. He served two terms in the U.S. Senate before he died in 1901. Hampton was known as a fearless leader who was the ideal subordinate. Warner, Generals in Gray, 122-123. The best full-length biography of Wade Hampton is Rod Andrew, Jr., *Wade Hampton: Confederate Warrior to Southern Redeemer.* (Chapel Hill: University of North Carolina Press, 2008.)
23. Freeman, *Lee's Lieutenants*, 3:639.
24. Wade Hampton to Louis T. Wigfall, January 20, 1865, Wigfall Family Papers, Manuscripts Division, Library of Congress, Washington, D.C.
25. Dunbar Rowland, ed., *Jefferson Davis, Constitutionalist: His Letters, Papers, and Speeches*, 10 vols. (Jackson, MS: Mississippi Department of Archives and History, 1923), 6:480. The promotion made Hampton the highest-ranking officer to ever serve in the Confederate cavalry, outranking even Nathan Bedford Forrest, whose date of commission as lieutenant general was February 28, 1865.
26. "Later from the North," *The Times-Picayune*, February 28, 1865.

lieutenant general had been commissioned in any command of Confederate cavalry. Hampton now outranked Wheeler. "[Lee] had me promoted so as to command [Wheeler] and all his cavalry," Hampton explained in a post-war letter. "The Genl refused to let me serve under Wheeler."[27]

While likely disappointed, Wheeler took the news gracefully. When the two officers met and Hampton advised him of the change in status, the diminutive cavalryman responded, "Certainly, general, I will receive your orders with pleasure."[28] Hampton showed equal graciousness toward his new subordinate. "It must be said in acknowledgment of the high-bred courtesy of Hampton that he studiously avoided any show of authority over Wheeler that was avoidable," the historian of Wheeler's cavalry corps observed. "He assumed the duties the government had assigned to him without his consent, but he gave Wheeler free rein. It was only one among other evidences of his greatness."[29]

Although Wheeler took the loss of overall command graciously, his troopers did not. They viewed the move as an insult to their commander. "His men can but feel that a grave wrong has been done one of the most gallant and meritorious officers in the service," one of Wheeler's horsemen noted. "They can but feel it was done on incorrect information, or by designing men who had other motives than the good of the service to influence them."[30] Every officer in one of Wheeler's divisions signed a resolution protesting the change. "While we would not underrate the distinguished services rendered or detract from the merited laurels won by General Hampton, we desire to say in most unmistakable terms that we entertain now, as we have always done, the most unbounded confidence in General Wheeler as a man and as an officer, and where he leads we will cheerfully follow," a document signed by more than 100 officers of Brigadier General William Y. C. Humes's division proclaimed.[31] Nevertheless, the petition changed nothing, and Hampton still assumed command.

No longer in overall command of the Southern cavalry, Wheeler hurried to try to interpose his command between Sherman's army and the South Carolina state capital at Columbia. He divided his force in

27. Wade Hampton to Edward L. Wells, April 9, 1900, Edward L. Wells Correspondence, Charleston Library Society, Charleston, South Carolina.
28. Dyer, *From Shiloh to San Juan*, 172.
29. John W. DuBose, "The Fayetteville Road Fight," *Confederate Veteran* 20 (1912), 84.
30. "An Interesting Letter," *Macon Daily Telegraph*, April 6, 1865.
31. Dodson, *Campaigns of Wheeler and His Cavalry*, 334-337 (emphasis in original).

an attempt to resist Sherman's approach, but dividing his small command only increased the odds against the Confederate cavalry, prompting one of Kilpatrick's troopers to note that "we run into [Wheeler] every now and then."[32] On February 14, some of Wheeler's men charged and broke through the Union army's rear guard, a skirmish line of the 14th Corps, capturing 40 prisoners and piercing the main battle line, before being driven away.[33]

On February 15, Beauregard ordered Wheeler to "concentrate forthwith for the defence [sic] of Columbia, either by joining your forces to those of General Hampton, or by attacking the enemy in flank and rear." Wheeler advanced on the left flank of Sherman's columns. The 14th and 20th corps arrived at Lexington on February 15, and Kilpatrick and his cavalry were about 10 miles to the west at Horse Creek, meaning that Columbia was largely cut off from reinforcements and left to its fate. Confederate cavalry attacked the Union infantry near Congaree Creek, resisting the advance of Sherman's right wing, while Wheeler and the rest of his command harassed their flank. Wheeler's command then joined Hampton's to defend Columbia.[34]

Although the Northern cavalry did not visit Aiken a second time, their first visit left its mark. "After the Yankees left, starvation stared this desolated section in the face, for all the food had been carried off or destroyed," Gasper Loren Toole II, who was about 10 years old at the time, recalled in 1865. "The people would gather up wasted corn from the abandoned camping grounds, sift and wash the sand from the kernels and use it in making bread. My father—who had had a well-stocked and tended farm, now had his family—but empty barns and fields. He obtained an old discarded mule, and with it and the colt the Yankees had failed to find, made his crop in 1865."[35] Kilpatrick's troopers captured a number of local male civilians and forced them to accompany the cavalry as it marched north.[36]

Not long after the Battle of Aiken, Sherman told Kilpatrick, "You may burn all cotton; spare dwelling houses that are occupied, and teach your men to be courteous to women; it goes a great way."[37] Sherman's staff officer Maj. Henry Hitchcock noted in his diary that while

---

32. Carter, *The Story of Joshua D. Breyfogle*, 322.
33. Dodson, *Campaigns of Wheeler and His Cavalry*, 326.
34. Ibid.
35. Toole, *Ninety Years in Aiken County*, 17.
36. Elmore, *Carnival of Destruction*, 145.
37. *OR* 47, 2:351.

Kilpatrick fought at Aiken he burned a residential property, angering Sherman, which was not his usual response.[38]

Consistent with their conduct throughout the March to the Sea, Wheeler's men also inflicted their fair share of damage. Henry William Ravenel owned a plantation called Hampton Hill. He had been away since January and returned to find that his beautiful home had been completely sacked by the Confederate cavalrymen, who had camped on and around the grounds. According to Ravenel, Wheeler's men took "all the corn...fodder, some salt, rifled the house, broke open all locks, and took away what they wanted, carpets, blankets, clothes, ...etc., etc." Wheeler's troopers broke into Ravenel's desk and haphazardly scattered important papers. Ravenel's sole consolation was that the house still stood and did not suffer the fate of nearby homes like those in towns such as Barnwell.[39]

The *Edgefield Advertiser* of Edgefield, South Carolina, ran an article complaining about the depredations of bands of cavalry roving across the state. Unfortunately, Wheeler's troopers committed the depredations. "We are not wont to tinker with the management and discipline of our armies, but, judging from the unbridled straggling, something must be demonstrably awry in military maters. Most of these marauders are cavalrymen, and are, or are generally said to be, 'Wheeler's men.' Now, the majority of Gen. Wheeler's men are, beyond a doubt, as brave and good and true as any soldiers in the service." The editorial continued, "These stragglers, from all accounts, never fight and never have fought; and while their better and braver companions are doing battle notably at the front, they are marauding and plundering through the country in rear of the army. Their outrages during the late military operations in South Carolina have been numerous and fearful." Concluding, the editorial did not mince words: "If a few of them were 'shot to death with musketry,' this terrible nuisance would soon be abated."[40]

However, Wheeler's conduct stemmed from Beauregard ordering him to destroy all supplies in hopes that they would not fall into the hands of Sherman's army. Further, Wheeler followed orders to forage off the land and to impress whatever supplies he needed from the

38. M. A. DeWolfe Howe, ed., *Marching with Sherman: Passages from the Letters and Campaign Diaries of Henry Hitchcock, Major and Assistant Adjutant General of Volunteers November 1864-May 1865* (New Haven: Yale University Press, 1927), 261.
39. Arney Robinson Childs, ed., *The Private Journal of Henry William Ravenel, 1859-1887* (Columbia: University of South Carolina Press, 1947), 224.
40. *Edgefield Advertiser*, February 15, 1865.

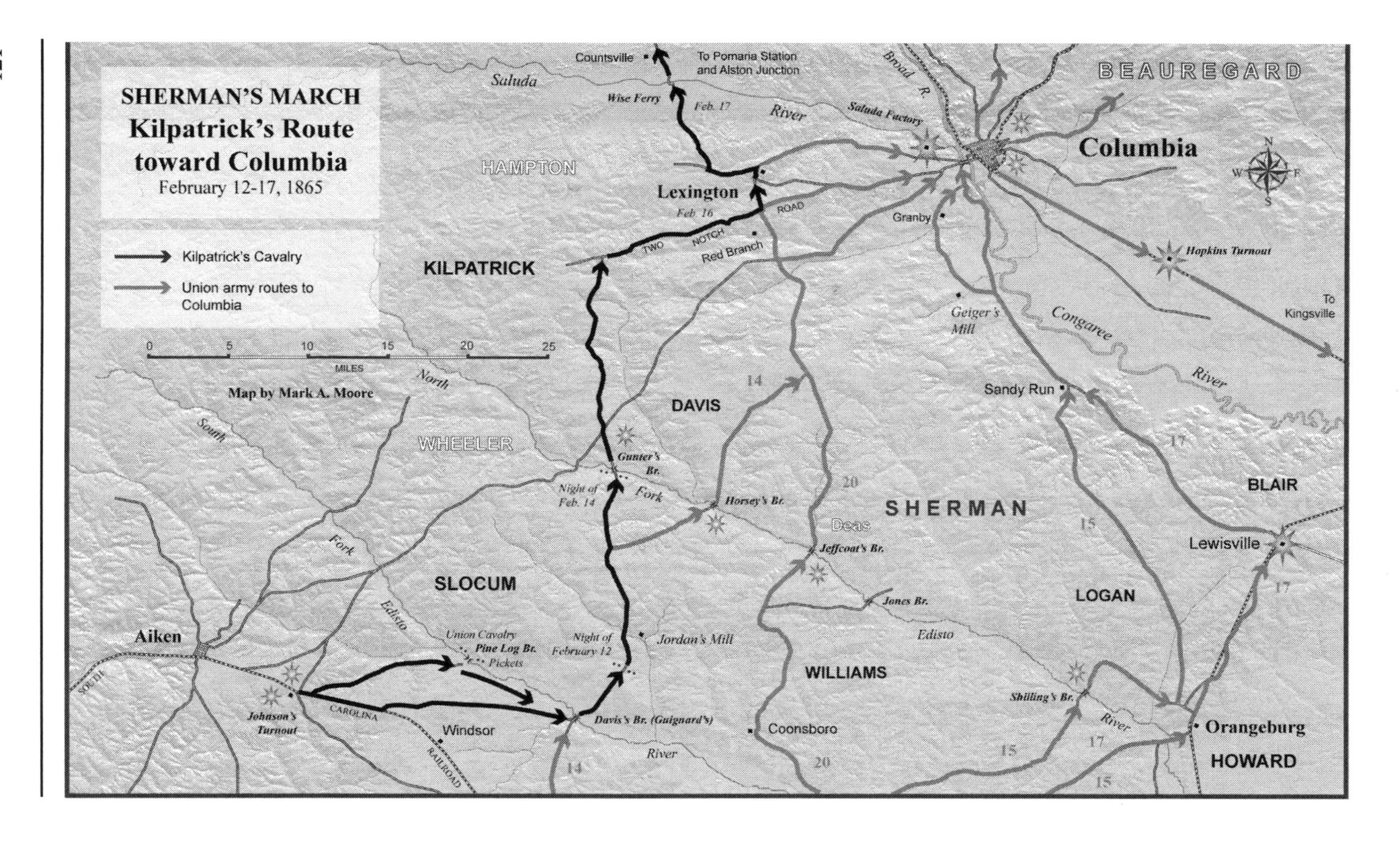
SHERMAN'S MARCH
Kilpatrick's Route
toward Columbia
February 12-17, 1865
Kilpatrick's Cavalry
Union army routes to Columbia
0 5 10 15 20 25
MILES
Map by Mark A. Moore
BEAUREGARD
Columbia
HAMPTON
KILPATRICK
WHEELER
SLOCUM
DAVIS
SHERMAN
WILLIAMS
LOGAN
BLAIR
HOWARD
Countsville
To Pomaria Station and Alston Junction
Saluda
Wise Ferry
Feb. 17
River
Saluda Factory
Broad R.
Lexington
Feb 16
TWO NOTCH ROAD
Red Branch
Granby
Hopkins Turnout
To Kingsville
Geiger's Mill
Congaree
River
Sandy Run
North
South
Fork
Edisto
Gunter's Br.
Night of Feb. 14
Horsey's Br.
Deas
Jeffcoat's Br.
Jones Br.
Lewisville
Aiken
Union Cavalry
Pine Log Br.
Pickets
Night of February 12
Jordan's Mill
Johnson's Turnout
CAROLINA
RAILROAD
SOUTH
Windsor
Davis's Br. (Guignard's)
Coonsboro
Shilling's Br.
Orangeburg
14
20
15
17

countryside.[41] Apparently, such orders were music to the ears of some men in his command, and they obliged with great enthusiasm. And lastly, his troopers had not been paid in more than a year; they had no money with which to purchase food or supplies, resorting to helping themselves to whatever they needed. Later, Wheeler became concerned about the toll his men had taken as they made their way across South Carolina, and the general offered either to return or to pay for any goods his men had stolen.[42]

While the Battle of Aiken played out, the rest of Sherman's army forced its way across the south fork of the Edisto River. The 17th Corps crossed the river on the night of February 9, coming within three miles of Orangeburg, which it occupied on February 12. Sherman's men ransacked the town and burned half of it to the ground before moving on. After destroying the railroad, the Federals advanced toward Columbia, and by February 15, they reached Lexington, less than 10 miles from the state capital. There, Kilpatrick's division rejoined the army, its unsuccessful expedition to Augusta over.[43]

When Kilpatrick rejoined Sherman's main body, his troopers again covered the army's left flank as it advanced; Wheeler and his Confederate cavalry harassed Sherman's advance as best it could. The Southern horse soldiers fought hard as they shadowed Sherman's army northward. Eventually, though, the sheer weight of Sherman's numbers overwhelmed Hampton's and Wheeler's small force, and Columbia fell on February 17, 1865.[44]

Sherman's intentions finally became clearer to the Confederates. On February 13, an Augusta newspaper accurately reported, "It is definitely ascertained that the main portion of the Federal forces have moved toward Columbia. They no longer occupy any points threatening this city and all apprehension of an attack here has passed for the present." The correspondent continued, "The policy of Sherman appears to be to harass interior points while he flanks Charleston. To accomplish this, he may make a push to Columbia as he did at Augusta, thus compelling our forces to evacuate Branchville and placing him within easy striking distance of the South Carolina Railroad: This accomplished, he will have the supplies of Charleston cut off, and they move on that coveted 'nest of rebellion' of with a portion of his Forces attempt to starve in time capitulation, while his

41. Joseph Wheeler to C. C. Jones, August 1, 1866, C. C. Jones Papers, Archives, Perkins Library, Duke University, Durham, North Carolina.
42. *Charleston News and Courier*, March 14, 1898. Apparently, Wheeler had few takers for his offer.
43. For a detailed discussion, see Sherman, *Memoirs*, 2:274-277.
44. McMurry, *An Ardent Secessionist*, 329.

main body proceeds toward Richmond."[45] The article precisely described Sherman's true intentions.

"This has been an anxious week for us all. The memory is burned into my brain," scientist Joseph LeConte, who lived in Columbia, wrote. "The enemy, swearing vengeance against South Carolina, the cradle of Secession, is approaching step by step, consternation and panic flight of women and children in front, and a blackened ruin behind." LeConte continued, "First we hear of them at Branchville, then at Orangeburg, then approaching Columbia by the Orangeburg Road. Still the authorities—Beauregard, Hampton &c.—seem confident that they cannot take Columbia and that they will not attempt it." But Sherman's army, indeed, was bearing down on Columbia.[46]

A few days later, LeConte wrote in his diary, "All day yesterday and today the booming of the enemy's guns seems to become nearer and nearer. Yesterday our front line of defence [sic] was carried. Today the second line was carried." He lamented, "Columbia is doomed!"[47]

Implementing Sherman's policy to destroy anything of value to the Confederate war effort, the Union razed the arsenal and many government warehouses that were jammed with military supplies. The Federals replenished their supply wagons with captured bags of corn meal and other commissary necessities.[48] As the capital of South Carolina, Columbia—viewed as the hated rebellion's birth-place—suffered a fate worse than any other city Sherman's men had occupied. A fire spread throughout the city caused by burning cotton bales, destroying both public and private property. The enemies never agreed about who was responsible for the inferno. Sherman blamed Confederate cavalry under Hampton for the firestorm, while Hampton pointed the finger at Sherman's men. Regardless of who caused the fire, it left many Columbians homeless, hungry, and unemployed.[49]

---

45. "Sherman's Progress," *Augusta Chronicle*, February 13, 1865.
46. Joseph LeConte, *Ware Sherman: A Journal of Three Months Personal Experience in the Last Days of the Confederacy* (Baton Rouge: Louisiana State University Press, 1999), 81.
47. Ibid., 83.
48. Sherman, *Memoirs*, 2:281.
49. The consensus, based on historic evidence, is that Sherman's men started the fire. Sherman blamed Hampton as a means of damaging public morale and diminishing confidence in Hampton and his troopers. While a Machiavellian ploy, it worked brilliantly, even though it enraged and forever alienated Wade Hampton and soured the tone of the rest of the war. For a detailed discussion about the fall and burning of Columbia, see William Gilmore Simms, *A City Laid Waste: The Capture, Sack, and Destruction of the City of Columbia* (Columbia: University of South Carolina Press, 2005).

Gen. Joseph E. Johnston, commander of all Confederate forces in North Carolina.

(Valentine Museum)

On February 25, 1865, Confederate General-in-Chief Robert E. Lee realized that the situation in the Carolinas was growing more desperate. Lee assigned 58-year-old Gen. Joseph E. Johnston, who was semi-retired, to command the available Confederate forces in North Carolina. Lee also tasked Johnston with cobbling together a cohesive command that would attempt to impede Sherman's efforts to reach Virginia via the Carolinas. President Jefferson Davis, who detested Johnston, only agreed to the plan "with the understanding that General Lee would supervise and control the operations."[50]

Major General Lafayette McLaws, who commanded a division in Hardee's corps, remarked, "The appointment appears to have been received with general favor by officers and troops."[51] Johnston assumed the responsibility "with no other hope of contributing to obtain favorable terms of peace; the only one that a rational being could then entertain. For the result of the war was evident in the fullest."[52] Johnston had about 20,000 infantry, along with Hampton's and Wheeler's combined cavalry forces, to dispute the advance of Sherman's 60,000 men. Trying to halt Sherman with meager resources proved to be a daunting task, at best. Johnston commanded the troops until surrendering to Sherman at the end of April 1865.[53]

On February 28, the governor of South Carolina, Andrew G. McGrath, sent the following letter of gratitude to Wheeler:

---

50. Jefferson Davis, *The Rise and Fall of the Confederate Government*, 2 vols. (New York: D. Appleton & Co., 1881), 2:631.
51. Oeffinger, *A Soldier's General*, 255.
52. Joseph E. Johnston, *Narrative of Military Operations, Directed, During the Late War Between the States* (New York: D. Appleton & Co., 1874), 372.
53. For a detailed discussion about the surrender of Johnston's army to Sherman at Bennett Place, near Durham, North Carolina, see Eric J. Wittenberg, *"We Ride a Whirlwind": Sherman and Johnston at Bennett Place* (Burlington, NC: Fox Run Publishing, 2017).

State of South Carolina,
Executive Department, Feb. 28, 1865

General:

I avail myself of the earliest opportunity to offer you in behalf of the State my thanks for the defence [sic] of the town of Aiken, and the protection given in that defence [sic] to the population of the town.

To be saved as was that town and its population from the ruthless foe by which it was attacked, calls not only for the thanks of those immediately exposed, but for the grateful remembrance of all classes of our citizens. To you, and through you that portion of your command which participated in the conflict for the possession of Aiken, I tender you the thanks of the State. I am, General,

Respectfully, etc.
A. G. McGrath, Governor.
TO GENERAL WHEELER.[54]

By the time McGrath wrote the letter, Sherman's blue juggernaut had rolled northward toward its ultimate destination, Goldsboro, North Carolina. It left a devastated wasteland wherever it went. Four major battles remained to be fought—Monroe's Crossroads on March 10, Wise's Forks from March 8-10, Averasboro from March 15-16, and Bentonville from March 19-21—but, finally, the end of the long, bloody war was in sight.[55]

Not surprisingly, Kilpatrick refused to admit that Wheeler defeated him at Aiken. "In the fight near Aiken, in which one of my regiments (the Ninety-second Illinois), one company of the Ninth Michigan, and small detachments from the Ninth and Tenth Ohio, and my staff and escort, were alone engaged against Humes' and Allen's divisions, commanded by Wheeler in person, I lost but 25 men killed and

54. Dubose, *Campaigns of Wheeler and His Cavalry*, 324.
55. For a detailed monograph of the Battle of Monroe's Crossroads, see Wittenberg, *Battle of Monroe's Crossroads*. For the best account of the Battle of Wise's Forks, see Wade Sokolosky and Mark A. Smith, *"To Prepare for Sherman's Coming": The Battle of Wise's Forks, March 1865* (El Dorado Hills, CA: Savas-Beatie, 2015). For the best account of the Battle of Averasboro, see Mark A. Smith and Wade Sokolosky, *"No Such Army Since the Days of Julius Caesar": Sherman's Carolinas Campaign from Fayetteville to Averasboro, March 1865* (El Dorado Hills, CA: Savas-Beatie, 2017). For the best account of the Battle of Bentonville, see Mark L. Bradley, *The Battle of Bentonville: Last Stand in the Carolinas* (Mason City, IA: Savas Publishing, 1996).
56. *OR* 47, 2:450.

wounded and less than 20 taken prisoners," Kilpatrick claimed, a few days after the fight. "It was not a general fight, but simply a reconnaissance. This party fell slowly back from Aiken before these two divisions, and at 11 a.m. Wheeler, with one brigade, feigned upon my left flank and charged me, mounted, with his entire command. I occupied a strong position, had no flanks, and he was most handsomely repulsed. His loss before he reached my barricades, in Allen's division alone, according to his official report, was 31 killed and upward of 160 wounded. I took upward of 60 prisoners, and have in my possession 5 battle-flags as proof of our superiority over his cavalry."

Kilpatrick had more to voice, though. "Wheeler has, as usual, reported a victory over my people, whose backs he has not yet seen," Kilpatrick inaccurately boasted, "and from all I can learn a portion of our army seems only too willing to believe such reports." He was unfazed by the news that Wade Hampton and a cavalry division from the Army of Northern Virginia had arrived to reinforce Wheeler. "I don't fear Wheeler and Hampton combined, even without supports," Little Kil boldly declared.[56]

At the end of February, Kilpatrick circulated a general order to his division. Praising his men's performance, he lauded, "Genl. Atkins' stubborn fight at Aiken and the subsequent splendid repulse given to the enemy by Col. Jordan and a portion of Lieut. Col. Way's command, at Johnson's Station. Our successful feint on Augusta, resulting in drawing Wheeler's entire corps moved far to our left and rear, with Cheatham's corps of infantry gave us Columbia without a struggle." Despite losing the battle at Aiken, Kilpatrick stubbornly claimed victory.[57]

Northern newspapers greeted Wheeler's victory with a good deal of skepticism. "But as Wheeler has frequently driven Kilpatrick, according to previous accounts, just exactly where he wanted to go, there is not much to be made out of this statement," *The Philadelphia Inquirer* sniffed. "It is simply a harmless device to keep up the spirits of the despondent at Richmond."[58]

John M. King, who served in the 92nd Illinois, asked his comrades, "When will you forget Aiken?" Continuing, he said, "Wheeler...had there prepared a trap for you, and Kilpatrick's dare-devil dash drove you squarely into the jaws of the trap, but when they sprung it and

57. General Order, Cavalry Division Headquarters, February 26, 1865, Thomas J. Jordan Papers, Historical Society of Pennsylvania, Philadelphia, Pennsylvania.
58. "The Operations at the South," *The Philadelphia Inquirer*, February 18, 1865.

thought they had you nicely, they found they had caught a tartar!"[59] King's exhortation to his comrades accurately reflects the attitude of the Union troopers who refused to acknowledge that Wheeler's corps had defeated them at Aiken.

Col. Thomas W. Sanderson, commander of the 10th Ohio Cavalry.

(New York State Archives)

Atkins admitted to 53 killed, wounded, and missing, but he asserted that Wheeler's command lost 72 killed that day.[60] Lieutenant Colonel Matthew Van Buskirk of the 92nd Illinois, whose troopers had borne the brunt of the fighting at Aiken, reported, "My casualties in this fight were 5 killed, 11 wounded, and 7 missing, including 2 officers."[61] Colonel William D. Hamilton, 9th Ohio Cavalry, reported 7 wounded and 4 captured.[62] Lieutenant Colonel Thomas W. Sanderson, 10th Ohio Cavalry, reported 2 killed, 4 wounded, and 10 captured.[63] Wheeler claimed 53 Federals killed, 270

59. Swedberg, *Three Years with the 92nd Illinois*, 235.
60. *OR* 47, 1:879-880.
61. Ibid., 882.
62. Ibid., 888.
63. Ibid., 891. Thomas W. Sanderson was born in Indiana, Pennsylvania, on October 17, 1829, as the son of Matthew D. Sanderson, a farmer of Scottish descent, and Mary Wakefield Sanderson, a British immigrant. In 1836, the family relocated to Youngstown, Ohio, where young Sanderson attended school. He later went to college at Bardstown, Kentucky. He then studied law in Youngstown, and in 1852 Sanderson was admitted to the bar. He also studied civil engineering. In 1854, he married Elizabeth Shoemaker of New Castle, Pennsylvania, and then started his own practice. In 1856, he was elected the prosecuting attorney for Mahoning County, Ohio. Sanderson gave up his law practice in 1861 to become lieutenant and adjutant of the 2nd Ohio Cavalry, remaining in the service for the entire four years of the Civil War. He was promoted to captain on October 7, 1861, and participated in the battles of Stones River, Chickamauga, and Chattanooga, as well as the Atlanta Campaign, the March to the Sea, and the Carolinas Campaign. When the 10th Ohio Cavalry was mustered in 1862, Sanderson transferred to the new regiment as a major. On January 30, 1864, he became its lieutenant colonel and then its colonel on May 22, 1866. He received a brevet to brigadier general of volunteers in March 1865. "He was regarded as one of the most daring and efficient officers in the volunteer service," an obituary stated. "As an organizer, tactician and strategist he had few superiors." When the 10th Ohio Cavalry mustered out in 1865, Sanderson returned to practicing

Graves of twenty Union soldiers killed in the Battle of Aiken in the graveyard of the First Baptist Church.

(Author's photo)

wounded, and 172 captured, who were allegedly "a number of officers of high rank."[64]

The number of Confederate casualties sustained at Aiken remains unknown, with neither side agreeing on a count. When he wrote his after-action report, Kilpatrick claimed that Wheeler "was handsomely repulsed with a loss of 31 killed, 160 wounded, and 60 taken prisoners."[65] Colonel Thomas J. Jordan, who commanded Kilpatrick's First Brigade, claimed that his men "repulsed [Wheeler] with his whole force at Johnson's Station 16 miles from Augusta and followed him taking 150 prisoners."[66] A trooper of the 10th Ohio claimed that "we lost yesterday in killed, wounded and missing some Hundred and fifty, the Rebels a great many more."[67]

law, ranking "as one of the leading lawyers" in Ohio. Active in Republican politics, he became delegate to the Republican National Convention in 1872, which nominated Ulysses S. Grant for a second term as president. In addition to practicing law, he also became vice president of a bank in Youngstown, where his colleagues held him in high esteem. He died in Youngstown on February 26, 1908, and was buried in Youngstown's Oak Hill Cemetery. See *Biographical History of Northeastern Ohio Embracing the Counties of Ashtabula, Trumbull and Mahoning* (Chicago: The Lewis Publishing Co., 1893), 656-657; "In Memoriam Companion Thomas Wakefield Sanderson." Military Order of the Loyal Legion of the United States, Commandery of the State of Ohio. Circular No. 13, Series of 1908, and Hunt and Brown, *Brevet Brigadier Generals in Blue*, 533.

64. *OR* 47, 2:450.
65. Ibid., 1:859.
66. Thomas J. Jordan to his wife, March 12, 1865, Jordan Papers.
67. Carter, *The Story of Joshua D. Breyfogle*, 322.

First Baptist Church, Aiken, South Carolina.

(Aiken Historical Society)

Reverend John H. Cornish of St. Thaddeus Church in Aiken recorded that on February 12 "we buried 30 odd of the enemy's dead, a staff officer of theirs, since captured, admits 80 killed. We took some 50 or more prisoners. Gen. Wheeler tells me that so far as he has learned our casualties in all, killed, wounded or missing did not exceed 40."[68]

Twenty Union battle dead from the Battle of Aiken still rest in the graveyard of the First Baptist Church. Four of the troopers remain unidentified, but one was a member of the 2nd Kentucky Cavalry of Jordan's First Brigade, and the rest are marked "5th U.S. Cavalry." Since the 5th U.S. Cavalry was a Regular Army unit that served with the Army of the Potomac's Cavalry Corps in Virginia, these men could not have come from that designated regiment.[69] It is unclear which Union unit the men might have served in. The 5th Ohio Cavalry had not taken sufficient casualties in the fighting at Johnson's Turnout, so the men likely did not come from that regiment.[70] Their unit will probably remain unknown. A marker in the First Baptist Church's graveyard commemorates the Confederate dead from the Battle of Aiken.

The people of Aiken never forgot that Joe Wheeler and his cavalrymen prevented the destruction of their town. When Wheeler passed away in 1906, J. B. Salley, who was then the mayor of Aiken, sent a telegram to Wheeler's home in Brooklyn, New York. "The people of Aiken mourn the death of General Wheeler, who saved our

68. Cornish diary, entry for February 12, 1865.
69. According to grave markers, the names of the identified Union cavalrymen buried in the graveyard of the First Baptist Church are: Henry Buhbrick, J. C. Burgen, C. M. Curtis, W. M. Driscoll, Matthew Ivory, W. M. Jackson, Martin Kelly, Fred K. Maple, James Massey, H. H. Reilley, Daniel Steele, W. M. Stonne, Fred K. Sweitzer, Otto Unrein, Joseph Vanzceptal, and W. I. Wiley.
70. See Dave Dougherty, *Making Georgia Howl! The 5th Ohio Volunteer Cavalry in Kilpatrick's Campaigns and the Diary of Sgt. William H. Harding* (Point Pleasant, NJ: Winged Hussar Publishing, 2016), 224, for a discussion of this issue.

The monument to the Battle of Aiken in the town of Aiken.

(Author's photo)

city from Kilpatrick's men, February 11, 1865," Salley declared.[71] But had it not been for Wheeler's aggressive and inspired defense of Aiken, the city likely would have met the same fate as Barnwell and other similar towns scattered across the South Carolina countryside.[72]

71. "About Wheeler," *The Montgomery Times*, February 15, 1906.
72. Discussed in Chapter One, Aiken was a resort area before the Civil War. It resumed that status after the war ended. During the Gilded Age, toward the end of the nineteenth century, Aiken gained fame as a favorite escape for wealthy Northeasterners seeking to flee harsh winters. Aiken boasted moderate weather, perfect areas for horse stables, and the Winter Colony, which became especially popular with equestrians. The town remains popular today. The many wealthy and famous Winter Colony residents included famous polo player Harry Payne Whitney and his wife, sculptress Gertrude Vanderbilt Whitney, founder of the Whitney Museum of Art in New York. See David M. Tavernier, *Stories of the Rich and Famous: Aiken's Winter Colony in the Gilded Age* (Parker, CO: Outskirts Press, 2012) and *More Stories of the Rich and Famous: Aiken's Winter Colony in the Gilded Age* (Parker, CO: Outskirts Press, 2014).

After the Civil War, Judson Kilpatrick received two separate appointments as U.S. ambassador to Chile. He served as ambassador from 1866-1870 and again in 1881, dying of Bright's Disease while serving in Santiago. During his first stint in Chile, he married a wealthy socialite. One of his granddaughters, Gloria Morgan, married a member of the wealthy Vanderbilt family. Gloria Morgan Vanderbilt's daughter, Gloria Vanderbilt, was born in 1924. In 1934, Gertrude Vanderbilt Whitney fought a highly publicized court battle with her sister-in-law, Gloria Morgan Vanderbilt, for custody of her ten-year-old niece, Gloria. Gertrude Vanderbilt Whitney won custody of her niece. See Helen Kennedy and Jay Maedar, "The Scandalous Custody Battle Between the Whitneys and the Vanderbilts Over 'Little Gloria'," *New York Daily News*, August 14, 2017. Gloria Vanderbilt spent long periods of her youth at the Whitney-Vanderbilt family's vacation home in Aiken, which still

In the years after the war, the city of Aiken erected a monument honoring the ferocious fight that took place in the town's streets on February 11, 1865. It sits at the corner of Richland and Newberry streets. The monument reads:

THE BATTLE OF AIKEN

NEAR THIS SITE ON FEBRUARY 11, 1865

WAS FOUGHT ONE OF THE FINAL CONFEDERATE

VICTORIES OF THE WAR BETWEEN THE STATES.

FEDERAL CAVALRY COMMAND BY MAJOR

GENERAL HUGH JUDSON KILPATRICK WERE

ATTACKED BY CONFEDERATE CAVALRY

COMMANDED BY MAJOR GENERAL JOSEPH

WHEELER WHEN THE FEDERALS ENTERED

AIKEN FROM THE SOUTHEAST ALONG THE

SOUTH CAROLINA RAILROAD. THE FEDERALS

RETREATED TO MONTMORENCI, WHERE THEIR

INFANTRY SUPPORT WAS STATIONED.

SUCCESSFUL DEFENSE OF AIKEN BY THE

CONFEDERATES PREVENTED THE POSSIBLE

DESTRUCTION OF THE CITIES OF AIKEN AND

AUGUSTA AND THE GRANITEVILLE MILL.

While not entirely historically accurate, the monument bears silent witness to the savage fighting that raged in the streets of Aiken on February 11, 1865.

---

stands. See, e.g., "The Colony," *Aiken Standard and Review*, July 29, 1938, for coverage of Aiken's social scene at the time. It specifically mentions Gloria Vanderbilt's doings as a teenager. Today, there is a street in Aiken called Vanderbilt Drive. Thus, Kilpatrick's great-granddaughter remains highly esteemed in Aiken, while her cavalryman ancestor remains a reviled figure. CNN television personality Anderson Cooper is Gloria Vanderbilt's son, meaning that he is Kilpatrick's great-great-grandson.

CONCLUSION

Battlefield victories were few and far between for the Confederates in 1865. This was particularly true during Maj. Gen. William T. Sherman's Carolinas Campaign when the Confederate armies suffered crushing defeat after crushing defeat. The Battle of Aiken was the one significant Confederate battlefield victory that the Rebels could claim during the Carolinas Campaign. That single battlefield triumph must be evaluated within the wider context of the Carolinas Campaign and within the even wider context of the Civil War in general. In defeating Bvt. Maj. Gen. Judson Kilpatrick's cavalry, Maj. Gen. Joseph Wheeler believed he had saved Augusta—and its powder works—as well as Aiken and the equally important mills at Graniteville from Union cavalry. But the Confederate victory at Aiken had much more serious consequences.

"Augusta was the largest city, most valuable depot, and contained more important government works than any place that escaped the enemy during the war. Yet it has been seen that Sherman, with his vast army, twice passed near in the hopes of taking it, but both times was opposed so strongly as to be compelled to turn his course," the historian of Wheeler's corps said, referring to both the Battle of Aiken and the December 4, 1864, Battle of Waynesboro, Georgia. "On both of these occasions the defender of this city, the one whose guns alone checked the advancing foe, was a brave young officer who fought to save his native heath and the scenes of his childhood, for Augusta was the birthplace and home of General Wheeler."[1]

This smokestack is the sole remaining element of the Augusta Powder Works, located in Augusta, Georgia.

(Author's photo)

---

1. Dodson, *Campaigns of Wheeler and His Cavalry*, 323-324.

"If General Wheeler had not checked the advance of the Yankees at Aiken, they would most probably have passed north further west, destroying the mill at Graniteville which they wanted to do very badly then going on through Edgefield and on to Columbia," James Andrew Jones, the Confederate mail rider who had met Wheeler on the morning of February 11, speculated.[2]

In 1888, Sherman told the editor of an Augusta newspaper, *The Chronicle*, why he elected not to enter Charleston or Augusta: "I did not want to drive out their garrisons [at Macon and Augusta] to accumulate ahead of me at Santee, Catawba, Peedee, Cape Fear, etc. The moment I passed by Columbia your factories, powder mills, and the old stuff accumulated at Augusta was lost to the only two Confederate armies left—i.e., Lee's and Hood's." The general concluded, "So if you have a military mind, you will see that I made a better use of Augusta than if I had captured it with all of its stores, for which I had no use."[3] In other words, by capturing Columbia, Sherman could cut the rail lines that connected Charleston and Augusta to Gen. Robert E. Lee's Army of Northern Virginia. By cutting the rail lines, Sherman rendered Charleston and Augusta useless to the Confederacy's military efforts. Considering that Sherman had no intention of capturing Augusta, Wheeler's victory over Kilpatrick is left somewhat hollow as a result.

Fighting Joe Wheeler seemed obsessed with defeating Little Kil, and Sherman apparently understood that. Once Sherman's grand army entered South Carolina, department commander Gen. P. G. T. Beauregard emphasized the importance of defending South Carolina by implementing a series of defensive positions based upon the location of rivers, namely the Salkehatchie and Edisto. And once the Union made its way across the Edisto, there were no terrain features to hinder Sherman's advance on Columbia. Beauregard intended to delay Sherman on the Edisto line, hoping that elements of the Army of Tennessee en route to South Carolina could be brought to bear on Sherman. Thus, Beauregard ordered Wheeler to join with Maj. Gen. Carter L. Stevenson's Army of Tennessee infantry, the first of the formation to arrive in South Carolina, to defend the line of the Edisto. However, Kilpatrick offered too tempting of a target to Wheeler. Once

2. Jones, "A Reminiscence of the Aiken Skirmish," 2.
3. A. Weller, "Sherman Talks Strategy," *Civil War Times Illustrated* 33, no. 3 (July-August 1994), 29. Historian Tom Elmore points out a popular Augusta legend that claims Sherman bypassed the town because a former sweetheart of his, named Cecilia Stovall, lived there. While her plantation was spared from the torch and Sherman left a note behind for her, there is no evidence suggesting any truth to the explanation for why Sherman spared Augusta. Elmore, *Carnival of Destruction*, 469, n. 113.

Wheeler realized that Kilpatrick's command was operating alone and unsupported in the vicinity of Aiken, Wheeler could not resist the temptation to try to defeat his former West Point chum on the battlefield. Wheeler disobeyed his orders, leaving the line of the Edisto behind, and went after Kilpatrick, defeating him on the field of battle at Aiken.

Although Sherman never said so, it appears that he knew by merely sending Kilpatrick's cavalry on a feint toward Augusta, he could draw Joe Wheeler out, even if that meant abandoning his responsibilities. Indeed, Sherman never intended to employ Kilpatrick to the front of his infantry columns, but rather as a screen on his left flank, including a feint toward Augusta. In short, it may be that Sherman wanted to bring on a large-scale cavalry battle somewhere in the vicinity of Aiken or Augusta in order to exploit the weakening of the Confederate defenses along the Edisto and to facilitate the advance on Columbia. If so, this was a brilliant move that Sherman made in the intricate chess game that marked the Carolinas Campaign.

Kilpatrick was characteristically rash in his dispositions at Aiken—and not for the first time. Major General Wade Hampton surprised him at Atlee's Station outside Richmond, Virginia, during the Kilpatrick-Dahlgren Raid, and then, of course, Wheeler stunned him at Aiken. More importantly, 27 days later, on March 10, Hampton's and Wheeler's combined forces pounced on Kilpatrick at Monroe's Crossroads, near Fayetteville, North Carolina. Kilpatrick had put out only a single company of videttes, and their capture left Kilpatrick's camp unguarded. Nearly 6,000 Confederate troopers swept down on the sleeping camp before dawn, and Kilpatrick barely escaped capture, beating a hasty retreat into a nearby swamp while wearing only his nightshirt. To Kilpatrick's credit, he rallied his troopers and eventually recaptured his camps. But the surprise attack cost him a day.

Kilpatrick's lack of vigilance combined with failing to take appropriate steps to provide security for his command resulted in numerous near captures. His behavior also caused the troopers to suffer needless casualties. But, somehow, Kilpatrick managed to avoid the worst possible outcome—once again.

Kilpatrick's command, particularly the 92nd Illinois Mounted Infantry, performed well at Aiken despite being surprised and ambushed. With only about 225 officers and men, the 92nd Illinois bore the brunt of the day's fighting. The Illinois men fought hard, extricating themselves from Wheeler's trap. Private John Wilcoxon, who served in Company D of the 92nd Illinois, bluntly assessed the situation at Aiken. "In the fight at Aiken, South Carolina, General

Atkins disobeyed the orders of Kilpatrick, and by so doing saved the 92nd from slaughter," Wilcoxon correctly asserted.[4] Other members of the 92nd Illinois credited their regimental commander with rescuing them at Aiken. "Lieutenant-Colonel Van Buskirk...ought to have been promoted to Brigadier General for his gallant and cool management of his little command at Aiken," the 92nd Illinois historian declared, years after the war.[5]

At the same time, Wheeler's Aiken victory meant that his command—the only viable, mobile force available to resist Sherman's advance after the Federals departed from Atlanta in the fall of 1864—was not available to resist the main Union army's advance toward Columbia. Without Wheeler's cavalry, there were a few thousand infantrymen from the remnant of the Army of Tennessee and Lt. Gen. William J. Hardee's command, a mixed lot of about 20,000 men who varied between rookies and veterans of the Civil War's most severe combat, available to defend the entire state of South Carolina.[6] Sherman had concentrated his forces along a very narrow front, while Beauregard had spread his available forces around South Carolina, guessing where Sherman intended to go.

Beauregard, in particular, had spent much of the last year of the war in South Carolina. Few understood better than Beauregard the importance of the Edisto River line and what would be required to hold it. For several days prior to the Battle of Aiken, he had emphasized the importance of defending the line of the Edisto in order to ensure that a substantial force was available to resist Sherman's advance on Columbia. Beauregard specifically ordered Wheeler and his cavalry to support the infantry holding the line of the Edisto for as

4. "Battle at Aiken, S.C., Feb. 11, '65." *Freeport Daily Journal*, March 4, 1909.
5. *92nd Illinois Mounted Infantry*, 217.
6. On February 3, Beauregard met with Hardee, Maj. Gen. D. H. Hill, and Maj. Gen. Gustavus W. Smith to discuss options for defeating Sherman. They tallied the following: (a) under Hardee in South Carolina, 8,500 men (mostly infantry, but including 2,000 artillerymen and 1,500 cavalry); (b) Georgia militia in and around Augusta, 1,450 men; (c) 22,450 infantry and 800 artillery from the Army of Tennessee, in transit (including 4,000 infantry of Lt. Gen. S. D. Lee's corps, under rank and first name Stevenson); (d) Wheeler's corps, 6,700 men. All told, once the Army of Tennessee arrived, the total would be 33,450 men—22,450 infantry, 2,800 artillerymen, and 8,200 cavalrymen. Because a garrison was left at Charleston, the effective number was about 20,000 men, spread across a wide front. The participants concluded, "In view of Sherman's present position, his manifest advance toward Branchville from Pocotaligo and Coosawhatchie, the weakness of our forces, and the expected arrival of the re-enforcements above referred to, it was deemed inadvisable to concentrate our forces at Branchville, and there offer battle to Sherman." See OR 47, 2:1084-1085.

long as possible. However, Wheeler disregarded the instructions. On February 12, Beauregard sent the following note to Hardee, expressing his frustration with Wheeler's obsession with Kilpatrick: "Wheeler reported he had gone toward Augusta in obedience to your instructions, leaving 1,400 men to support Stevenson and McLaws...Present management of the cavalry surpasses my understanding."[7]

Mounted cavalry battles in urban settings were rare during the Civil War. Urban settings are not typically conducive to the drama of mounted charges and countercharges; cavalry actions, by nature, are better suited to open fields without obstructions. The only four instances of such combat east of the Mississippi River during the war were: the August 2, 1862, Battle of Orange Court House, Virginia; the June 30, 1863, Battle of Hanover, Pennsylvania, during the Gettysburg Campaign; and the July 6, 1863, Battle of Hagerstown, Maryland, during the retreat from Gettysburg.[8] Ironically, Kilpatrick was the Union commander at both Hanover and Hagerstown, meaning that he commanded three of the four notable instances of urban mounted cavalry combat. Hence, in addition to the other interesting aspects of the Battle of Aiken, it was also unique for occurring in an urban area.

While Wheeler saved Augusta, Aiken, and Graniteville from Kilpatrick's horsemen burning them to the ground, their absence from Sherman's front cleared the way for the Union army's advance on Columbia. Wheeler's decision to attack Kilpatrick at Aiken left the road to Columbia nearly unobstructed, although it resulted in a battlefield victory and saved Aiken and Graniteville. Wheeler's men outnumbered Kilpatrick's by nearly two to one at Johnson's Turnout on February 12, but they failed to attack in force, allowing Kilpatrick's entire division to escape. After the losses at Aiken, Wheeler did not move to try to interpose his command between Sherman and Columbia until February 14, despite receiving repeated requests to do so from the Confederate authorities.[9] Accordingly, Wheeler must bear a significant portion of the blame for the disaster that befell Columbia once Sherman captured it.

---

7. *OR* 47, 2:1166.
8. Historians have largely forgotten the cavalry fight at Orange Court House. On August 2, 1862, a Union cavalry brigade, in some of the first brigade-level cavalry fighting of the Civil War in the Eastern Theater, charged Col. William E. "Grumble" Jones's 7th Virginia Cavalry in the streets of Orange Court House, driving the Confederates from the center of town after fierce mounted fighting. For further discussion, see Laurence H. Freiheit, *Boots and Saddles: Cavalry During the Maryland Campaign of September 1862* (Iowa City, IA: Camp Pope Publishing, 2012), 94.
9. *OR* 47, 2:1186.

In the end, Hampton superseded Wheeler and played a critical role during the remainder of the Carolinas Campaign. Wheeler did not command troops in battle, or taste victory again, until the Spanish-American War in Cuba at the July 1, 1898, Battle of Kettle Hill, often misnamed the Battle of San Juan Hill. While Kilpatrick ultimately won the Battle of Monroe's Crossroads, his propensity for recklessness and failure to secure his command nearly caused him the embarrassment of being captured and cost his division heavy, but mostly unnecessary, casualties throughout the campaign. By contrast, Wheeler defeated Kilpatrick at Aiken, making the battle just one of the Union general's many failures throughout the Carolinas Campaign. However, victory allows the victor to be magnanimous, and Sherman never relieved Kilpatrick of command. Both Wheeler and Kilpatrick retained their commands until the end of the war in April 1865, clashing numerous times along the way.

Aiken marked a significant event during Sherman's brilliant campaign in South Carolina. Sherman's cleverly designed strategy allowed his army to make its way across South Carolina's rivers and swamps without having to fight a single large-scale battle, much like the ones the Federals fought in North Carolina at Averasboro on March 16 and at Bentonville from March 19-21. By using Kilpatrick's cavalry to draw Wheeler away from his assigned position along the Edisto, Sherman neutralized Beauregard's chosen defensive position and advanced on Columbia, almost unhindered. His strategy led to cutting the railroad lines that connected Charleston and Augusta to Lee's army in Virginia, rendering Augusta and Charleston worthless to the Confederacy, without having to assault either well-defended bastion. Wheeler took Sherman's bait—he attacked and defeated Kilpatrick at Aiken, opening the door for Columbia's destruction.

APPENDIX A

ORDER OF BATTLE
THE BATTLE OF AIKEN
FEBRUARY 11, 1865

UNION FORCES
DEPARTMENT OF THE MISSISSIPPI
Maj. Gen. William T. Sherman

ARMY OF THE TENNESSEE

Maj. Gen. O. O. Howard

Third Cavalry Division
Bvt. Maj. Gen. Judson Kilpatrick

Special Scouts (Capt. Theodore F. Northrop)

First Brigade
Brig. Gen. Thomas J. Jordan

3rd Indiana Cavalry Battalion (Capt. Charles U. Patton)
8th Indiana Cavalry (Col. Fielder A. Jones)
2nd Kentucky Cavalry (Maj. Owen Starr)
3rd Kentucky Cavalry (Lt. Col. Robert H. King)
9th Pennsylvania Cavalry (Lt. Col. David H. Kimmel)

Second Brigade
Brig. Gen. Smith D. Atkins

92nd Illinois Mounted Infantry (Lt. Col. Matthew Van Buskirk)
9th Michigan Cavalry (Col. George Acker)
9th Ohio Cavalry (Col. Douglas Hamilton)
10th Ohio Cavalry (Col. Thomas W. Sanderson)
1st Ohio Independent Cavalry Squadron (also known as McLaughlin's Independent Cavalry Squadron) (Maj. Richard Rice)

Third Brigade
Col. George E. Spencer

1st Alabama Cavalry (U.S.)(Maj. Francis L. Cramer)
5th Kentucky Cavalry (Maj. Christopher T. Cheek)
5th Ohio Cavalry (Maj. George H. Rader)

Fourth Provisional Brigade (dismounted)
Lt. Col. William B. Way

1st Regiment (Maj. Charles A. Appel)
2nd Regiment (Lt. Col. William Stough)
3rd Regiment (Capt. John B. Riggs)

10th Wisconsin Battery (Lt. Ebenezer Stetson)

CONFEDERATE FORCES
MILITARY DEPARTMENT OF THE WEST
Gen. P. G. T. Beauregard

ARMY OF TENNESSEE
Lt. Gen. Alexander P. Stewart

WHEELER'S CAVALRY CORPS

Maj. Gen. Joseph Wheeler

Allen's Division
Brig. Gen. William Wirt Allen

Anderson's Brigade
Brig. Gen. Robert H. Anderson

3rd Confederate Cavalry (Col. R. H. Rice)
8th Confederate Cavalry (Lt. Col. John S. Prather)
10th Confederate Cavalry (Capt. W. Vason)
5th Georgia Cavalry (Col. Edward Bird)

Hagan's Brigade
Col. James Hagan

1st Alabama Cavalry (Col. David T. Blakely)
3rd Alabama Cavalry (Lt. Col. Josiah Robins)
9th Alabama Cavalry (Capt. S. H. Dodds)
12th Alabama Cavalry (Lt. Col. Marcellus Pointer)
51st Alabama Cavalry (Col. M. L. Kirkpatrick)

Crews's Brigade
Col. Charles C. Crews

1st Georgia Cavalry (Lt. Col. George T. Watts)
2nd Georgia Cavalry (Capt. George C. Looney)
3rd Georgia Cavalry (Lt. Col. Robert Thompson)
6th Georgia Cavalry (Col. John R. Hart)

Humes's Division
Brig. Gen. William Y. C. Humes

Dibrell's Brigade
Col. William S. McLemore

4th Tennessee Cavalry[1]
11th Tennessee Cavalry
Shaw's Tennessee Battalion

Ashby's Brigade
Col. Henry Ashby

1st Tennessee Cavalry (Lt. Col. James T. Wheeler)
2nd Tennessee Cavalry (Lt. Col. John H. Kuhn)
5th Tennessee Cavalry (Col. George W. McKenzie)
9th Tennessee Cavalry (Maj. James H. Akin)

Harrison's Brigade
Brig. Gen. Thomas Harrison

3rd Arkansas Cavalry (Maj. William H. Blackwell)
8th Tennessee Cavalry
8th Texas Cavalry (Terry's Texas Rangers)(Capt. Doc Matthews)
11th Texas Cavalry

1. There were actually two different regiments designated as the 4th Tennessee. One regiment had been raised by rank Nathan Bedford Forrest and was part of Col. William S. McLemore's brigade. The other 4th Tennessee was part of Maj. Gen. Joseph Wheeler's command and was the regiment that served in rank and full name Harrison's brigade. It was consolidated with the small remnant of the 8th Tennessee Cavalry. The reader should be careful not to confuse these two regiments.

APPENDIX B

KNOWN CONFEDERATE CASUALTIES FROM THE BATTLE OF AIKEN

The following are the known Confederate casualties sustained at the Battle of Aiken. By the winter of 1865, the Confederacy's recordkeeping had deteriorated; this list is probably not complete and should not be counted upon as such. Rather, it marks an attempt to identify those Confederates who were reported as casualties in the Battle of Aiken.[1]

Name	Regiment	Status
Pvt. Jesse B. Robinson II	Co. K, 8th Alabama Cavalry	WIA[2]
Pvt. John Cullen Duncan	Co. A, 8th Confederate Cavalry	WIA
Pvt. Darwin D. Smith	Co. D, 51st Alabama Cavalry	WIA
Sgt. James Bird	F&S, 5th Georgia Cavalry	WIA
Pvt. James P. Young	Co. A, 5th Georgia Cavalry	KIA[3]
Pvt. Irbin B. Carmichael	Co. E, 5th Georgia Cavalry	WIA
Sgt. William A. Hodges	Co. E, 5th Georgia Cavalry	WIA
Pvt. Phillip N. Clifton	Co. F, 5th Georgia Cavalry	WIA
Pvt. James N. Newton	Co. F, 5th Georgia Cavalry	WIA
Pvt. James Usher	Co. F, 5th Georgia Cavalry	WIA
Pvt. Orlando D. Chester	Co. G, 5th Georgia Cavalry	WIA
Pvt. Chester O. Devant	Co. G, 5th Georgia Cavalry	WIA
Pvt. Malachi Johns	Co. G, 5th Georgia Cavalry	WIA
Pvt. Henry A. Russell	Co. G, 5th Georgia Cavalry	WIA

1. The author is grateful to Wade Sokolosky for sharing his voluminous research on Confederate casualties during the Carolinas Campaign and for permitting it to be recounted in this work.
2. "WIA" means wounded in action. Please contact the Bentonville Battlefield State Historic Site for additional information regarding Mr. Sokolosky's documentation of casualties during the 1865 Carolinas Campaign.
3. "KIA" means killed in action. This also includes those who were mortally wounded and died of their wounds later.

Name	Regiment	Status
Pvt. Nehemiah Sharp	Co. I, 1st Tennessee Cavalry	KIA
Lt. John McMahan	Co. D, 2nd Tennessee Cavalry	KIA
Pvt. Jesse Morris	Co. G, 2nd Tennessee Cavalry	KIA
Pvt. James Cox	Co. B, 4th Tennessee Cavalry	KIA
Pvt. Matthew Deadman	Co. C, 4th Tennessee Cavalry	KIA
Pvt. Joseph Hares	Co. E, 4th Tennessee Cavalry	KIA
Pvt. John R. Rushing	Co. E, 4th Tennessee Cavalry	WIA
Sgt. John Nealy	Co. E, 4th Tennessee Cavalry	KIA
Pvt. Legran Walkup	Co. E, 4th Tennessee Cavalry	KIA
Pvt. Samuel L. Richards	Co. A, 8th Texas Cavalry	WIA
Pvt. James M. Brannon	Co. D, 8th Texas Cavalry	WIA
Pvt. John A. Gage	Co. D, 8th Texas Cavalry	WIA
Pvt. Peyton R. Kennedy	Co. D, 8th Texas Cavalry	KIA
Pvt. Kyle R. Polk	Co. D, 8th Texas Cavalry	WIA
Pvt. James P. McArthur	Co. D, 8th Texas Cavalry	WIA
Pvt. George T. McGehee	Co. D, 8th Texas Cavalry	WIA
Pvt. David Nunn	Co. D, 8th Texas Cavalry	KIA
Pvt. Samuel H. Screws	Co. D, 8th Texas Cavalry	KIA
Pvt. Paul J. Watkins	Co. D, 8th Texas Cavalry	WIA
Pvt. Jim Wynn	Co. D, 8th Texas Cavalry	KIA
Pvt. Oscar W. Alexander	Co. F, 8th Texas Cavalry	WIA
Pvt. Fritz Lindenburg	Co. F, 8th Texas Cavalry	WIA
Capt. William R. Jarmon	Co. F, 8th Texas Cavalry	WIA
Pvt. James W. Pope	Co. F, 8th Texas Cavalry	WIA
Pvt. William C. Freeman Jr.	Co. H, 8th Texas Cavalry	WIA
Lt. J. W. Haskell	Co. K, 8th Texas Cavalry	KIA

APPENDIX C

DEFENDING AUGUSTA: A TALE OF TWO BATTLES

After the fall of Atlanta, Lt. Gen. John Bell Hood first went to work against Maj. Gen. William T. Sherman's supply lines. But in late October, the Army of Tennessee retired into Alabama. Sherman, sensing from statements Confederate President Jefferson Davis made about Hood's intention to invade Tennessee, saw an opportunity. Instead of chasing Hood, Sherman planned a march through Georgia. After dispatching Maj. Gen. George H. Thomas's Army of the Cumberland, except for two corps, to defend Tennessee, Sherman embarked on an epic march to Savannah, Georgia, with four corps. Then, after Sherman began the March to Sea on November 15, Hood invaded Tennessee with his army, hoping to defeat the two scattered wings of the Army of the Cumberland, separated by 75 miles, in detail.

Hood's invasion led to disaster; he suffered severe defeats at Franklin on November 30, 1864, and then at Nashville from December 15-16. The Army of Tennessee suffered about 15,000 casualties, leaving only 20,000 demoralized men in its ranks after the Battle of Nashville. Hood was relieved of command at his own request, and the remnants of the Army of Tennessee were ultimately scattered, with some sent to North Carolina in the winter of 1865. The surviving fragments of the Army of Tennessee surrendered to Sherman's army at Bennett Place, near Durham, North Carolina, on April 26, 1865.

When Hood decided to invade Tennessee, about 45,000 men of Lt. Gen. William J. Hardee's Department of South Carolina, Georgia, and Florida and Maj. Gen. Joseph Wheeler's Cavalry Corps were available to resist Sherman's horde of more than 60,000 men. This included all of the garrisons that Hardee controlled, but many of the men were not veterans or reliable troops.

Hardee did what he could, but his efforts largely proved futile. As demonstrated in Chapter One, Hardee evacuated Savannah, which fell to Sherman on December 24, 1864, and Hardee's bedraggled command made its way north to Charleston, South Carolina. Wheeler's men constantly harassed Sherman's army, annoying the temperamental general and inflicting losses along the way. As noted in Chapter Three, Wheeler's men earned the reputation of being as destructive to Georgia as Sherman's army, and Georgia citizens came to loathe and fear the

Confederate troopers as much as they did Sherman's notorious bummers.

As discussed in Chapter One, Augusta, Georgia, was a major industrial center for the Confederacy. The Confederacy's largest powder works were located in Augusta, as well as significant textile mills. Further, the Georgia Railroad had its terminus at Augusta. The line ended on the Tennessee River at Chattanooga, Tennessee, and it provided access from interior Georgia to the Mississippi River until it was cut when Sherman captured Atlanta. Finally, Fighting Joe Wheeler's hometown was Augusta, which he had an incentive to defend. However, Sherman never intended to directly attack Augusta; instead he planned feints in order to tie down Confederate forces. He hoped to draw Wheeler's cavalry out so that it would not be available to resist the advance of his infantry columns.

Wheeler successfully defended his hometown twice from Bvt. Maj. Gen. Judson Kilpatrick in about a 90-day period at Waynesboro, Georgia, on December 4, 1864, and again during the February 11, 1865, Battle of Aiken. This appendix will give some information about the Battle of Waynesboro, and then compare and contrast the two actions.

The Union column began its advance on the morning of December 1. Brevet Major General Absalom Baird's Third Division of the Fourteenth Corps accompanied Kilpatrick's division in order to support the efforts of the cavalry. Marching out from Louisville, Georgia, that morning, the two divisions took the road northeast toward Waynesboro. Although Wheeler's main body remained in position behind Rocky Creek, several of his detachments contested the advance. Baird recorded, "During the day considerable skirmishing with the enemy's cavalry, with a loss on our side of 3 men killed and 10 wounded."[1] On the other hand, Kilpatrick described the day's march as "without a severe skirmish."[2]

Wheeler became convinced that Kilpatrick was headed toward Augusta, and he was determined to stop him from doing so. "The enemy immediately started toward Augusta on the lower Augusta road. On reaching the house where General Kilpatrick had staid [sic] I learned that he and his officers had been overheard talking a great deal in private about Augusta," Wheeler stated. "It was the opinion of citizens that this move was intended as a raid upon that place. Being mindful of the great damage that could be done by the enemy's burning the valuable mills and property which were not protected by

1. *OR* 44, 204.
2. Ibid., 364.

fortifications, including the factories in the vicinity, the large portion of the city outside of the fortifications, the arsenal and sand hills, I hoped by pressing him hard he might be turned from his purpose." Wheeler "also learned that the night previous he had sent a party of some 500 men to Waynesborough to destroy the railroad bridge, which convinced me that Augusta and not Waynesborough was Kilpatrick's destination, as had the latter place been the point he designed striking he would not have sent a small party there on the preceding day." Thus, Wheeler pushed his tired command in pursuit of the Union cavalry.[3]

On the far left of the advance, Baird and Kilpatrick continued their combined effort to deal with Wheeler's cavalry. They crossed Buck Head Creek and pushed the Confederate pickets. A saber charge by a battalion from the 5th Ohio Cavalry cleared the way. Reaching Rocky Creek, Kilpatrick's cavalry gave way to permit an infantry attack. Baird extended his lines and found a crossing point. After the 74th Indiana crossed the creek, Wheeler withdrew toward Waynesboro. Once across the creek, Baird turned the column southeast toward Thomas Station. For the second time, Wheeler boasted that he'd "turned" a Federal column threatening Augusta.[4]

On December 3, Wheeler moved back down through Waynesboro and engaged the Federal picket line, alerting the Union to his return. Kilpatrick and Baird had orders to turn north toward Wheeler's position. The flanking column was to "destroy the bridge over Briar Creek" on December 4, which set the stage for the second cavalry clash around Waynesboro.[5]

During the restless night, Baird sent a status report to Maj. Gen. Jefferson C. Davis, the Fourteenth Corps commander. Earlier, Baird had expressed his disdain for the cavalry, which seemed to be leaning too much on the infantry for support. Now he alerted his commander about Wheeler's increased activity, the presence of Confederate artillery, and signs of entrenching: "Kilpatrick thinks that the fight of the campaign will take place here to-day. I do not see it in that light, but will support him."[6] However, Baird experienced severe limitations as to how much he could do since his ammunition supplies were desperately low.

On the morning of December 4, 1864, knowing that Wheeler's corps was in his front, Kilpatrick ordered his command to advance on

3. Ibid., 407.
4. Ibid., 408.
5. Ibid., 365.
6. Ibid.,625.

Waynesboro. Troopers overheard Kilpatrick warn "to prepare for a fight; that he was going out to whip Wheeler."[7] With the 10th Ohio Cavalry leading the way, Kilpatrick moved out toward Waynesboro. Almost immediately after moving out, the Buckeyes encountered a series of three barricades that dismounted Confederate cavalry manned. The barricades might not hold against a set piece assault, but any adversary would pay a price to gain them. Wheeler looked to lure the Federals into a close fight the next morning, where he could negate any numerical advantage they enjoyed. The Confederates' initial volley forced the Ohio men to fall back.

The Union cavalry deployed and advanced again, finding the first barricade abandoned. About three hundred yards farther, they came upon Wheeler's main position, described as "a splendid defensive position with heavy rail barricade, with a swamp on one flank and the railway embankment on the other."[8] In short, Wheeler used the small detachment of men at the first barricade to draw Kilpatrick into a bottleneck from which the Federals could not easily escape once they were engaged.

Kilpatrick ordered Brig. Gen. Smith Atkins's Second Brigade to take the second barricade. Atkins decided to pin down the enemy with severe fire while his mounted elements turned the flanks. Atkins assigned the 92nd Illinois Mounted Infantry to pin down Wheeler's men at the barricade with the massed firepower of their Spencer rifles, while the 9th Ohio Cavalry swept around Wheeler's right flank and the 9th Michigan Cavalry and 10th Ohio Cavalry tried the left. While his men deployed, Kilpatrick taunted his West Point classmate. He grabbed his battle flag, stepped in front of the skirmish line, and called out to Wheeler, "Come on now, you cowardly scoundrel! Your [news] organs claim you have thrashed Kilpatrick every time. Here's Kil himself. Come out, and I'll not leave enough of you to thrash a corporal's guard!"[9]

The troopers of the 92nd Illinois laid down a heavy suppressing fire while the men of the 9th Ohio put spurs to their horses and dashed around Wheeler's right flank. Colonel William D. Hamilton led them. "I ordered my bugler to sound the charge," Hamilton recalled. "The companies began to move in an awkward irregular line, looking back for me." Hamilton waved his hat and cried, "'come on, boys.' A shout went up all along the line, and the glitter of their sabers

7. A. K. Miller, "Driving Wheeler: A Leaf from a Sergeant's Diary at Waynesboro," *National Tribune*, December 8, 1887.
8. "Sherman. The Gallop Through Georgia," *New York Herald*, December 22, 1864.
9. Ibid.

following the fire of the carbines showed the mettle of the men, when the charge was on."[10] One of Hamilton's troopers said, "Away we went on the gallop, carbines firing, sabers flashing."[11]

While the 9th Ohio Cavalry attacked the right, the 10th Ohio pounced on the left. Just before charging, 22-year-old Capt. Samuel E. Norton, who commanded Company D of the 10th Ohio Cavalry, shouted, "Now for a name for our regiment."[12] The 10th Ohio dashed forward. "At the word of command 200 bright blades leaped from their scabbards, and with a yell away we flew," a trooper of the 10th Ohio recollected, "like the sweeping cyclone, until the intervening space had been passed." He continued, "Moments seemed like hours," recalled another trooper of the 10th Ohio. "Suddenly a sheet of flames shot out from the...barricade...and as suddenly horses and riders were in the last agonies of death, blocking the way."[13] Unfortunately, Captain Norton, a favorite of Kilpatrick's, was seriously wounded while leading the charge. Another Buckeye watched a Confederate officer dashing up and down the enemy line of battle with his saber raised, calling on his brave men to defend against the enemy invaders. The Ohioans later learned that the Confederate officer was Fighting Joe Wheeler himself.[14] The 9th Michigan Cavalry joined the attack on the Confederate left.

While the flank attacks proceeded, the men of the 92nd Illinois charged the barricade, overrunning it as they "pumped their Spencers at the backs of the retreating rebel soldiers."[15] The color bearer of the 92nd Illinois was shot down during the melee at the barricade, and a Confederate officer seized the flag. An Illinoisan grabbed the flagstaff, and the two men wrestled for possession of the banner until the Illinois man freed his revolver, aimed at the Confederate, and compelled him to surrender.[16]

Wheeler "made several counter-charges to save his dismounted men and check our rapid advance," Kilpatrick noted.[17] At that moment, Kilpatrick committed his reserve, the 5th Ohio Cavalry, and ordered, "Col. Heath, take your regiment; charge by column of fours down that

10. Hamilton, *Recollections of a Cavalryman*, 163.
11. Elliott B. McKeever, "Atlanta to the Sea," unpublished manuscript, Archives, Western Reserve Historical Society, Cleveland, Ohio.
12. *OR* 44, 392.
13. John T. Frederick, "The Battle of Waynesboro," *National Tribune*, February 12, 1891.
14. J. B. Kilbourne, "The March to the Sea. Kilpatrick's Cavalry on the March Through Georgia," *National Tribune*, May 17, 1883.
15. *92nd Illinois Mounted Infantry*, 191.
16. Trudeau, *Southern Storm*, 339.
17. *OR* 44, 365.

road and give those fellows a start."[18] Kilpatrick personally led the Buckeye charge. "They rode over the rebel barricade, hewed men down and used their pistols in a close engagement."[19] Some of Baird's infantrymen, who were not engaged in this fighting, arrived just in time to witness the charge. "The charge by our cavalry across the open field was a most sublimely grand, never-to-be-forgotten scene," an Ohio infantryman recounted, "no words of the writer can describe or paint the picture."[20] The presence of these infantrymen drew the attention of the Confederate cavalry. An Indiana soldier watched as some of the Rebels "had to retreat across a large swamp about a mile and the road was graded high and about wide enough for three or four men to ride abreast. They was in such a hurry they crowded each other off."[21]

There was a third, stronger barricade just outside the town of Waynesboro, and his men fell back to that spot, taking position behind it. Kilpatrick moved his First Brigade into position to assault the third barricade, which was supported by artillery. Kilpatrick realized that he could not flank Wheeler out of this position, as his "flanks [were] so far extended that it was useless to attempt to turn them. I therefore determined to break his center."[22]

The First Brigade, then commanded by Col. Eli H. Murray of the 3rd Kentucky Cavalry, advanced while mounted.[23] The 3rd Kentucky assaulted the Confederate left, the 9th Pennsylvania Cavalry headed for the right flank, and the 8th Indiana Cavalry, dismounted, attacked the center, with the 2nd and 5th Kentucky Cavalry held in reserve, all of which were supported by Capt. Yates Beebe of the 10th Wisconsin Battery and six three-inch ordnance rifles. Because the 3rd Kentucky attacked first, it drew the full attention of Wheeler's troopers. Their muzzles blazed. "No body of men ever stood fire more resolutely, not

18. J. A. Gilberg, "With the Cavalry. Kilpatrick Tilting with Wheeler Down in Georgia," *National Tribune*, August 20, 1903.
19. "Sherman. The Gallop Through Georgia."
20. William C. Johnson, "The March to the Sea," *G. A. R. War Papers: Papers Read Before the Fred C. Jones Post, No. 401* (Cincinnati: Fred C. Jones Post, 1891), 327.
21. William B. Miller diary, entry for December 4, 1864, Gibson County Civil War Papers, Archives, Indiana Historical Society, Indianapolis, Indiana.
22. *OR* 44, 365.
23. On February 13, 1865, Sherman ordered Colonel Murray to assume command of the Second Cavalry Division assigned to the Department of Kentucky. Murray had already left the command by the time the Battle of Aiken had occurred. Colonel Thomas J. Jordan assumed command of the First Brigade when Murray departed. Murray was breveted to brigadier general of volunteers for meritorious service at the end of the Civil War. Special Orders 33, February 13, 1865, included in Murray service records, RG 93, NARA.

a man faltered," the commander of the 3rd Kentucky remembered. "At length, the enemy's fire becoming fierce and many of their comrades falling around them, they disregarded the restraints of discipline and rushed, with wild shouts, upon the enemy in their front."[24] The 9th Pennsylvania then made a mounted charge on the Confederate right flank.

While the dismounted troopers of the 8th Indiana Cavalry fired volley after volley at the center of Wheeler's line, the Union horse artillery shelled it. At that moment, Murray committed the 2nd Kentucky, which drew sabers and charged the center of the Confederate barricade. They smashed through the Confederate line, and Wheeler's position collapsed, driving his beaten troopers back into and through the town of Waynesboro. Wheeler admitted that his troopers "were so warmly pressed that it was with difficulty we succeeded in withdrawing."[25] A victorious Judson Kilpatrick relished the moment. He rushed "around like a child with a new toy, saying: 'I knew I could lick Wheeler! I can do it again!'"[26] Kilpatrick and Baird then withdrew and bivouacked for the night. They resumed their march the next day. A few days later, they were crossing Ebenezer Creek as the rear guard with Wheeler hot on their tail. In turn, Davis, the Fourteenth Corps commander, decided to pull up bridges and leave the long column of contrabands following his troops to their fates.

Backed by at least one battery of horse artillery, Wheeler smartly and professionally reformed his command on the north side of Briar Creek to defend the bridges. Atkins's Second Brigade pursued the retreating Confederates right up to the creek, and the 5th Ohio Cavalry destroyed the railroad bridge. The wagon bridges were not severely damaged.

The Confederates retreated after taking approximately 250 casualties in the vicious fight. Wheeler claimed that he inflicted 197 casualties upon Kilpatrick's command.[27] Kilpatrick had, in fact, thrashed Wheeler. Kilpatrick's feint fooled Wheeler into thinking that the Federal cavalry was headed to Augusta. Wheeler believed that the severe fight at Waynesboro prevented Kilpatrick from marching on Augusta, and, by taking the fight to Kilpatrick, he managed to save his hometown for the first time—including the town's important powder works. The Battle of Aiken, 76 days later, marked the second time that

---

24. *OR* 44, 380.
25. Ibid., 410.
26. Leroy S. Fallis, "With the Cavalry. Fights at Buck Head Creek, Millers Grove and Reynolds Plantation," *National Tribune*, November 26, 1903.
27. *OR* 44, 635.

Kilpatrick's feint fooled Wheeler into defending Augusta, when the Federals never intended to go there in the first place.

In fact, the feint tricked Wheeler into committing his cavalry to a defensive action at Waynesboro, while Sherman's main body worked around Maj. Gen. Lafayette McLaws's line of resistance along the Ogeechee River without any significant fight—much like how the fight at Aiken permitted Sherman's army to bypass the intended defensive line at the Edisto River.

At Waynesboro, Wheeler implemented a well-designed and well-executed delaying action that drew Kilpatrick into attacking three prepared defensive positions, which stymied his advance and inflicted losses. At Aiken, Wheeler used decoys to entice Kilpatrick to attack, relying upon the element of surprise and superior numbers to defeat the Union cavalry. In both instances, Wheeler relied upon his knowledge and understanding of Kilpatrick's aggressive nature; he knew that once enticed into giving battle, his adversary would commit his entire force to the fight.

Kilpatrick won the battle at Waynesboro by successfully assaulting Wheeler's position with simultaneous attacks on both flanks and the center of the Confederate line. Once Wheeler's decoys drew him in at Aiken, Kilpatrick fought an almost entirely defensive battle. He then conducted a fighting withdrawal and fell back upon the rest of his division at Johnson's Turnout, where the entire command conducted a stout defensive action. On March 10, 1865, Lt. Gen. Wade Hampton and Wheeler again relied upon Kilpatrick's known personality traits—recklessness and lack of diligence—to catch his command unaware and unprepared at dawn, nearly capturing Little Kil in the process.

In losing at Waynesboro and winning at Aiken, Wheeler believed he had saved his hometown of Augusta twice. In reality, Sherman had twice duped Wheeler by using Kilpatrick to draw the Confederate cavalry away from the main Federal advance.

BIBLIOGRAPHY

PRIMARY SOURCES

NEWSPAPERS:

Aiken Standard
Aiken Standard and Review
Atlanta Southern Confederacy
Augusta Chronicle
Charleston Mercury
Charleston News and Courier
Charleston Sunday News
Daily Confederate (Raleigh, North Carolina)
Detroit Free Press
Edgefield Advertiser (Edgefield, South Carolina)
Freeport Daily Journal (Freeport, Illinois)
The Journal and Review (Aiken, South Carolina)
Kalamazoo Daily Telegraph
Macon Daily Telegraph
Mansfield News (Mansfield, Ohio)
The Montgomery Times (Montgomery, Alabama)
The National Tribune
New York Daily News
New York Herald
Ohio State Journal (Columbus, Ohio)
The People Sentinel (Barnwell, South Carolina)
The Philadelphia Inquirer
Richmond Dispatch
Sussex Independent (Deckertown, New Jersey)
Sussex Register (Deckertown, New Jersey)
The Times-Picayune (New Orleans, Louisiana)
The Tri-Weekly Journal (Camden, South Carolina)
Wantage Recorder (Deckertown, New Jersey)

MANUSCRIPT SOURCES:

Archives, Aiken County Historical Museum, Aiken, South Carolina:
Elizabeth C. Teague, "The Battle of Aiken."

Archives, Aiken County Historical Society, Aiken, South Carolina:
Rev. John Hamilton Cornish Diary

Archives, Charleston Library Society, Charleston, South Carolina:
Edward L. Wells Correspondence

Archives, Perkins Library, Duke University, Durham, North Carolina:
C. C. Jones Papers

Archives, Historical Society of Pennsylvania, Philadelphia, Pennsylvania:
Thomas J. Jordan Papers

Archives, Indiana Historical Society, Indianapolis, Indiana:
Gibson County Civil War Papers
William B. Miller Diary
Williamson D. Ward Diary

Manuscripts Division, Library of Congress, Washington, D.C.:
Alfred Roman Papers
Wigfall Family Papers

Kevin D. McLemore Collection, Fort Campbell, Kentucky:
Diary of Bethenia McLemore
Nathan Bedford Forrest Letter of August 30, 1863

National Archives and Records Administration, Washington, D.C.:
RG 93, Compiled Service Records
RG 94, Records of the Adjutant General's Office 1780-1917, Theodore F. Northrop, Captain of Volunteers File, File No. 1674 vs. 1676, Box 1200

Archives, United States Army Heritage and Education Center, Carlisle, Pennsylvania:
Civil War Miscellaneous Collection
William W. Pritchard Diary

Southern Historical Collection, Wilson Library, University of North Carolina, Chapel Hill, North Carolina:
O. P. Hargis Reminiscences

Archives, Western Reserve Historical Society, Cleveland, Ohio:
Elliott B. McKeever unpublished manuscript, "Atlanta to the Sea."

PUBLISHED SOURCES:

"*A Staff Officer.*" *Synopsis of the Military Career of Gen. Joseph Wheeler, Commander of the Cavalry Corps, Army of the West.* New York: n.p., 1865.

"A Member of the Aiken Mounted Infantry," "For the Advertiser," *Edgefield Advertiser*, January 25, 1865.

"A 10th Ohio Cavalryman," "Campaign Through the Carolinas. From Savannah to Goldsboro With Kilpatrick's Cavalry. Obstacles Overcome. Crossing the Savannah on a Swaying Pontoon Bridge. Hand-to-Hand Fighting. Destroying the Property of a Bloodhound-Keeper," *National Tribune*, April 28, 1892.

"About Wheeler." *The Montgomery Times*, February 15, 1906.

"An Interesting Letter," *Macon Daily Telegraph*, April 6, 1865.

Adams, Charles Francis. *A Cycle of Adams Letters, 1861-1865.* Ed. by Worthington C. Ford. 2 vols. Boston: Houghton-Mifflin, 1920.

Agassiz, George R., ed. *Meade's Headquarters 1863-1865: Letters of Colonel Theodore Lyman from the Wilderness to Appomattox.* Boston: The Atlantic Monthly Press, 1922.

Angle, Paul M., ed. *Three Years in the Army of the Cumberland: The Letters and Diary of Major James A. Connolly.* Bloomington: University of Indiana Press, 1959.

"Anniversary Aiken Fight. Fifty-Two Years Ago Wheeler and Kilpatrick Fought Here." *The Journal and Review*, February 14, 1917.

Barnwell, John, ed. "Hamlet to Hotspur: Letters of Robert Woodward Barnwell to Robert Barnwell Rhett." *South Carolina Historical Magazine* 77 (October 1976): 236-37, 247.

Basler, Roy, ed. *Collected Works of Abraham Lincoln.* 8 vols. New Brunswick, NJ: Rutgers University Press, 1953.

Bates, Samuel P. *Martial Deeds of Pennsylvania.* Philadelphia: T. H. Davis & Co., 1875.

"Battle at Aiken, S.C., Feb. 11, '65." *Freeport Daily Journal*, March 4, 1909.

Berkenes, Robert E., ed. *Private William Boddy's Civil War Journal: Empty Saddles—Empty Sleeves.* Altoona, IA: TiffCor Publishing House, 1996.

Boies, Andrew J. *Record of the Thirty-Third Massachusetts Volunteer Infantry, from Aug. 1862 to Aug. 1865.* Fitchburg, MA: Sentinel Printing Co., 1880.

Bradley, Rev. G. S. *The Star Corps; Or, Notes of an Army Chaplain, During Sherman's Famous "March to the Sea."* Milwaukee, WI: Jermain & Brightman, 1865.

Calhoun, Charles M. "Credit to Wheeler Claimed by Others," *Confederate Veteran* 20 (1912): 82-83.

Camburn, T. E. "Capture of Col. Rhett," *National Tribune*, August 23, 1906.

Carter, George E., ed. *The Story of Joshua D. Breyfogle, Private, 4th Ohio Infantry (10th Ohio Cavalry) and the Civil War.* Lewiston, NY: Edward Mellen Press, 2001.

Cauthen, Charles E., ed. *Family Letters of the Three Wade Hamptons, 1782-1901.* Columbia: University of South Carolina Press, 1953.

Childs, Arney Robinson, ed. *The Private Journal of Henry William Ravenel, 1859-1887.* Columbia: University of South Carolina Press, 1947.

Coffin, James P. "Col. Henry M. Ashby." *Confederate Veteran* 14 (1906): 121.

Cox, Jacob D. *Reminiscences of the Civil War.* 2 vols. New York: Charles Scribner's Sons, 1900.

Davis, Jefferson. *The Rise and Fall of the Confederate Government.* 2 vols. New York: D. Appleton & Co., 1881.

"Death of Capt. Northrop," *Sussex Independent*, February 1, 1918.

"Death of Civil War Veteran on Sunday," *Wantage Recorder*, February 1, 1918.

Dodson, W. C., ed. *Campaigns of Wheeler's Cavalry 1862-1865.* Atlanta: Hudgins Publishing Co., 1899.

DuBose, John W. "The Fayetteville Road Fight." *Confederate Veteran* 20 (1912): 84-86.

Evans, Clement A., ed. *Confederate Military History: A Library of Confederate States History, Written by Distinguished Men of the South.* 12 vols. Atlanta: Confederate Publishing Co., 1899.

Fallis, Leroy S. "With the Cavalry. Fights at Buck Head Creek, Millers Grove and Reynolds Plantation." *National Tribune*, November 26, 1903.

Frederick, John T. "The Battle of Waynesboro." *National Tribune*, February 12, 1891.

Freeman, Douglas Southall, ed. *Lee's Dispatches: Unpublished Letters of General Robert E. Lee to Jefferson Davis and the War Department of the Confederate States of America 1862-65.* New York: G. P. Putnam's Sons, 1915.

"From South Carolina—Sherman's Movements." *Richmond Dispatch*, February 16, 1865.

Garber, Michael C., Jr. "Reminiscences of the Burning of Columbia, South Carolina," *Indiana Magazine of History*, Vol. 11, No. 4 (1915): 285-300.

Gilberg, J. A. "With the Cavalry. Kilpatrick Tilting with Wheeler Down in Georgia." *National Tribune*, August 20, 1903.

Gray, Alonzo. *Cavalry Tactics as Illustrated by the War of the Rebellion Together With Many Interesting Facts Important for Cavalry to Know. In 2 parts.* Fort Leavenworth, KS: U.S. Cavalry Assoc., 1910.

Guild, George B. *A Brief Narrative of the Fourth Tennessee Cavalry, Wheeler's Corps, Army of Tennessee.* Nashville: privately published, 1913.

Hamilton, Posey. "Incidents of the Fighting at Aiken, S.C." *Confederate Veteran* 32 (February 1924): 58.

Hamilton, William Douglas. *Recollections of a Cavalryman of the Civil War After Fifty Years, 1861-1865.* Columbus, OH: The F. J. Heer Printing Co., 1915.

Henderson, P. F. *A Short History of Aiken and Aiken County.* Columbia: The R. L. Bryan Co., 1951.

Hinman, Wilbur F. *The Story of the Sherman Brigade, the Camp, the March, the Bivouac, the Battle and How the Boys Lived and Died During Four Years of Active Field Service*. Alliance, OH: privately published, 1897.

Howard, Oliver Otis. *Autobiography of Oliver Otis Howard, Major General, United States Army*. 2 vols. New York: Baker & Taylor Co., 1907.

Howe, M. A. DeWolfe, ed. *Home Letters of General Sherman*. New York: Charles Scribner's Sons, 1909.

--------------------------------. *Marching with Sherman: Passages from the Letters and Campaign Diaries of Henry Hitchcock, Major and Assistant Adjutant General of Volunteers November 1864-May 1865*. New Haven, CT: Yale University Press, 1927.

Hughes, Daniel J., ed. *Moltke on the Art of War: Selected Writings*. New York: Presidio Press, 1993.

"In Memoriam Companion Thomas Wakefield Sanderson." Military Order of the Loyal Legion of the United States, Commandery of the State of Ohio. Circular No. 13, Series of 1908.

Johnson, William C. "The March to the Sea." *G. A. R. War Papers: Papers Read Before the Fred C. Jones Post, No. 401*. Cincinnati: Fred C. Jones Post, 1891: 309-336.

Johnson, Suzanne Stone and Robert Allison Johnson, eds. *Bitter Freedom—William Stone's Record of Service in the Freedmen's Bureau*. Columbia: University of South Carolina Press, 2008.

Johnston, Joseph E. *Narrative of Military Operations, Directed, During the Late War Between the States*. New York: D. Appleton & Co., 1874.

Jones, J. Keith, ed. *Boys of Diamond Hill: The Lives and Civil War Letters of the Boyd Family of Abbeville County, South Carolina*. Jefferson, NC: McFarland, 2011.

Jones, James A. "A Reminiscence of the Aiken Skirmish," *Aiken County Historical Society Journal*. Vol. 3, No. 3 (October 1988): 1-2.

Jones, William B. "The Late Maj. Gen. William Wirt Allen." *Confederate Veteran* 2 (1894): 324.

Kidd, James H. *Personal Recollections of a Cavalryman in Custer's Michigan Brigade*. Ionia, MI: Sentinel Publishing Co., 1908.

Kilbourne, J. B. "The March to the Sea. Kilpatrick's Cavalry on the March Through Georgia." *National Tribune*, May 17, 1883.

Kirwan, A. D., ed. *Johnny Green of the Orphan Brigade*. Lexington: University of Kentucky Press, 1956.

Knepp, Gary L., ed. *To Crown Myself with Honor: The Wartime Letters of Captain Asbury Gatch*. Milford, OH: Little Miami Publishing Co., 2011.

"Later from the North," *The Times-Picayune*, February 28, 1865.

LeConte, Joseph. *Ware Sherman: A Journal of Three Months Personal Experience in the Last Days of the Confederacy*. Baton Rouge: Louisiana State University Press, 1999.

Luce, Stephen B. "Naval Administration, III." *Proceedings*, U. S. Naval Institute 29, no. 4 (December 1903): 809-821.

Mahan, Dennis H. *An Elementary Treatise on Advanced-Guard, Out-Post, and Detachment Service of Troops, and the Manner of Posting and Handling Them in the Presence of an Enemy*. New York: John Wiley, 1861.

McKeever, J. H., ed. *He Rode with Sherman from Atlanta to the Sea*. Aberdeen, SD: McKeever Press, 1947.

McMaster, J. N. "A Correction," *National Tribune*, September 13, 1888.

----------------. "How They Surprised a Rebel Camp." *National Tribune*, February 28, 1888.

----------------. "Kilpatrick's Cavalry at Aiken, S. C.," *National Tribune*, July 26, 1888.

McMurry, Richard M., ed. *An Uncompromising Secessionist: The Civil War of George Knox Miller, Eighth (Wade's) Confederate Cavalry*. Tuscaloosa: University of Alabama Press, 2007.

Meyer, Henry C. *Civil War Experiences Under Bayard, Gregg, Kilpatrick, Custer, Raulston, and Newbury, 1862, 1863, 1864*. New York: Knickerbocker Press, 1911.

Miller, A. K. "Driving Wheeler: A Leaf from a Sergeant's Diary at Waynesboro." *National Tribune*, December 8, 1887.

Morgan, D. B. "Incidents of the Fighting at Aiken, S. C." *Confederate Veteran* 22 (1924): 300.

Morris, William H. "Ohio Veteran Doesn't Like the Rebel Yell," *Confederate Veteran* 18 (1910): 61-62.

"Neighborhood News. Lexington," *Mansfield News*, May 8, 1900.

Nichols, George Ward. *The Story of the Great March, from the Diary of a Staff Officer*. New York: Harper & Bros., 1865.

Ninety-Second Illinois Volunteers. Freeport, IL: Journal Steam Publishing House and Bookbindery, 1875.

Northrop, Theodore F. "Capture of Gen. Rhett," *National Tribune*, January 18, 1906.

"Outrages of Wheeler's Command," *Charleston Mercury*, January 14, 1865.

Pepper, George W. *Personal Recollections of Sherman's Campaigns in Georgia and the Carolinas*. Zanesville, OH: Hugh Dunne, 1866.

Quiner, E. B. *The Military History of Wisconsin: A Record of the Civil and Military of the Patriotism of the State in the War for the Union*. Chicago: Clarke & Co., 1866.

Reed, John. "The Battle at Aiken, S. C." *National Tribune*, August 30, 1888.

Reid, Whitelaw. *Ohio in the War: Her Statesmen Generals and Soldiers*. 2 vols. Cincinnati: The Robert Clarke Co., 1865.

Ridley, B. L. "Chat with Col. W. S. McLemore." *Confederate Veteran* 8 (1900): 262-264.

Robertson, John, comp. *Michigan in the War*. Lansing: W. S. George & Co., 1882.

Robertson, Mary D., ed. *A Confederate Lady Comes of Age: The Journal of Pauline DeCaradeuc Heyward, 1863-1888*. Columbia: University of South Carolina Press, 1992.

Rowland, Dunbar, ed. *Jefferson Davis, Constitutionalist: His Letters, Papers, and Speeches*. 10 vols. Jackson: Mississippi Department of Archives and History, 1923.

Schofield, John M. *Forty-Six Years in the Army*. New York: The Century Co., 1897.

Scott, Douglas D. and William J. Hunt, Jr. *The Civil War Battle of Monroe's Crossroads: A Historical Archaeological Perspective*. Fort Bragg, NC: U.S. Army, 1998.

Sea, Andrew M. "Destruction of the Broad River Bridge." *Confederate Veteran* 21 (November 1913): 542.

"Sherman. The Gallop Through Georgia." *New York Herald*, December 22, 1864.

Sherman, William T. *Memoirs of Gen. W. T. Sherman*. 2 vols. New York: Charles L. Webster & Co., 1891.

"Sherman's Progress," *Augusta Chronicle*, February 13, 1865.

Simms, William Gilmore. *A City Laid Waste: The Capture, Sack, and Destruction of the City of Columbia*. Columbia: University of South Carolina Press, 2005.

Smith, Frank. "A Maine Boy in the Tenth Ohio Cavalry." *First Maine Bugle* Vol. 4, No. 1 (January 1897): 11-21.

"South Carolina." *Daily Confederate*, February 17, 1865.

Swedberg, Claire E., ed. *Three Years with the 92nd Illinois: The Civil War Diary of John M. King*. Mechanicsburg, PA: Stackpole Books, 1999.

Toole, Gasper Loren, II. *Ninety Years in Aiken County: Memoirs of Aiken County and Its People*. Aiken, SC: self-published, 1958.

"The Late General Acker," *Kalamazoo Daily Telegraph*, September 8, 1879.

"The Operations at the South," *The Philadelphia Inquirer*, February 18, 1865.

The War of the Rebellion: A Compilation of the Official Records of the Union and Confederate Armies. 128 volumes in 3 series. Washington, D.C.: United States Government Printing Office, 1889.

"Troublous Times in Edgefield." *Edgefield Advertiser*, February 14, 1865.

Ulmer, J. B. "Ruffin Dragoons with A. S. Johnston." *Confederate Veteran* 17 (1909): 597.

"Unlawful Impressments," *Edgefield Advertiser*, February 22, 1865.

"Unveiling of Confederate Monument at Montgomery, AL: Major Falkner's Words," *Charleston Sunday News*, November 20, 1898.

Wyeth, J. A. "Gen. Joseph Wheeler," *Confederate Veteran* 6 (1898): 361.

Vale, Joseph G. *Minty and His Cavalry: A History of Cavalry Campaigns in the Western Armies*. Harrisburg, PA: E. K. Meyers, 1886.

Wainwright, Charles S. *A Diary of Battle: The Personal Journals of Colonel Charles S. Wainwright, 1861-1865*. Ed. by Alan Nevins. New York: Harcourt, Brace & World, 1962.

Weller, A. "Sherman Talks Strategy." *Civil War Times Illustrated* 33, no. 3 (July-August 1994): 28-29 and 76.

Wheeler, Joseph. *A Revised System of Cavalry Tactics, for the Use of the Cavalry and Mounted Infantry, C.S.A.* Mobile, AL: S. H. Goetzel & Co., 1863.

Wilson, James Harrison. *Under the Old Flag: Recollections of Military Operations in the War for the Union, the Spanish War, the Boxer Rebellion, Etc.* 2 vols. New York: D. Appleton, 1912.

SECONDARY SOURCES:

Allardice, Bruce S. *More Generals in Gray.* Baton Rouge: Louisiana State University Press, 1995.

Andrew, Rod, Jr. *Wade Hampton: Confederate Warrior to Southern Redeemer.* Chapel Hill: University of North Carolina Press, 2008.

Austerman, Wayne R. "C. S. Cavalry Arms—1865." *North South Trader*, vol. XII, no. 2 (January-February 1985): 22-27.

Baumgartner, Richard A. *Blue Lightning: Wilder's Mounted Infantry Brigade at the Battle of Chickamauga.* Second ed. Huntington, WV: Blue Acorn Press, 1999.

Biographical History of Northeastern Ohio Embracing the Counties of Ashtabula, Trumbull and Mahoning. Chicago: The Lewis Publishing Co., 1893.

Boylston, Raymond P., Jr. *Battle of Aiken.* Columbia: Boylston Enterprises, 2003.

Bradley, Mark L. *The Battle of Bentonville: Last Stand in the Carolinas.* Mason City, IA: Savas Publishing, 1996.

Brockington, William S., Jr. and Judith T. Van Steenburg, eds. *Historical Sketches on Aiken.* Aiken, SC: The Sesquicentennial Committee of Aiken, 1985.

Bush, Bryan S. *Terry's Texas Rangers: The 8th Texas Cavalry.* Paducah, KY: Turner Publishing Co., 2002.

Campbell, Jacqueline Glass. *When Sherman Marched North from the Sea: Resistance on the Confederate Home Front.* Chapel Hill: University of North Carolina Press, 2003.

Cavender, Michael Bowers. *The First Georgia Cavalry in the Civil War: A History and Roster.* Jefferson, NC: McFarland, 2006.

Cobb, J. Michael, Edward Hicks, and Wythe Holt. *Battle of Big Bethel: Crucial Clash in Early Civil War Virginia.* El Dorado Hills, CA: Savas-Beatie, 2013.

Collier, Calvin L. *The War Child's Children: The Story of the Third Regiment, Arkansas Cavalry, Confederate States Army.* Little Rock, AR: privately published, 1965.

Connelly, Thomas L. *Autumn of Glory: The Army of Tennessee, 1862-1865.* Baton Rouge: Louisiana State University Press, 1971.

Cornish, Joseph E. *The History and Genealogy of the Cornish Families in America.* Boston: Geo. H. Ellis Co., 1907.

Daiss, Timothy. *In the Saddle: Exploits of the 5th Georgia Cavalry During the Civil War.* Atglen, PA: Schiffer Publishing, 1999.

Davis, Burke. *Sherman's March*. New York: Random House, 1980.

DeLeon, T. C. *Joseph Wheeler, the Man, the Statesman, the Soldier, Seen in Semi-Biographical Sketches*. Atlanta: Byrd Printing, 1899.

Dougherty, Dave. *Making Georgia Howl! The 5th Ohio Volunteer Cavalry in Kilpatrick's Campaigns and the Diary of Sgt. William H. Harding*. Point Pleasant, NJ: Winged Hussar Publishing, 2016.

Dyer, John P. *From Shiloh to San Juan: The Life of "Fightin' Joe" Wheeler*. Baton Rouge: Louisiana State University Press, 1961.

Elmore, Tom. *Carnival of Destruction: Sherman's Invasion of South Carolina*. Charleston: Joggling Board Press, 2012.

Evans, David. *Sherman's Horsemen: Union Cavalry Operations in the Atlanta Campaign*. Bloomington: Indiana University Press, 1996.

Fisher, John E. *They Rode with Forrest and Wheeler: A Chronicle of Five Tennessee Brothers' Service in the Confederate Western Cavalry*. Jefferson, NC: McFarland, 1995.

Freeman, Douglas Southall. *Lee's Lieutenants: A Study in Command*. 3 vols. New York: Charles Scribner's Sons, 1942-1944.

Freiheit, Laurence H. *Boots and Saddles: Cavalry During the Maryland Campaign of September 1862*. Iowa City, IA: Camp Pope Publishing, 2012.

Henderson, P. F. *A Short History of Aiken and Aiken County*. Columbia: R. L. Bryan Co., 1951.

"Historical marker set up for Camp Butler," *Aiken Standard*, November 24, 2012.

History of Hardin County, Iowa. Springfield, IL: Union Publishing Co., 1883.

Hunt, Roger D. and Jack R. Brown. *Brevet Brigadier Generals in Blue*. Gaithersburg, MD: Olde Soldier Books, 1989.

Jones, R. Wayne and Thomas D. Perry. *The Battle of Aiken South Carolina. Kilpatrick vs. Wheeler February 11, 1865*. Ararat, VA: Laurel Hill Publishing, 2011.

Kennedy, Helen and Jay Maedar. "The Scandalous Custody Battle Between the Whitneys and the Vanderbilts Over 'Little Gloria'," *New York Daily News*, August 14, 2017.

King, G. Wayne. "General Judson Kilpatrick," *New Jersey History*, vol. XCI, no. 1 (Spring 1973): 35-52.

Longacre, Edward G. *A Soldier to the Last: Maj. Gen. Joseph Wheeler in Blue and Gray*. Dulles, VA: Potomac Books, 2006.

------------------------. "Judson Kilpatrick," *Civil War Times Illustrated 10* (April 1971): 25-33.

Martin, Samuel J. *"Kill-Cavalry:" Sherman's Merchant of Terror—The Life of Union General Hugh Judson Kilpatrick*. Cranbury, NJ: Associated University Press, 1996.

--------------------. *Southern Hero: Matthew Calbraith Butler: Confederate General, Hampton Red Shirt, and U.S. Senator*. Mechanicsburg, PA: Stackpole Books, 2001.

McClaren, H. Addison. *St. Thaddeus of Aiken: A Church and Its City*. Spartanburg, SC: The Reprint Co., 1994.

McMurry, Richard M. *Virginia Military Institute Alumni in the Civil War: In Bello Praesidium*. Lynchburg, VA: H. E. Howard Co., 1999.

Mohon, James L. "Henry Ashby's 2nd Tennessee Cavalry in the Confederate Heartland." *Civil War Regiments: A Journal of the American Civil War*, vol. 4, no. 1 (1994): 1-43.

Moir, William J., ed. *Past and Present of Hardin County Iowa*. Indianapolis: B. F. Bowen & Co., 1911.

Morris, Jerry. "Trail of Fire: The Nineteen." *The People Sentinel*, March 19, 2015.

Mowery, David L. *Morgan's Great Raid: The Remarkable Expedition from Kentucky to Ohio*. Charleston: The History Press, 2013.

Murrah, Jeffrey D. *None But Texians: A History of Terry's Texas Rangers*. Austin, TX: Eakin Press, 2001.

Peters, Pete. *The Battle of Aiken Commemorative Program, 131st Anniversary of the Battle of Aiken*. Aiken, SC: Brig. Gen. Barnard E. Bee Camp, Sons of Confederate Veterans, 1996.

Pohanka, Brian C. and Patrick A. Schroeder. *History of the 5th New York Volunteer Infantry: Vortex of Hell*. Lynchburg, VA: Schroeder Publications, 2012.

Poole, John Randolph. *Cracker Cavaliers: The 2nd Georgia Cavalry under Wheeler and Forrest*. Macon, GA: Mercer University Press, 2000.

Powell, David A. *Failure in the Saddle: Nathan Bedford Forrest, Joe Wheeler, and the Confederate Cavalry in the Chickamauga Campaign*. El Dorado Hills, CA: Savas-Beatie, 2010.

Richland County, Ohio Civil War Veterans Extracted from *Hardesty's Historical and Genealogical Encyclopedia*. Mansfield, OH: Richland County Historical Society, 1998.

Rowell, John W. *Yankee Cavalrymen: Through the Civil War with the Ninth Pennsylvania Cavalry*. Knoxville: University of Tennessee Press, 1971.

Savas, Theodore P. "Heart of the Southern War Machine: The Augusta Powder Works was an Unparalleled Accomplishment of Military Industry." *Civil War Times 56* (June 2017): 34-43.

------------------------. "The War's Biggest Blunder: William T. Sherman had Many Opportunities to Capture Augusta's Ordnance Complex and Didn't Even Try." *Civil War Times 56* (August 2017): 30-35.

Smith, Mark A. and Wade Sokolosky. *"No Such Army Since the Days of Julius Caesar": Sherman's Carolinas Campaign from Fayetteville to Averasboro, March 1865*. El Dorado Hills, CA: Savas-Beatie, 2017.

Sokolosky, Wade and Mark A. Smith. *"To Prepare for Sherman's Coming": The Battle of Wise's Forks, March 1865*. El Dorado Hills, CA: Savas-Beatie, 2015.

Starr, Stephen Z. *The Union Cavalry in the Civil War*. 3 vols. Baton Rouge: Louisiana State University Press, 1981.

Tavernier, David M. More *Stories of the Rich and Famous: Aiken's Winter Colony in the Gilded Age*. Parker, CO: Outskirts Press, 2014.

-------------------------. *Stories of the Rich and Famous: Aiken's Winter Colony in the Gilded Age*. Parker, CO: Outskirts Press, 2012.

"The Colony," *Aiken Standard and Review*, July 29, 1938.

Todd, Glenda McWhirter. *First Alabama Cavalry, USA: Homage to Patriotism*. Bowie, MD: Heritage Books, 1999.

Trudeau, Noah Andre. *Southern Storm: Sherman's March to the Sea*. New York: Harper, 2007.

Vandervelde, Isabel. *The Battle of Aiken*. Aiken, SC: Art Studio Press, n.d.

Venter, Bruce M. *Kill Jeff Davis: The Union Raid on Richmond, 1864*. Norman: University of Oklahoma Press, 2016.

Warner, Ezra J. *Generals in Blue: Lives of the Union Commanders*. Baton Rouge: Louisiana State University Press, 1964.

-----------------. *Generals in Gray: Lives of the Confederate Commanders*. Baton Rouge: Louisiana State University Press, 1959.

Wittenberg, Eric J. *Gettysburg's Forgotten Cavalry Actions: Farnsworth's Charge, South Cavalry Field, and the Battle of Fairfield*. El Dorado Hills, CA: Savas-Beatie, 2011.

---------------------. *Like a Meteor Blazing Brightly: The Short but Controversial Life of Colonel Ulric Dahlgren*. Roseville, MN: Edinborough Press, 2009.

---------------------. *The Battle of Monroe's Crossroads and the Civil War's Final Campaign*. El Dorado Hills, CA: Savas-Beatie, 2006.

---------------------. *"We Ride a Whirlwind": Sherman and Johnston at Bennett Place*. Burlington, NC: Fox Run Publishing, 2017.

WEBSITES:

Episcopal Church of the Holy Apostles website, history section: http://www.holyapostles-sc.org/about/

Lt. Col. Matthew Van Buskirk listing: https://www.findagrave.com/memorial/37645239/matthew-van_buskirk

Index

Photograph by Scott Cunningham

About the Author

Eric J. Wittenberg is an award-winning Civil War historian, speaker and tour guide. A native of southeastern Pennsylvania, he has been hooked on the Civil War since a third-grade trip to Gettysburg. Wittenberg is deeply involved in battlefield preservation efforts with the Civil War Trust. He is a graduate of Dickinson College and the University of Pittsburgh School of Law. He is an attorney in private practice in Columbus, Ohio, where he resides with his wife Susan and their three golden retrievers.